NUCLEAR CATHOLICS AND OTHER ESSAYS

NUCLEAR CATHOLICS ——

and other essays ————————

J. M. CAMERON

WILLIAM B. EERDMANS PUBLISHING COMPANY
GRAND RAPIDS, MICHIGAN

Copyright © 1989 by Wm. B. Eerdmans Publishing Co.
255 Jefferson Ave. S.E., Grand Rapids, Mich. 49503

Library of Congress Cataloging-in-Publication Data

Cameron, James Munro, 1910–
    Nuclear Catholics and other essays / J.M. Cameron.
      p.   cm.
    ISBN 0-8028-3667-4
    1. Christian ethics—Catholic authors. 2. Education, Humanistic.
   3. Education (Christian theology) 4. Criticism. 5. Catholic
   Church—History—1965–. I. Title.
   BJ1249.C166   1989
   081—dc20   89-28096
                                                   CIP

En vieillissant on devient plus fou et plus sage

As we grow older, we become madder and saner

—*The Maxims of La Rochefoucauld, no. 209*

Contents

CONTENTS

Acknowledgments

Most of these essays were first published in *The New York Review of Books, Commonweal, The University of Toronto Quarterly,* and *English Studies in Canada.* "The Idea of Christendom" was first published by the University of Notre Dame Press in a volume entitled *The Autonomy of Religious Belief,* edited by Frederick Crosson. "Poetry and Dialectic" was first published by the University of Leeds Press.

My friend and colleague Sam Solecki has encouraged me in this as in other ventures. My friend Isabelle Noradunkian Robinson has been of immense help to me, especially in criticizing the first draft of the Introduction and in checking the proofs.

Toronto   J. M. CAMERON
July 1989

Introduction ———————————————————

More than twenty years ago I published a selection of my occasional writings. *The Night Battle,* as I called the book, was well received at the time and achieved a reputation that went rather beyond its merits. Two pieces on the poetry of Pope went into the critical anthologies; and an argument in one of the essays—"Poetry and Dialectic," my Inaugural Lecture at the University of Leeds—was brought, approvingly, into the metacritical work of Professor David Lodge. The argument was, crudely, that it followed from the nature of poetic fictions that paraphrase is always impossible and that there is no state of affairs of which the poetic fiction could be true or false. Some years ago I told David Lodge I had come to doubt the thesis, at least in the form in which I had expressed it. He was a trifle alarmed, as though I had kicked away a supporting piece of his structure of argument. But I have now rejected the doubt I entertained briefly—I hope I have not merely suppressed it—and this may relieve David Lodge's anxiety. Indeed, through the urging of some readers and friends, I have reprinted "Poetry and Dialectic" in this volume. *The Night Battle* is out of print and unlikely to be reprinted, and "Poetry and Dialectic," which was contained in it, has become hard to find.

The essays in the present volume fall into two sections.

Those in the first section are essentially occasional and are written for the general educated public. They are mostly book reviews, and many of them first appeared in *The New York Review of Books*. Over the years *The New York Review* has been kind to me in giving me congenial topics to write about and viewing what I have written with great generosity of spirit. Those in the second section, on the other hand, are written for particular publics, for example, those interested in the work of Dickens or Henry James. But the division between the work in the two sections is not always clear, and I am sure the essays in the second section are intelligible to the same public I have in mind in the first section.

I have been compelled to consider how far I stand by the positions I have set forth here. In general my views on social and political questions have not changed greatly; for example, I am still just as much opposed as I was to the kind of argument I attack in "Nuclear Catholics."

The essay about which I feel the greatest qualms—"Sex in the Head"—is one that was much admired and praised at the time, especially in quarters where I don't commonly look for praise. I intended it as a serious attack on fashionable and progressive views on sexuality, and I wanted it to be amusing at the same time, touching lightly on topics that both progressive and conservative people tend to discuss in solemn tones. I don't disagree with the essentials of the argument. But I now find it somewhat harsh in tone and lacking in sympathy for many of those who are not just victims of current sophistries but are genuinely troubled over what to think on matters of sexual morality. I think I was unnecessarily brisk on the question of male and female homosexuality. On the question of marriage I simplified unduly what is a more complicated question than I allowed.

Two considerations in particular have caused me to want to say something more complex and up to date. It is now well known that among Roman Catholics the disciplines of separation and annulment have greatly changed in recent years. Many who in earlier years would have had little chance of getting a decree now have their marriages annulled—and annulment is a declaration that the parties in the case were never in fact married. Perhaps the most interesting ground for annulment is the notion of "psychological immaturity," or incapacity. Here it is argued that for reasons of age or inexperience, or something else of this sort, the original marriage vow was defective; the fundamental elements of an unforced, free consent were lacking.

The other matter that has begun to get in the way of my thinking decisively has been the history (very obscure and much controverted by historians) of marriage in the first thousand years of Christianity. Something like divorce seems to have happened from time to time. The famous "Matthean exception" (Matthew 5:31-32), where it seemed that divorce was allowed for adultery, was taken seriously. By contrast, the doctrine of the Western canon lawyers since the Middle Ages has been that a consummated union preceded by promises freely exchanged is absolutely indissoluble; and this contrasts with the rather grudging permission to remarry within the Orthodox tradition. Perhaps it should also be noted that on some other matters, the remarriage of widows, for instance, the Orthodox tradition is more severe than that in the West.

I don't assert any position in these matters. I simply state that doubts I am bound to consider reasonable have arisen in my mind in the years since I wrote the article. I should like to write another, more comprehensive article, but I don't find this within my power at the present time.

Perhaps I may add a general comment. I think there is much confusion over matters of sexuality in my own mind and in the minds of many others who have written about this topic. We have not yet digested the many possible consequences of vast secular changes in human practice. The common use in the opulent societies of various methods of contraception and the common view among Christians and others that a primary justification of sexual relations is that they delight the partners, quite apart from any consequent generation of offspring, have influenced even the most conservative thinkers. To take one example, Paul VI's encyclical *Humanae Vitae* is notably different in style and tone from earlier Roman pronouncements. In particular, the brutal and legalistic view of the marriage debt, something that prevailed in the work of theologians until then, is substantially changed. It is perhaps to be desired, now, that pronouncements on sexual ethics ought not to be multiplied beyond necessity.

Sexual mores are influenced by the life of the street, by the popular media, by sermons, and, in Western societies, by the imaginative treatment of sexuality in the arts, and especially in literature. In the European past this last was commonly the work of Christians, though of Christians who would have been thought a little to the side of the main theological tradition. We think of Chaucer, of Rabelais, of Montaigne, of Donne, of Molière, of Blake. The influence of Shakespeare is so powerful that it seems absurd to include him in a list. In the modern English-speaking world, the principal shapers of our imagination have been James Joyce and D. H. Lawrence. Joyce perhaps counts as a Christian writer, for though he tells us that he lost his faith (but not his reason), Catholic theology as he had come across it in his years at school and university overarched the whole of his work. In a strange way Lawrence, not a Christian, came closer and was more sympathetic to the element in Christianity that takes sexuality to be a form of the sacred than overtly Christian writers, who often find it hard to get rid of the Manichaean in them. The late Gerald Vann once said to me that copies of Lawrence's pamphlet "A Propos of *Lady Chatterley*" ought to be presented to newly married couples at the church door as they leave. But in the main the sexual outlook of Christians, and especially of Catholics in the Anglo-Hibernian tradition, was that of the Victorian middle class. In the reaction that followed the Second Vatican Council there was a good deal of new writing about sexuality. But it tended to be—still is—of a slightly shame-making, sentimental, romantic character—Dr. Dominian's much admired, and justly admired, writings are at times marred by this saccharine approach. Such writing is, I suspect, remote from the experience of most Christians, who are less analytical and less high-minded in their approaches to sex.

It seems to me just a fact of modern life that "the multitude," to use the New Testament phrase and concept, is simply deaf to what religious mentors have to say on such matters as contraception and on such practices as were at one time thought to be perversions (oral sex is the principal example), finding them without authority or expertise. This is not a voluntary deafness in most cases; it is an established condition. There was a time when the multitude, whatever their practice, took for granted the Mosaic Law. That the multitude doesn't have this character any more, and because we have the idea that perhaps springs from a sort of perspective effect that there was a recent time when it *did* take the principles of the Mosaic Law as axiomatic, this is a ground of irritation among many Christians, especially Roman Catholics. One sees the spokesmen of the traditional morality, that still promulgated by various Roman authorities, finding in the deafness or incomprehension of the masses an element of willful delusion combined with a vast stupidity. In consequence the spokesmen of authority fall into an angry despair with the sincere, immensely confused, members of the multitude.

I think this response is mistaken. There is in the whole field of sexual morals a great desire to do well, and better, but a great confusion over what this could be. Much of the interest in sexual matters, and some of the anxieties over what is proper, are no doubt induced for base reasons by the various media. Even if this is true, the interest and the anxieties are there and strongly felt. It is, after all, a perfectly defensible position that none of us should have fallen in love but for the literary fictions about it. But this doesn't invalidate the soul-rending sentiments that ravage us.

Perhaps people are coming to think alike, and to share common anxieties, on some questions. The institution of serial monogamy that is devouring the middle class, especially the professional middle class, is coming to be seen as a source of problems and tensions, not a cure for them. There is a tendency for the young to make their sexual debut at such a tender age that by the time they reach late adolescence they are shut off from many enchanting experiences and are pushed into asking the question, just because romantic feeling is so important an ingredient of our culture: Is that all? The claim to have dominion over life and over the processes of life—this shows itself in such practices as abortion, the insemination of women from sperm banks, a great and growing variety of interventions in the production of genetic material, and the demand for euthanasia at the beginning and the end of life—produces a vague sense of guilt, for there is something hubristic about the implied claims to dominion.

If I leave "Sex in the Head" just as I wrote it in 1976, it is as in part a period piece. My criticisms of the silly progressive writing about sex still, I believe, stand; but the tone of knowingness and certainty that lies behind much of what I write strikes me as excessive.

As to other themes in what I have written, especially those themes in which philosophy and the criticism of literature come together (as, for example, "Dickens and the Angels" and "The Description of Feeling"), these are problems and questions that have been working in my mind for many years. If I have an opportunity, I should like to treat some of them at greater length and more systematically. "Newman the Liberal" is one of a number of pieces on Newman I have written over the years; here too there is scope for a more extended treatment.

One of the essays here reprinted is in large part a summary of something that first appeared in a more extended form. The central ideas, and their treatment, in "The Idea of a Liberal Education," are drawn from my *On the Idea of a University* (Toronto University Press, 1978). The positions I argue for in that book have not had much influence on educational theory and practice. I still believe strongly in them and hope that this time round they will receive a sympathetic hearing, and introduce some readers to ideas they may have missed when they first appeared. I may add that my ideas on university education have been received most warmly by the young, those who are closest to a vivid experience of university education today and most conscious of its gaps and shortcomings. I am grateful to those undergraduate and graduate students, and those who are older but keep a sharp impression of their student years, who have, since I came to North America in 1971, combined affection with criticism and have given me so much pleasure and have been for me a source of good sense and enthusiasm.

PART I
OCCASIONAL PIECES

Sex in the Head ————————————————————

"Revolution," like "tragedy," is a bit overused; but there can't be any doubt that we are in the course of, perhaps at the end of, a revolution in sexual mores. From Sweden there has come a report that a government committee has recommended that children be legally free to make their hetero- or homosexual debuts at fourteen, that all legal prohibitions of incest be lifted, and that the word "homosexual" be dropped from the terminology of the law. As to what goes on, it is easy to say what has happened in our society, and I will attempt a short account presently, but it isn't and can't be clear how far behavior that is in one sense characteristic represents how most people conduct their lives.

Other questions even harder to answer are: how far the

From *The New York Review of Books* (May 13, 1976); reviews of Eugene C. Bianchi and Rosemary Radford Ruether, *From Machismo to Mutuality: Essays on Sexism and Woman-Man Liberation* (Paulist Press); Nancy Friday, comp., *My Secret Garden: Women's Sexual Fantasies* (Trident Press, Pocket Books); Richard Ginder, *Binding with Briars: Sex and Sin in the Catholic Church* (Prentice-Hall); Morton Hunt, *Sexual Behavior in the 1970s* (Playboy, Dell); D. D. R. Owen, *Noble Lovers* (Phaidon); Paul Robinson, *The Modernization of Sex* (Harper & Row); C. A. Tripp, *The Homosexual Matrix* (McGraw-Hill).

revolution has added to human happiness or misery, and if to both how the proportions are distributed; what the effects on civilization and culture will be; what the connections are between the revolution and other things that go on in the opulent societies of the West, things both good and bad. Finally, we must surely ask what we are now to think of what has been, in the matter of sexual morality, the central tradition of our culture; this comes from Deuteronomy and was given a circulation outside the Jewish tradition by the first Christians. It forbids fornication, adultery, incest, homosexuality, sexual connection with the brutes, and sacred prostitution (in our own day this last could perhaps be understood as sex as theater).

The content of the sexual revolution seems as follows.

1. In sexual practice virtually everything is interesting and nothing is grave. It is still thought wrong to force people, especially the young, to engage in sexual practices against their will, though there is sometimes to be heard a Pecksniffian voice claiming that rape is really a protest against a repressive social order. Apart from this, pretty well anything goes so long as it doesn't *harm* other people. What is to count as harm isn't easy to determine, for sadism and masochism are interesting too. It is supposed, strangely, that what is harmful is immediately evident. Whatever gives sexual pleasure is all right; the burden of proving that it isn't rests upon the objector.

2. Masturbation is the prototype of all sexual activity, the most harmless, even the "best." Proficiency in masturbation was a necessary condition of fitness for taking part in the Masters and Johnson experiments. Paul Robinson observes in *The Modernization of Sex* that "from this pathogenic status among the Victorians, masturbation has arisen to the position of final sexual arbiter"; its rewards are held by some to be superior to those of any other sexual activity. In particular, female masturbation is the badge of sexual independence. Virtually all the sexual fantasies in Nancy Friday's compilation are used in masturbation as well as in other activities. It is now commonly known that the nineteenth-century belief that (male) masturba-

tion causes a variety of physical and mental ills is groundless. There isn't absolute unanimity that masturbation is without bad emotional consequences, but most students of sex think it at least harmless, like chewing gum or back-scratching.

3. Oral sex—fellatio and cunnilingus—is now a very big activity. Morton Hunt finds there is a great increase of these practices among the married. Such practices, once called perversions, live in a legal twilight in many countries. Even more noteworthy is the fairly wide acceptance of buggery between heterosexual partners. (It is curious that "buggery" is seldom used, though the vernacular terms for other acts and for the male and female genitalia are often used and their use is taken to be a mark of emancipation; but for "buggery" is commonly substituted the prim "anal penetration.") The acceptance by so many of the practice of buggery makes very plain one of the messages of the sexual revolution: that there are now in sexual matters no common principles of decorum.

4. Homosexuality, male and female, is now thought to be a native sexual orientation, not a genetic endowment but in most cases as firm and as unalterable as though it were genetic. Homosexual men and women are often pictured as members of an oppressed third sex in need of emancipation.

5. In many cities of the Western world there are openly advertised emporia that stock curious "objects." These are such things as vibrators (Morton Hunt has a sad and hilarious story about a lady whose Acapulco holiday was ruined because she had forgotten to pack her vibrator), dildos, boots, chains, underclothes of unusual cut, books, photographs, even (though these are perhaps more often procured by mail order) life-size plastic dolls in female shape with which the shy and lonely may cohabit. These emporia correspond in their own field to gourmet shops for lovers of rare foods, and it is characteristic of our time that the publication of gourmet books on sexual techniques reinforces the analogy.

6. Such periodicals as *Playboy* and *Penthouse* and their proliferating imitations should be mentioned. Their appearance

both satisfies and stimulates demand. They represent big money and their proprietors have a strong interest in persuading readers to accept the picture of the sexually liberated human being they offer. Such periodicals are beginning to achieve a kind of respectability and are not too slowly moving into the picture of the normal American home, along with the *Reader's Digest*, cola beverages, contraceptive pills, laxatives, instant coffee, and stuff to make the floor shine.

No doubt these six "notes" of the sexual revolution could be added to and subdivided in various ways; but as they stand they provide enough material for discussion. It is also clear that the revolution as I have described it is confined to Western, free, middle-class, capitalist societies of some degree of opulence. The governments of even the more prosperous socialist societies proscribe most of its manifestations as signs of a bourgeois corruption against which they wish to protect their citizens.

As for the poor societies, of whatever political complexion, these are delights they can't afford. In them the much derided (in the West) *machismo* of the males keeps an uncomplicated heterosexuality as the predominant pattern; and even where, as in some of the Arab countries, male homosexuality is traditional, the business of procreation is well attended to. Here homosexuality seems not so much a way of life as a kind of gentlemanly relaxation. This is how it must have seemed to Maynard Keynes, who, before the First World War, wrote to Lytton Strachey to recommend Tunis as a place where "bed and boy" were not dear.[1] (It is curious that in none of the books under review is Bloomsbury given even the modest place it deserves in the prehistory of the sexual revolution.)

In 1948 Lionel Trilling published in *Partisan Review* a comment on the first Kinsey Report. It is a classic statement, calm, judicious, prescient. Trilling was the first to remark on the bland assurance implied in the chosen title of the Report: *Sexual Behavior in the Human Male*. A cross section, not even complete, of

----

1. Michael Holroyd, *Lytton Strachey* (Holt, Rinehart & Winston, 1968), Vol. II, p. 80.

North American males was to serve as material for generalizing about all human males. The article is still worth reading: indeed, it may be said to have gathered weight in the almost thirty years since it appeared. I wish to mention two of its points. First, there is what might be called the vulgar democratic (on the analogy of "vulgar Marxist") view of social research.

> We might say that those who most explicitly assert and wish to practice the democratic virtues have taken it as their assumption that all social facts—with the exception of exclusion and economic hardship—must be *accepted*, not merely in the scientific sense but also in the social sense, in the sense, that is, that no judgment must be passed on them, that any conclusion drawn from them which perceives values and consequences will turn out to be "undemocratic."[2]

All the books under review (setting apart, obviously, Mr. Owen's study of courtly love) are influenced in some degree by this assumption.

Then Trilling spoke of "the large permissive effect the Report is likely to have." It was, in fact, as he saw, a powerful agent of revolution; it changed the sexual more of the time. Its scientism, its half-concealed complacency toward mechanical models of the life of feeling and action, the bad faith which presented as a purely technical work what it was foreknown would be widely read by an audience quite unable to weigh its claims, all these gave it a unique authority wherever it was read. Without Kinsey's work other writings about sexual matters would have taken a different form. Perhaps none of our authors except Father Ginder and Dr. Tripp takes Kinsey's conceptual apparatus quite seriously—the idea of "outlet" in particular is much blown upon—but they are all of them influenced by Kinsey's investigative techniques and "democratic" assumptions.

2. Lionel Trilling, *The Liberal Imagination* (Doubleday Anchor, 1957), p. 234.

Morton Hunt's *Sexual Behavior in the 1970s* is the outcome of a "national sex survey" *(sic)* conducted under the auspices of the Playboy Foundation. Thoughts of lung cancer research by the makers of cigarettes may trouble the mind; but I think we may accept without fretting Hunt's assurance that no pressure was put upon him by any of the Playboy entrepreneurs or personalities to come up with what they wanted. What the survey shows is no doubt much the same as what the Kinsey Institute for Sex Research would have found had they conducted the survey (they were in fact invited to do so but declined).

The year 1966, in which *Human Sexual Response* by Masters and Johnson was published, is a critical date. Morton Hunt comments that the study "was considered obscene only by a few intellectual troglodytes." This seems to mean that the principle that sexual performances should be studied by witnesses, photographed, monitored by machines, and that these performances should be between partners provided for experimental purposes, is not open to moral objection. There is a curious inconsistency—perhaps a remnant of the troglodyte mentality?—in the Masters and Johnson procedures: male subjects were sometimes provided with surrogate partners, that is, females with whom they had had no earlier emotional or sexual involvement; female subjects never.

Voyeuristic attitudes to sexual activity were being popularized at the same time, through X-rated movies and such spectaculars as *Oh! Calcutta!;* the works of the Marquis de Sade and Genet (these two were given awards for moral pioneering by unimpeachable authorities) were to be had in cheap editions; innumerable popular works combining descriptive material with how-to instructions were being published. Things went hard with the troglodytes in those years. We had left behind the period in which it could be a matter for thrilling moral dispute whether or not to put *The Catcher in the Rye* on reading lists for adolescents.

Morton Hunt is able to establish that since the time of Kinsey there have been some important changes in activities and attitudes: a decline in petting among adolescents and young adults and an increase in copulation; a blurring of the distinction—this had been one of the most emphatic and surprising of the Kinsey findings—between working-class and middle-class sexual behavior; a substantial increase in extramarital sexual activity among young couples under twenty-five—this seems to go with a lessening of guilt feelings and anxiety over adultery, whereas among older couples, even among the liberated practitioners of serial monogamy, adultery is still a grave matter; a slight but significant increase in sadistic and masochistic practices, and a notable increase in sadistic and masochistic elements in sexual fantasies.

Marital swinging, that is, group sexual activities—the swinging party blurs into the orgy—seems to fascinate Americans and there is a vast amount of folklore about what goes on in the suburbs, but it doesn't seem to be increasing. The increased acceptance of fellatio, cunnilingus, and buggery has already been noted. Religion—Catholicism, Orthodox Judaism, old-fashioned Protestantism—still has some restraining influence on the disposition to be sexually adventurous, but it does not seem decisive in the samples studied.

Like many books commenting on sexual behavior—Paul Robinson's book is an exception—Morton Hunt's is confused, in a way almost impossible to clarify except at tedious length, when it raises larger moral or anthropological questions. Hunt assumes that moral and anthropological problems are readily soluble. The following passage is not picked out as especially simple-minded but as altogether representative of his standard of analysis.

> Merely because a practice has been observed in a number of societies does not mean that it has been *functional* for all those involved in it. Slave prostitution, the castration of captured enemies and the rape of the enemies' women have all been fairly common in the annals of human history, but distinctly dysfunctional, biologically and psychologically, for the victims. Moreover, since such be-

havior is far from universal, it cannot be instinctive ... but must be the product of specific social conditions; in any society where it is not sanctioned, its normality depends on the degree to which it is in conflict with the cultural norms of that society. What one can legitimately say, therefore, is that any sexual act that has been observed in many societies, and that has few or no adverse effects upon most of the persons involved in it or upon the societies themselves, may be considered natural or normal even when practiced in a milieu in which it is mildly to moderately deviant.

The Modernization of Sex is clearly written and often theoretically acute. In choosing Havelock Ellis, Kinsey, and Masters and Johnson as the chief shapers of sexual modernism, and in paying attention to Freud but noting that in this connection his role is ambiguous, Robinson seems right. Freud is on the whole, from the standpoint of sexual liberation, a menacing figure. That energy which gives the Oedipal situation its power and is a perpetual source of ecstasy, pain, and guilt, all three tightly bound together, is plainly the tremendous and fascinating mystery hedged about historically with rituals and taboos. Freud thought the best we could hope for was to temper the sadness of human life. Others, Marcuse in one way, Norman O. Brown in another, have drawn from Freud's description of infantile sexuality a message of sexual liberation (not at all the kind of liberation talked about in the how-to and gourmet books now current). This is to suggest that sexual repression is an option, not the necessary agony, the foundation and safeguard of all the institutions of civility, Freud thought it was.

Havelock Ellis was the first systematic student of sexual behavior to attempt something far-ranging and comprehensive. He was not preoccupied with the pathological, as were Acton and Krafft-Ebing; his books were filled with a winning, slightly dotty crusading spirit, and in this he is a true grandfather of sexual liberation. He is perhaps the last of the major writers on sex whose prose is elegant and easily understood. He was a cultivated man, with a humane education, who was interested in a variety of topics (he wrote a fine book on Spain).

Robinson gives us horrific specimens of the dense jargon of modern writers; it isn't, very often, especially in the case of Masters and Johnson, a question of determining what has been said, but rather of finding out if anything at all has been said. Robinson follows his account of Havelock Ellis with a masterly, judicious, and penetrating study of the work of Kinsey. He seems to me to show, though I think he might not agree, that Masters and Johnson are the most effective revolutionaries of all. Their impenetrable jargon—Robinson misses this—is an important rhetorical weapon (compare the prose of the literature put out by the Church of Scientology); it softens up the half-educated public who are grown accustomed to the idea that what is important and improving is always framed in obscure incantatory prose, whose passion for "meaningful communication," "new values," "new parameters of significance," is a kind of intellectual masochism, so that when something intelligible does come through it is embraced with sobbing relief.

Robinson is inclined to think Masters and Johnson conservative because, as he shows in a fine piece of exegesis, they are firmly loyal to what they think to be the domestic ideals of the post-Christian suburban middle class. But what Masters and Johnson want to bring about and what historically it will appear they did bring about may be different things. At any rate, they have fostered a vast industry of sexual therapy to propagate and nourish their distinctive attitudes. It is in their attachment to the therapeutic that they are distinct from Kinsey and closer to the aims of Havelock Ellis.

The combination of lucidity and analytical power in Robinson's work is impressive. What I find disappointing is his failure (scarcely a refusal, for I don't think he sees the necessity) to give a critical account of his own position. For example, he writes: "Masters and Johnson's tough-minded, materialistic examination of human sexual response can be said to serve progressive ends. But their materialism can also become reactionary, especially when it results in transforming sex into labor." I can see that progressive means good and reactionary bad, but I'm not clear what the criteria involved are. I suppose he doesn't see any point in discussing whether or not a society which is "liberated" and hedonistic in its view of sexuality is superior to a sexually repressive and conservative society or in discussing how far these alternatives are the only choices open to us.

He sees, I think, that, in the past, modes of sexual behavior have been one thread in the web of culture, and that the pattern and integrity of the web depend upon the disposition of every thread; yet he isn't inclined to speculate about the remoter consequences for our culture of deep changes in sexual mores. Like Hunt he seems to think moral questions are not too troublesome within the realm of sexuality and that sensible men get along well enough with a doctrine that makes the rightness and wrongness of actions depend upon their anticipated consequences. Consequences as they are anticipated are certainly among the criteria we use in deciding what we ought to do. But they can't be decisive in crucial cases. First, in many situations, predicting consequences is an idle occupation just because we can't know; to claim that we can is to play at being God. The decisions to bomb Hiroshima and Nagasaki are melancholy evidence of this; the torture of political prisoners to extract information from them, something that goes on all over the world under both "progressive" and "reactionary" regimes, provides another example. Second, whether or not a man has a given virtue (veracity, for example, or justice) is settled by noting how he behaves in some of those cases where calculation about consequences doesn't seem to matter and might even appear, in an affair of such moment, ludicrous (Thomas More or Bonhoeffer or those doctors who in the death camps refused to perform medical experiments, even though they knew these experiments would be performed by others).

I may be wrong in thinking that Robinson's cool approach to sexual theories—he calls rival theories ideologies in conflict—carries with it any information about the author's moral attitude. The moral presuppositions of Havelock Ellis, Kinsey, and Masters and Johnson are pretty evident, and not to comment on them (beyond saying that sexual issues are "emotionally charged") seems to imply that here, at any rate, they are not plainly open to criticism. It is also true that there is a deeply rooted view in the modern philosophical schools that what is the case, how the world is, what exists "according to nature," never imply anything about morality; and Robinson's restriction of the field of inquiry would on this view be evidence of a commendable intellectual austerity.

It is at least conceivable that the attitudes and practices commended by the *sansculottes* and *tricoteuses* of the sexual revolution exhibit relations of manipulation and exploitation that spill over into other activities. For Nancy Friday, women's ability to frame sexual fantasies is a badge of their liberation, a sign of their independent sexual power. It doesn't seem to worry her that a persistent feature of many of the fantasies related is a sadomasochistic view of what is desirable in sexual relations. There are fantasies of rape, beating, violation by dogs and donkeys, intercourse with statues, fantasies of being tortured in concentration camps. The sadness and triviality of this book are almost unbearable. One can't forget the girl of seventeen who relates that she has given up lesbian fantasies and fantasies of orgies, for, "Now I'm into emotion . . ."; or the woman who in the transports of the marriage bed calls out the name of her lover; fortunately, she tells us, "My husband is deaf in one ear!" One wonders about this last example, as about some other of the items in the collection; perhaps the striking impression of verisimilitude belongs to art rather than life.

The Homosexual Matrix defeats me. If Monsieur Homais could have written a book, this is the kind of book he might have written. Kinsey and Morton Hunt are vulgar democrats; Dr. Tripp is a vulgar *encyclopédiste*. His book professes to be an inductive study founded upon the observation of a group of fifty-two persons, eight of whom Tripp came to know well. These persons are mentioned in the first pages, then virtually disappear, though it may be that the confident generalizations that distinguish the book owe something, though we are never told what, to Tripp's acquaintance with his sample. His evidence is largely literary and there is an extraordinary dependence upon the Kinsey volumes. They are cited as authoritative, even though they have been critically studied for almost thirty years and even though there is good reason to think that the sexual scene has changed a good deal since the 1940s. (A curious feature of Tripp's references is that page numbers are given only when the reference is to a periodical.)

Tripp was closely connected with the original Kinsey research and plainly idolizes Kinsey. He shares many of Kinsey's prejudices and has some of his own. Unlike most workers in this field, for whom Christianity, with its supposedly Manichaean streak, is the great poisoner of the wells of truth, Tripp thinks Judaism the most dangerously repressive moral system, Christianity being only a channel of Jewish influence. He doesn't understand Judaism. For example, he writes: "The invention of the post-exilic Judeo-Christian tradition was to establish the claim that sex was *only* for reproduction and to label all other uses as perversions." There is a confusion, shared by most writers in the field, here between the view that the *function* of sex is reproduction and the view, never maintained by any serious person, so far as I know, that the *justification* for each sexual act is reproduction. It has rarely been held that it is wrong as such for the involuntarily sterile or those past the age of childbearing to copulate. In any case, Tripp might care to look at the Mishnah. According to Eliezer the Great, "the *duty of marriage* enjoined in the Law is: every day for them that are unoccupied; twice a week for labourers; once a week for ass-drivers; once every thirty days for camel drivers; and once every six months for sailors."[3] All this seems a bit excessive for reproductive purposes.

3. *The Mishnah*, translated from the Hebrew by Herbert Danby (Oxford, 1933), p. 252.

Tripp's attitude to history is, to put it gently, careless. He tells us that "at the Council of Mâcon held near the end of the sixth century a major issue raised was whether or not women were human beings. After careful deliberation, and then by a narrow margin, it was decided that they probably are human." Westermarck (no page numbers given) is the cited authority for this strange anecdote, and Westermarck cites Gregory of Tours as printed in Migne. Tripp ought first to have used his common sense. He knows perfectly well what the Latin theologians then thought of the place of Mary in the scheme of salvation. He ought to have known that the bishops would have been familiar with and would have taken as authoritative the Roman martyrologies which included the names of such women as Cecilia, Anastasia, Perpetua. There is something excessively strange about the story. If Tripp had gone to Migne he would have discovered that Gregory tells us *one* bishop raised the question as to whether "human" should be applied to women in the same sense as to men (what his motives, logical or other, were in putting the question isn't clear) and that his colleagues thought he was wrong.

Many women will find Tripp's work offensive; most readers will find it at least curious. He has a chapter entitled "The Origins of Homosexuality." One reads the chapter with growing disbelief. It is all about the origins of *male* homosexuality; there are a few parenthetical remarks about female homosexuality. Indeed, the whole book is predominantly about male homosexuality. There are some good things in the book, notably some interesting theoretical analyses, but most of the good things are rather the *obiter dicta* of a reflective man of some experience than the judgments of a social scientist. The chapter "The Question of Psychotherapy" contains much shrewd comment. He has a good argument to show that perfect rapport between sexual partners may deprive the relationship of strains and tensions that tend to intensify the interest of the partners in each other. Since he holds that there are deep differences between male and female psychology, he endorses the view that

15

heterosexual partnerships rather than homosexual are likely to remain interesting and rewarding over a long period. His clarification of the concepts of inversion and transvestism is useful and discredits much of the folklore.

Aristotle (*Nicomachean Ethics*, v. 7) remarks that "of political [here "political" has a greater breadth than in its modern use] justice part is natural, part legal—natural, that which everywhere has the same force and does not exist by people thinking this or that; legal, that which is originally indifferent, e.g. . . . that a goat and not two sheep shall be sacrificed."[4] Aristotle doesn't think it is easy to distinguish one kind of justice from another. He is claiming that we are compelled to make a distinction between what is required or forbidden simply in virtue of the culture we live in and what is required or forbidden in a more stringent sense. An ability to make this distinction may even be a mark of sanity. One who thought how we are to pick our teeth in public a grave matter would be deranged; so would one who thought the requirements of the Nuremberg Laws under Hitler were brute features of the national culture about which further questions couldn't be raised. No decent or sane man, we should be inclined to say without formality, could have accepted such requirements as morally binding. It is also plain that what is in itself indifferent, e.g., whether to drive on the right or the left, may become a stringent requirement through agreement.

That is, there are three things: what is required or forbidden by a culture where falling in with the culture or not doesn't seem greatly to matter; what is required or forbidden belongs to the culture but its being agreed upon makes it morally obligatory—I must drive on the right, I must keep poisons in *blue* bottles; what has prescriptive or interdictory force "but does not exist by people thinking this or that." It is interesting that Aristotle, on the whole not very interested in absolutes, should have bruised himself against this problem. In the biblical tradi-

4. *The Nicomachean Ethics*, translated by Sir David Ross (London: World's Classics, 1969), p. 124.

tion there are three things a man may not do, even to save the city or his own life: he must not worship false gods, he must not spill innocent blood, he must not commit any of the sexual sins forbidden by the Law. Leon Roth remarks that these prohibitions "are specifically distinguished from ritual and social commandments," that is, their force "does not exist by people thinking this or that."[5]

It is very common now for people to find such a discussion boring and stupid. They are confident there is a hedonistic calculus that will get them out of their moral difficulties and they have a strong impression that somehow or other it has been shown, to all except a few religious freaks, that *all* moral requirements "exist by people thinking this or that." To argue that there must be such a thing as being in the right if it is possible for a man to think he is in the right seems to them mere logic-chopping.[6] It isn't then surprising that in the works so far discussed there is no serious consideration of the moral problems that may be raised by changes in the sexual mores of our society; still less is the notion ever canvassed of the possibility of there being in this field absolute interdictions. Very occasionally, perhaps, this is discussed, but with derision, as modern chemists would talk about phlogiston.

It is as though somewhere in life there must be a happy corner where menacing authorities, sad consequences, agonizing choices, tragic blunders don't exist or don't count. Elsewhere in modern society everything is harsh, acrid, dark, and no one can wish away what is disagreeable. Once there were those who offered mescaline or LSD or other magical substances as the ultimates in happy corners. The dark and the acrid turned up there, too. Free sexual activity seems at first glance to offer a happy corner where all is sweetness and light. A second or a third glance leaves one a bit unsure. It may occur to us that the makers of the how-to and gourmet books, and the prophets

5. Cf. Leon Roth, *Judaism: A Portrait* (London, 1960), p. 68.
6. I think I got this argument from Professor G. E. M. Anscombe, in conversation.

upon whom they rely, are absurdly trying to make the erotic tractable and domestic. The student of the Song of Songs or of the *Symposium* isn't likely to make this mistake, even if he offers no cure for our disquiets.

Christians and Jews have been pressed very hard in recent years. They are the only remaining public representatives of the old ethos set out in Deuteronomy. Orthodox Jews no doubt remain intransigent, but on the whole their witness is within their own community. Other Jews and many Protestants have been pushovers for the new ethos. Roman Catholics have been perhaps a little more resistant; but if the books by Father Ginder, Mr. Bianchi, and Ms. Ruether are in any way symptomatic, the Catholic attitude, at any rate in North America, is beginning to shift. Both books are important as symptoms rather than as new intellectual departures. Their standards of argument are poor and their understanding of history is defective.

Ginder is on the whole a very conservative priest, an un-reconstructed Tridentine, except in one respect. He has come to doubt the common opinions of moral theologians in matters of sexual morality and here he attempts to say why. His writing is free from high-minded and mystifying verbiage and the tone is engaging.

He has one good general point to make: that the Church has been false to its own message where and when it has picked out for severe treatment sexual sins but has treated sins against charity and justice lightly. In the classic tradition of Catholicism, charity—*agape*—is *the* virtue, and the rich and the oppressors of the poor, the proud and the hard of heart, are those most in danger of damnation. In Anglo-Hibernian and in American Catholicism sexual sins came to fill almost the whole picture. For Catholics fornication and contraception were what liquor and gambling were for the Methodists and Baptists.

This is the Church speaking from the pulpit and in the pious press. In its functioning, and especially in the confessional, the regime was much less burdensome, and some actions—masturbation is the example most adduced by Ginder—were in practice, though not in theory, treated as peccadilloes. Ginder thinks the Church has in such matters been split-minded and ought to square her public doctrine with her tolerant practice. He argues that masturbation and premarital copulation are not sins at all; homosexual activities aren't sinful either; and incest isn't so great a matter as people used to think it.

What makes Ginder a singular case is the setting in which these views are advanced. He doesn't in any sense belong to the Catholic avant-garde. He thinks abortion is always murder. He has nothing to say about war or racial problems. He seems to admire American society just as it is. If only the Church would change the established moral theology of sex, if only Paul VI would withdraw *Humanae Vitae*, a happy life would be there for all. (He even seems to believe, I can't think why, that if the Pope changed his mind on contraception this would affect the population explosion in the Indian subcontinent; most rural Indians don't even know the Pope exists.) He has no sense of the complexity of moral and anthropological issues, and no feeling for the immensely old human tradition of venerating the powers of sexuality and hedging them about with taboos, myths, piety; an attitude for which the sexual is not an extra, a relaxation, a consolation, a relief of tension, though it may also be all these things, but a part of the sacred order of the cosmos.

In the end the indictment of liberated sexuality of the kind raised by Ginder is that it makes sex trivial and empties life of its difficult mystery. Here is Ginder at his most reductive.

> When stimulated by friction of one kind or another, the human sex organs produce pleasure, relieve boredom, relax visceral tension, and tranquilize the nerves.

This is a trivializing view—if it were right we could look forward to the invention of the sex pill which would do away with all the troublesome interpersonal business. He combines it with a belief that only sexual problems stand between us and the coming utopia.

[After the appearance of the first contraceptive pills on the market] for the first time in history, a happy society based on power over nature was within the grasp of men.

Lest we should fear that lots of happy, consequence-free sexual activity would eat away our moral feelings, he affirms that the United States is a great place.

Though more openly sensual and pleasure-seeking in their sex activities than past generations, modern Americans are more other-conscious in their relations than ever before.

He doesn't intend the bitter truth in these words.
The Bianchi-Ruether volume starts off badly.

... the new awareness and activity against sexism in our culture constitute a probe to the underlying core of oppression that also manifests itself in totalitarianism, racism and militarism.

This is a representative sentence. It expresses a syndrome rather than a thought. It is assumed that there is a strong analogy and some kind of interconnection between "sexism" and "racism." This is simply a muddle.[7] It is to be feared "we shall get pictures of father ironing and little girls playing with trains long before we shall get much accurate and rational presentation of African, Asian and Caribbean peoples in children's books."[8]
As to probing "to a core," and a core that manifests itself, these seem strange matters. We probe to find out if something is there, and if we find a core we expose it or leave it where it is. Perhaps Bianchi would consider which of the following alternatives to "core" he would choose: "root," "foundation," "cause," "basis," "principle". . . . Given the kind of sentence it is, of course it doesn't matter; this is what is so depressing and even

7. Cf. Ann Dummett, "Racism and Sexism: a False Analogy," *New Blackfriars* (Oxford), November 1975.
8. Dummett, p. 485.

frightening, for the corruption of language is the worst corruption of culture.

After this sad start we have to push our way through pages besprinkled with isms of all kinds and with *identity, perspective, dimension, privatize,* and such. In this respect Ms. Ruether and Mr. Bianchi share the same kind of prose. Ruether doesn't think, as does Bianchi, that "deprecate" means "depreciate," "tenuous," "tentative." Her infelicities are more complicated. My favorite is: "[about 1900] the contradiction between an intensified domesticity and a sexually repressive culture became so violent that the underside of Victorian society exploded in the Freudian revolution." The idea of psychoanalysis as the great fart of late Victorian society has a crazy charm, but I fear this isn't what Ruether is getting at.

The intention of *From Machismo to Mutuality* is to give a general historical sketch of relations between men and women "from remote pre-history, whose roots are lost in the mists of time" *(sic)*, down to the present day of reckoning for sexism; and to follow this with proposals for the shaping of Western society in the light of Christian principles as these are understood by the two authors. The abolition of sexism involves the abolition or transformation of all other social institutions in the direction of a socialist-anarchist community.

History is a difficult matter, the balance of truth is hard to come by, generalizations may turn out to be ill-founded even where they at first seem most plausible. Even if history were not so hard to get right, a conscientious writer heeds Voltaire's *On doit la vérité aux morts*. None of these maxims is heeded. Ruether's chapter on women during the rise of industrial society is a model of how not to write a historical sketch. It is full of loose and often highly misleading generalizations—e.g., "With the loss of a servant class, who entered socialized work at the end of the nineteenth century"—and she writes down, in the vehemence of her anger against patriarchs and capitalists, statements that she would know to be false if she were to reflect for even half a second—e.g., "The very fact that children were

21

produced by sexual intercourse between the parents became the well-concealed scandal of *every* Victorian household" (my italics).

What a *mean* view of the past Ruether gives us! The kind of public—not very critical, eager to be *au courant* with new ideas, anxious over gnawing moral problems—Bianchi and Ruether write for deserves something richer and more nuanced than the chronicle of domestic slavery and human exploitation it is offered. The nineteenth century is one of the *great* centuries of Western civilization: we think of George Eliot's calm intelligence, of the strongly lived, reflective lives of Newman and Mill, of such women as Josephine Butler and Florence Nightingale, of such historians as Maitland and Parkman, of Darwin. Ruether writes about the nineteenth century as the Enlightenment historians used to write about the Middle Ages. She may say she is concerned with one theme and can't put everything in; the point is that most of her readers have no setting in which to place what she so bleakly and inaccurately tells them, and are therefore likely to stay in a condition of idiotic complacency about our life now.

Bianchi and Ruether have some sharp things to say about sexual liberation taken as a sign of liberation from all servitudes; in this they are shrewder than Ginder. They don't at all commend sexual liberation in any of the popular contemporary senses. They view marriage in the way now fashionable in much Catholic writing: ideally it is a rather jolly and affectionate relationship of equal comrades who recognize each other as persons in their own right. This seems somehow not so much wrong as cerebral; and avoids what is deepest in the Jewish and Christian traditions of marriage; that in marriage the partners are *one flesh*. There is a lot of Gnosticism, a false spirituality, an excessive concern with what Lawrence called "sex in the head" (this is characteristic of the entire sexual revolution). The excessively spiritual attitude is perfectly exemplified in Bianchi's comment on adultery (a coarse expression he avoids): "My own conviction is that the overwhelming majority of married people cannot cope creatively with extra-marital sex." Presumably their consciousness hasn't been "raised."

Bianchi and Ruether write professedly as Christians but they have little attachment to the concrete tradition. Ruether traces the "betrayal at the heart of the Gospel" back to the earliest times and fixes responsibility for this on the apostolic age. This is intelligible, even the ABC of the matter, if we too take ourselves to be traitors; but proclaimed solemnly, without humor or irony, as a condemnation of the apostolic age by the creative copers of the Western world, it is a bad joke.

Courtly love was one aspect of medieval asceticism, and yet it tempered it, deepening and complicating sexual feeling. The two most influential books on the matter are C. S. Lewis's *The Allegory of Love* and Denis de Rougemont's *L'Amour et l'- Occident* (published here as *Love in the Western World*). The origins of the cult are obscure and the features of its development matters of controversy; what there can be no doubt about are the large consequences of the cult as, through poetry and, later, the novel, the romantic sensibility came to be shared by more and more people. Mr. Owen has given us a useful popular history and a pleasant picture book. He sees that the really interesting problem about courtly love is its legacy rather than its origin. The most obvious facts of the legacy's history no one could dispute over: Ronsard, Shakespeare, Cervantes, the novel from *Clarissa* to *A Farewell to Arms* or *The Heart of the Matter*, all these and much ephemeral stuff enlivened European culture.

The complex picture of male and female sensibility we find in the tradition isn't easily judged. What is certain is that without the tradition we shouldn't have had the heroic woman. As I think about Rosalind *(As You Like It)*, Beatrice *(Much Ado About Nothing)*, about Elizabeth Bennet and Lucy Snowe and even Trollope's Lily Dale, I become more and more dissatisfied with our stereotypes of female exploitation and oppression, and with such repeated general statements as that sexual feeling was not, in the Victorian age, supposed to exist in respectable women.

Trollope was a popular novelist who depicted and even shaped *les moeurs de province,* and he is therefore good evidence for what people thought and felt in the mid-Victorian period. Now, it is plain that most of his heroines glow with sexual feeling. The liberationists judge the past badly and this coarsens their judgment of the present.

It is impossible to say whether or not there is in the Western world a growing synthesis of ideas on sexual behavior. There is evidence that the loosely associated ideas held by sexual liberationists are deeply affecting groups that have traditionally accepted the biblical prohibitions of fornication, adultery, and the rest. Father Ginder's book and *From Machismo to Mutuality* may represent what is going on in the minds of some religious believers in our society. How far such changes speak of a collapse before current fashion we need not determine. We must assume that there is a felt logical compulsion in any line of thought that ends with the acceptance of modes of sexual activity that have always been thought forbidden among orthodox Jews, most Protestants, and almost all Roman Catholics. Bianchi and Ruether stress as a premise of their argument a special view of the marriage relation and would, I think, argue that their view is a legitimate development of what is implicit in the Christian view of sexuality. Bianchi writes:

> Mutuality for us men points towards a threefold acceptance that is denied in contemporary society. It means that we cultivate the feminine dimensions of our male selves, that we respect the diversity of homosexuality and that we come to live with women as diverse but equal others who do not exist for our aggrandizement but for our mutual growth as persons.

This rests upon what I have already called Gnosticism. The belief is that in a union of love between two people, personal, nonsexual relations are fundamental and that to these relations, between males and females, males and males, females and females, there may be added sexual relations, as relaxation, play, signs of affection, on occasion as means to procreation. In the biblical tradition, by contrast, it is the sexual relation between man and woman that constitutes the relation of marriage, and the love of friendship—this can exist outside marriage and without sexual relations—is an added grace that belongs to the perfection of marriage but isn't constitutive of it. The sexual relation of marriage lies within the protection of covenant: the communally gratified exchange of promises establishing mutual and exclusive rights to sexual activity between the parties. Thus, for the partners in marriage conceived in this way, adultery resembles self-contradiction.

If Jewish-Christian prescriptions about marriage and sexuality are in retreat, this is in part a consequence of the secularization of social life. *Pietas* toward natural processes and established institutions is rare in our society and not often counted as a virtue. The absence of *pietas* toward some natural processes is beginning to disturb us; this is evident in the growth of movements to protect and purify the natural environment. *Pietas* toward sexuality, so strong a feature of the entire human past, seems much diminished. If there is sense in Freud, if anything of what Lawrence says in "A Propos of *Lady Chatterley*" and *Fantasia of the Unconscious* is to the point, too easy and familiar an approach to sex risks more than we can understand. The taboos of the past, the touch of hysteria men of today discover in past religious pronouncements on the topic, speak of the uncannily powerful in sexuality; and it seems an implication of what Freud thought that the ending of sexual repression could unravel the web of culture. This may be what the Marxist regimes obscurely understand. No high culture without guilt, as Philip Rieff would say.

A culture without guilt, in which all conceivable sexual practices are innocent, such is the happy arrangement many believe to be already practicable. There may be guilt over one's inadequacies as a sexual performer (this is what Robinson has in mind when he remarks that the Masters and Johnson program tends to transform sexual activity into labor); but the great guilt

25

and the dread that went with the violation of the taboos will have gone.

In such a culture it would come to be thought that all sexual mores essentially resemble those other things that are in themselves indifferent. (Of course, *some* sexual mores are plainly of this kind: the male-superior position in coitus would be an example of a local and temporal peculiarity.) But it may be that other things (the prohibition of incest, for example) can't be settled "by people thinking this or that." If everything is interesting and nothing is grave, satire cannot bite and tragedy gives way to the social illness of maladjustment. For many, human life under such conditions would lose its music. It may be that life can't in any case be like this and that the hurt of guilt and the pity and terror of tragedy are ineluctably with us, as much in our sexual relations as in all other dealings between members of the family of man.

Can We Live the Good Life? ————

The elective system in most North American universities and colleges means that undergraduates may, within limits, make up their own combinations of subjects during their three or four years of study. In the better institutions there may be much guidance, even direction. But the ethos expressed in the system relies upon the idea that by right the undergraduate chooses for himself the subjects that compose his course, just as the customer chooses dishes as he passes along the cafeteria line.

This is an image of how moral education and moral growth are often presented, and Alasdair MacIntyre is concerned to combat what this image represents. Especially in schools of education and in institutions for the training of social therapists, we find it asserted that children must be free to choose their own values and that the exercise of choosing is a means of growing up morally. Such thoughts may have odd consequences for the curriculum. Boys and girls who couldn't write on a sheet of paper, or put into speech, even the rudest outline of what Christians or Jews believe and who couldn't recount

---

From *The New York Review of Books* (November 5, 1981); review of Alasdair MacIntyre, *After Virtue: A Study in Moral Theory* (University of Notre Dame Press).

accurately a single story from the Old or the New Testament, may be given instruction in Hindu and Buddhist metaphysics; this, lest the teachers commit the offense of proselytizing on behalf of the traditional European culture.

Sex education may consist in presenting in picture and word a variety of "lifestyles" from which the pupils may choose what they prefer and what they want to try out. Those who argue for the freedom to choose values and lifestyles are commonly in bad faith. It is tacitly understood that certain values are not to be chosen, those of racism or sexism, for example. This presents difficulties. If the values of racism and sexism are not matters for legitimate choice, why isn't this true of other values too? If there are criteria, as seems to be supposed, for deciding that common decency excludes our judging people by their skin color or keeping women out of the professions of medicine and mechanical engineering, why may there not be criteria for deciding that chastity is a virtue or acquisitiveness a vice?

Where does the notion that values may be chosen come from? At first sight, it seems strange to say that whether or not veracity or courage is to count as a virtue is a matter of how one chooses. It isn't clear that a person who maintained that mendacity is a virtue or a harmless quirk of character would be maintaining anything intelligible. All the same, many are thoroughly convinced that somehow it has been settled by educated people, and especially by philosophers, that moral principles are, and can only be, matters of choice; for in this field true and false have no legitimate application. It may be true that most people think that x is right/wrong/good/bad; but it is commonly held to be a mistake to suppose that "x is right/wrong/good/bad" *can* be true or false.

Moral judgments, according to the reigning view, are either expressions of feeling or are derived from or justified by general principles for which no higher reasons can be given. It follows that important moral differences can be clarified but not settled dialectically, for there is no matter of fact (apart from the fact that particular people make particular moral judgments) involved in the discussion, no question of truth or falsity. In this respect moral questions can no more be matters of dispute than can questions of taste. This may be hidden from us because in a culture of any strength there will be a practical concurrence of moral judgments or because, as Hume thought was at least probable, there is "some internal sense or feeling, which nature has made universal in the whole species" (*An Enquiry Concerning the Principles of Morals,* Section I).

It may be argued, and is argued by Professor MacIntyre, that this belief—generally called by him "emotivism"—about the nature of morality and about the logic of moral discourse is fundamentally the same in the thought of moral philosophers who at first strike one as maintaining very different accounts of these topics: Hume, Price, Sidgwick, G. E. Moore, Stevenson, Hare.[1]

What all these thinkers have in common is the belief that no account of "good," or "right," or whatever other concepts may be thought central in moral discourse, can be given such that this account can legitimately be inferred from any set of true statements about how things are with men in the world. No functional account can be given of man (as the Aristotelians have, it is thought, mistakenly believed was possible). We can say that a watch is a good one if it goes on telling the correct time; but we can say this because a functional account of a watch can be given; indeed, we shouldn't grasp what a watch is unless we already had implicit knowledge of its function. We can say of a watch's appearance that it is pleasing, and from

---

1. G. E. Moore, certainly when he published *Principia Ethica,* argued that "*x* is good" can be true or false, since it is a judgment that a given state of affairs has the property of being good and that its having this property is independent of what the person making the judgment thinks. But it turns out that for Moore such a property is "non-natural" and that this means that there are no acceptable procedures, as there would be for the ascription of "is six feet tall" or "is the professor of philosophy at the University of Laputa," for settling the truth of "*x* is good" in any given case.

this verdict no appeal can go out. But our knowing that a given object is a *watch* rests upon our already knowing what its function is, and with it goes the factual, verifiable application of "good" to it.

Now, if those philosophers are right who maintain that no functional account of man as moral agent can be given, it seems that they are advancing, not a thesis in philosophy, but a necessary truth; and if this is so, then to want to apply "true" and "false" to moral judgments, or to statements of general moral principle, is as intellectually disreputable as to assert that phlogiston exists. It is worse, perhaps, for that is a mere empirical matter, and to err in such a matter is just to be mistaken, whereas to make a logical howler, once its howlerishness has been plainly exhibited, is to choose to be intellectually self-stultified, as were those medieval philosophers who held there could be propositions that were true in philosophy and false in theology, and vice versa.

Professor Alasdair MacIntyre has always been bold. In attacking in *After Virtue* what has become a ruling orthodoxy in moral philosophy, both at the academic heights and in the lower depths of the educated public ("true for me," "right for me," "choosing one's own values," and so on), he is attacking a tradition well established in the universities and a way of discussing public policy that shows itself in the work of sociologists, jurisprudents, political scientists, and in the practice of an army of therapists. *After Virtue* is a striking work. It is clearly written and readable. The nonprofessional who would nod over Rawls on justice, or simply give up, will find MacIntyre perspicuous and lively. In this respect MacIntyre stands within the best modern traditions of writing on such matters. He treats his readers as Hume did, or Adam Smith, and although his dissent from the conclusions of these philosophers is nearly complete, he has them in mind in resisting the complication of discourse that has accompanied the professionalizing of moral philosophy and the social sciences.

His argument is, in the first place, that philosophers have

been mistaken in supposing that the ultimate premises of moral argument are arbitrary, and necessarily so. In our culture, as in the history of mankind, there seem to be many conflicting moral principles, and it is commonly argued that this plurality simply has to be accepted, so far, that is, as thinking is concerned. Of course, the acceptance of such plurality in modern liberal societies itself constitutes a common ethos of these societies. MacIntyre believes that our moral discourse contains fragments and traces of concepts and arguments that make sense within a different, largely forgotten scheme of thought and practice, and that this is what accounts for the intractable character of some problems in modern ethical discussion, the inconclusiveness, the seemingly interminable character of the arguments over the logical nature of ethics. "We have lost . . . our comprehension, both theoretical and practical, of morality."

It is no use, if we want to get back our comprehension, asking the analytical philosophers to work harder. That a sense of desperation characterizes much of their work, both on abstract ethical questions and on the problems of war and peace, and on social and sexual relations, as in the periodical *Philosophy and Public Affairs,* is a consequence of the disintegration of a coherent moral discourse. Some of the concepts most in use issue in paradox: they seem to belong to a scheme in which it is understood that there are nonarbitrary standards in morality, and ways of settling clashes of principle while leaving the principles in question unreconciled.

To give an example in what I think to be the spirit of MacIntyre, Max Weber in his essay "Politics as a Vocation" argues that there is an irreconcilable conflict between the imperatives of politics and those of morality. He is aware, and says so, that this involves a paradox: that the man of politics *ought* (that is, he is morally obliged), in virtue of his commitment to his calling, to flout the highest demands of morality; and Weber cites with approval Machiavelli's praise for the citizen who prefers the greatness and safety of the city to the salvation of his soul. Ever since Kierkegaard, to say that something is paradoxical, that we live agonizingly within the paradox, somehow implies—this isn't Kierkegaard's fault—that the speaker is profound, courageous, and exceptionally sensitive. Perhaps—this would be MacIntyre's argument—we ought to be deflationary and substitute for "paradox," "paralogism," or even "sophism."

The moral tradition we now possess only in fragments is most adequately, though imperfectly, expressed in the *Nicomachean Ethics* of Aristotle; and MacIntyre is prepared to call himself an Aristotelian, even though he thinks some important parts of Aristotle's analysis are mistaken and that the analysis generally is embedded in a teleological biology that we need no longer believe. How this classical tradition was fragmented is a question of history; it is hard to answer, for modern history is written "after the Fall," that is, after the fragmenting of the tradition, and is therefore governed in its style and in its canons of judgment by the pluralism on which the practical ethos of liberal society is grounded. (To come across a historian, Acton, for instance, who will have nothing to do with moral pluralism, or one who finds the advance into the bureaucratic individualism of modern society something tragic and not hopeful, as Burckhardt did, is often a cause of irritation and perplexity. Only now, perhaps, after the experiences of National Socialism and Stalinism, are we disposed to think there may be something in the moral intransigence and dislike of modernity of such historians.)

A partial explanation of what MacIntyre takes to be the loss—roughly, since the eighteenth century in Europe—of any grasp of a rational and consistent set of moral concepts, with the consequence of arbitrariness already mentioned, may be explained by his aphorism: "A moral philosophy . . . characteristically presupposes a sociology." This is so because action is necessarily intentional and strives to embody what it seeks, not discretely but in a connected way, in institutions and practices. This is what Plato and Aristotle, Aquinas, Hume, Adam Smith, understood; and they therefore thought it a part of the task of moral philosophy to give an account of the social expression of intentions. Adam Smith's *Inquiry into the Nature and Causes of the Wealth of Nations* followed quite naturally his *Theory of Moral Sentiments*. Intentions embody themselves in institutions and practices and in reflective, systematic accounts of the ensemble of social relations at a given time and in a given region. (Examples of such accounts would be the *Nicomachean Ethics* and the *Politics* of Aristotle, and the *De Monarchia*.)

Today, even when philosophers have a strong interest in the working out of the social implications of a chosen moral standpoint, they are, if they are liberals, committed to finding the standpoints of their opponents at least interesting; and they are drawn into debate over the violently different inferences made from what appear to be the same moral principles. For example, some of those for whom "equality" is a major value may be supporters of socialism and others may want to restore competitive capitalism; here it isn't clear which of the two parties has made the big mistake, or, indeed, whether it can properly be said that any mistake has been made.

MacIntyre believes that the impossibility of deriving moral principles or judgments from statements about the world of men has seemed to many an unassailable necessary truth because they have lacked a sufficient historical consciousness. They have considered the moment of transition from the old view of man as finding his fulfillment in his social role to the new view of man "as an individual prior to and apart from all roles"—the transition, as Sir Henry Maine put it, "from status to contract"—as the freeing of man from historical limitations that held him back from realizing his full nature. This mistake, as MacIntyre would consider it, parallels, and is historically connected with, the belief that the breaking of the network of institutions and practices that held back the development of capitalism under the old regime, and the forsaking of some moral beliefs (that acquisitiveness is a vice, for example, or usury a sin) of precapitalist society, brought into existence for the first time a society of free individuals. This new society is thought to be a "natural" society whose laws of existence transcend the limitations of the historical.

The most powerful criticism of the new view came from Marx and Engels, who argued for the historicity and mortality of all social and economic formations; but MacIntyre is able to show that Marxism also shares the prejudices of the liberal age. The separation of the individual from any necessary connection with his social role links the neoconservatism of the Reagan and Thatcher administrations with those who are cast as their ideological opponents. This explains the sense of unreality that often seizes us when we view the political confrontations of our time. "The creatures outside looked from pig to man, and from man to pig, and from pig to man again; but already it was impossible to say which was which."

The transition from man as identified with his social role to man as having an individuality prior to and outside all social roles is historically and in thought complicated. For MacIntyre in heroic society (the society celebrated in epic) "morality and social structure are in fact one and the same. . . . There is only one set of social bonds. . . . Evaluative questions *are* questions of social fact." In fifth-century Athens Homeric models are still influential, but now "the conception of a virtue has . . . become strikingly detached from that of any *particular* social role." This makes moral analysis more difficult, and some of its "cases" are reflected in the drama of the period. All the same, it is within the setting of the *polis* that moral injunctions and the virtues are intelligible. But great as are the contrasts between different historical periods, it is only with the late-eighteenth and early-nineteenth centuries in Europe that we arrive at the notion of man as having moral substance apart from and prior to *all* social roles, as, for example, in the work of James Mill.

That the older morality survives only in fragments, then, helps to account for the inconclusiveness of philosophical arguments over moral matters and for the curious character of a wisdom which tells us that heroic individuals may be summoned, in the name of morality, to disregard the commands of morality.

The latter point isn't just a matter of theoretical interest: it arises in our own period in connection with decisions to use nuclear weapons, in the use of torture in cases where this is employed with reluctance, in the fighting of guerrilla wars and in military responses to them, in some kinds of medical research, in lying for the sake of what is taken to be some great public good—all the topics, that is, that are treated with such candor, such sharpness, by Machiavelli, though the cases examined by him are naturally different.

Now, we might simply note that this is so, and accept that the moral pluralism of our society is the historical successor of varying moral traditions, of, for example, the heroic moralities presented in ancient epic, of the ethical debate in fifth-century Greece, of the prophetic morality of the Old Testament, of the ethics projected by the New Testament. After all, no one seriously doubts the intellectual patrimony of the European cultures. But MacIntyre goes further: he argues that the modern world has made a mistake; that there is a human *telos*, an end or object, which enables us to give an account of the virtues and of moral judgment that is *right*, as against the *mistaken* accounts current in our present culture; that the medieval Aristotelians, in adding to the premise that goodness lies in what fulfills the human *telos* a second premise, that what fulfills the human *telos* is commanded by God, rightly draw our attention to the stringency and imperative character of moral rules; that the authentic core of the complex Jewish, Christian, and Islamic tradition has a claim upon us that liberals thought to have been set aside forever.

This makes MacIntyre sound like a romantic, a praiser of the far away and long ago, one who wishes to put us all to sleep under the rule of pope and emperor, a de Maistre of our time who improbably teaches philosophy at a North American university. Any filleted or boiled-down version of *After Virtue*, and a review can scarcely avoid some filleting or boiling-down, may convey such an impression—one that greatly misleads. MacIntyre is less ideological than I may have made him sound, and in his approach to the fundamental problems of moral philosophy he is by no means alone among his contemporaries. Philippa Foot,[2] Elizabeth Anscombe, and others share his uneasiness over the general drift of academic ethics.

Many important aspects of his argument can only be referred to glancingly. There is for example the brilliant use he makes of contemporary work in sociology and anthropology. Given his general thesis, the exploration of such work is necessary; and in what he writes he shows himself unique, among those who philosophize in the English language, in his grasp of theory in the social sciences, and in the subtlety of his analyses. A good example is his bringing together of the thought of Weber with that of the moral philosophers whose work he (MacIntyre) criticizes.

> . . . Weber's thought embodies just those dichotomies which emotivism embodies, and obliterates just those distinctions to which emotivism has to be blind. Questions of ends are questions of values, and on values reason is silent; conflict between rival values cannot be rationally settled. Instead one must simply choose—between parties, classes, nations, causes, ideals. *Entscheidung* [decision] plays the part in Weber's thought that choice of principles plays in that of Hare or Sartre. "Values," says Raymond Aron in his exposition of Weber's view, "are created by human decisions . . ." and again he ascribes to Weber the view that "each man's conscience is irrefutable" and that values rest on "a choice whose justification is purely subjective."

There is passion in the book, above all in what he writes about Greek, Icelandic, and Gaelic epic; the ethos of the heroic cultures he evidently finds close to his own feeling about human life, though of course he doesn't deny the limitations of this ethos. He has some important reflections on tragedy and on its per-

---

2. Her work is, strangely, not referred to in the bibliography or in the text.

tinence to ethics, especially in what he has to say about Aristotle, whose view that all conflict is in principle eliminable from human life is shown to involve a misreading of the Greek tragedians. His treatment of such topics could only be discussed adequately at some length; I mention these matters to give some impression of the richness and density of the book.

About two things something must be said. How can there be an argument to show that there is a human *telos* and that virtue consists in its fulfillment? And how, granted that such an argument has some plausibility, can the argument be morally relevant in the societies, liberal or not, of today, bureaucratic and individualist as they undoubtedly are? Here, in a very schematic form, is what I think MacIntyre to be saying on these two questions.

Moral pluralism—Sir Isaiah Berlin is perhaps its best and most thoughtful exponent—denies that questions about the good life for man can be given only one set of coherent answers; there simply are radically different choices within morals, and within liberal society we have to put up with this variety. Our willingness to put up with moral variety may be thought a test of our liberal virtue, and this may suggest MacIntyre is right in finding a deep inconsistency in liberalism. To maintain that there is a good for humankind may in our world seem almost unintelligible, or to be understood only after a strenuous effort of the historical imagination; for, as MacIntyre emphasizes, "the presupposition which [Plato, Aristotle, and Aquinas] share is that there exists a cosmic order which dictates the place of each virtue in a total harmonious scheme of human life. Truth in the moral sphere consists in the conformity of moral judgment to the order of this scheme."

How can there be a cosmic order that requires us to pursue certain ends? Obviously, it can't be a merely external order. The order must show itself in what human beings characteristically seek. This seeking can only show itself in the concrete, in the behavior and proclamations of particular communities as they persist through time, with those traditions which are a communal memory. Any serious discussion about morality must therefore begin with what people say, spontaneously or reflectively, about what things are worth aiming at.

This feature of Aristotle's discussion in the *Nicomachean Ethics,* and of Plato's discussion in several dialogues—"What do men say that justice is? What do men say is the good for man?"—is, MacIntyre suggests, not Greek parochialism, or not only that: moral philosophy has no choice but to begin with the subject matter of (in Aristotle's sense) the political scientist. That moral philosophy begins with the forms of life within which men live in particular places and at particular times doesn't mean that it is not also concerned with the universal, the formal. The form is only to be found—here Aristotle differs from Plato—in the particular. It is to be found as much in those states of affairs that are the subjects of moral appraisal as in those forms of nature ("humanity," "animality," "psyche," etc.) we encounter in experience and sort out in thought. For Aristotle and for MacIntyre, what men characteristically seek, and say they seek, is *eudaimonia* ("happiness" is the usual—too thin—translation). What this may be is elucidated in many ways; but it will evidently include the free activity of reason, for it is reason that distinguishes man from the other animals.

The virtues are acquired, steady dispositions which enable us to lead lives of free, rational activity. It is thus not arbitrary that justice, courage, veracity, and so on are counted as virtues, capacities necessarily connected with the good life. Aristotle strikes us as deficient in one respect: he talks, not about the human *telos,* but about the *telos* of free Greek males, a *telos* they do not share with slaves, women, and barbarians (those who are not Greeks, don't live in city-states, and make ugly noises when they speak). One of Christianity's historical achievements is to have rescued Aristotle from some of these parochialisms.

The virtues are not just instruments for producing the end, *eudaimonia;* they are, in their exercise, a part of the end. Similarly, what is wrong with the vices—the dispositions to take innocent life, to steal, to lie, to betray—is that their exercise is not only a means to unhappiness: a life characterized by these vices is the worst life conceivable, the tyrannical life described by Plato. Such a life, even if it is filled with a variety of pleasures, is utterly hateful, whereas the life of virtue, even if it is accompanied by great pain and ends in public disgrace, is intrinsically desirable. (This is Plato: Aristotle doesn't fully face this grim possibility; we could say that he doesn't accept the possibility of tragedy, which may always disrupt the progress in happiness of the good life.)

To understand what MacIntyre makes of Aristotle we have to look at what he (MacIntyre) calls a *practice*. A practice is a cooperative human activity which has its own standards of excellence; in part these standards go with the nature of the activity, in part they define and circumscribe the activity, making it *this* activity. Games, farming, furniture-making, the pursuit of the natural sciences, the art of politics in small communities, the group of arts involved in making and sustaining family life, these are all practices. Sometimes they serve goods outside themselves, as when one plays a game for health or pursues a science for money; but they require for their well-being an understanding of those satisfactions which are internal to the practice. Try to think of a great musical performer—Schnabel, say—who was motivated only by the prospects of money and fame.

It follows from what a practice is—it isn't even necessary to argue that a good life depends upon our engaging in some practices and benefiting from the practices of others—that it cannot be successfully pursued without certain cardinal virtues. For MacIntyre a virtue is an acquired human quality the possession and exercise of which tends to enable us to achieve those goods that are internal to practices, and the lack of which effectively prevents us from achieving any such goods.

As he writes:

> It belongs to the concept of a practice as I have outlined it . . . that its goods can only be achieved by subordinating ourselves to the best standard so far achieved, and that en-

tails subordinating ourselves within the practice in our relationship to other practitioners. We have to learn to recognise what is due to whom; we have to be prepared to take whatever self-endangering risks are demanded along the way; and we have to listen carefully to what we are told about our own inadequacies and to reply with the same carefulness for the facts. In other words we have to accept as necessary components of any practice with internal goods and standards of excellence the virtues of justice, courage and honesty.

Given that practices are central in human life, it is thus possible to deduce the major virtues from the conditions for the successful pursuit of the practices.

MacIntyre does not argue that an account of the virtues as getting their point from their roles in the furthering of practices is an exhaustive one. He writes:

> . . . unless there is a *telos* which transcends the limited goods of practices by constituting the good of a whole human life . . . a human life conceived as a unity, it will *both* be the case that a certain subversive arbitrariness will invade the moral life *and* that we shall be unable to specify the context of certain virtues adequately. . . . [T]here is at least one virtue recognised by the tradition which cannot be specified at all except with reference to the wholeness of a human life—the virtue of integrity or constancy.

The completed picture contains many puzzles. One question is how far the variety of human life and possibility can be brought within such an account. I think MacIntyre examines this question with skill, especially in his elucidations of such novelists as Jane Austen and Henry James and in his attention to dark corners of history. For example, in discussing a virtue not easy to describe, the virtue "of having an adequate sense of the traditions to which one belongs or which confront one," he startles us, and at the same time clarifies the virtue, by writing that "Cardinal Pole possessed it, Mary Tudor did not; Montrose possessed it, Charles I did not." Another question (emphasized by MacIntyre) is that posed in the *Antigone*: may it not be the case that moral principles, each of undoubted authority, are irreconcilable with each other? Perhaps the greatest difficulty is what we are to do within a bureaucratic and individualistic society, whose educational theories and practices, and its jurisprudence, are made and governed by those who think major moral principles are arbitrary. What is it to be a good man in such a society? Isn't MacIntyre just giving us a social anthropological account of forms of life that have charm just because they are gone forever?

From the "classical" standpoint it is the task of the polity to lead its members into virtue. But "the power of the liberal individualist standpoint partly derives," in MacIntyre's view, "from the evident fact that the modern state is indeed totally unfitted to act as the moral educator of any community." This may be too extreme. Court decisions, as in *Brown* v. *Board of Education*, have done much to improve the moral attitudes of American society. But in general MacIntyre seems to be right. There is something odd about the state's offering moral guidance if it is in many fields committed to the thesis that there are no moral truths to be determined. The modern citizen lacks a homeland, a *patria*, for the political authority is merely

> a set of institutional arrangements for imposing a bureaucratised unity on a society which lacks genuine moral consensus. . . . Loyalty to my country, to my community—which remains unalterably a central virtue—becomes detached from obedience to the government which happens to rule me.

What then are we to do? Some of us may be fortunate in belonging to marginal communities with strong traditions (some Jews, some Catholics, some Orthodox, Mennonites, Hutterites). More of us can in some degree live within a historical tradition, represented chiefly by a mass of texts and commentaries, written and unwritten—poems, fairy stories, fables, religious histories, philosophical classics—that can still nourish the attentive reader. It is highly important that children should be given stories of lost children, wise animals, wicked step-mothers, fortunate younger sons; without them they are left, MacIntyre writes,

> unscripted, anxious stutterers in their actions as in their words. . . . Vico was right and so was Joyce. And so too of course is that moral tradition from heroic society to its medieval heirs according to which the telling of stories has a key part in educating us into the virtues.

We have to look, he continues, for "the construction of local forms of community within which civility and the intellectual and moral life can be sustained through the new dark ages. . . . We are waiting not for a Godot, but for another—doubtless very different—St. Benedict."

The Benedictine communities were able to conserve what belonged to the past and civilize the present because they cared more for the good life, lived at first in simple, unpretentious ways, than for civilization. Perhaps this is one of the things Mac-Intyre wants us to take away from our reading of his book. Many will hate the book and its line of thought, finding it "reactionary" and unenlightened. But it is something to have a book, devoted to certain quite central technical philosophical questions, which is likely to produce so passionate a response.

Morality and War ————————————

There are two doctrines about war which often look like two sides of the same doctrine: absolute pacifism; and the doctrine represented in the American Civil War by General Sherman, that war is absolutely hellish and cannot be refined, and that therefore in the fighting of wars that are justly engaged in there are theoretically no limits beyond which the righteous side may not go. Absolute pacifists similarly argue that war is hellish and that to fight it in any way is the moral equivalent of fighting it in every way; killing a solider is not in the end morally distinguishable from killing a civilian, bombing an arms factory (or trying hard to be accurate in doing so) is not really different from bombing a residential neighborhood. In for a penny, in for a pound, if stealing a lamb will get one hanged one may as well steal a flock of sheep: proverbial wisdom is used to suggest that if one abandons the position of absolute pacifism, distinguishing among different kinds of killing is a piece of moral imbecility.

This running together of the two doctrines may even have

From *The New York Review of Books* (December 8, 1977); review of Michael Walzer, *Just and Unjust Wars: A Moral Argument with Historical Illustrations* (Basic Books).

political force in some situations. The British Campaign for Nuclear Disarmament of the 1950s, and the consequent pressure within the Labour Party to "ban the bomb" had a complicated background, and many considerations, moral and political, influenced its supporters and opponents. Supporters of the Campaign included absolute pacifists who were against bombs and weapons of every kind, as well as a few who didn't really object to the bomb but objected to its being under the control of a non-communist government. They also included a number of people who supported the theory of the just war and argued that in no conceivable circumstances, or at least in no circumstances at all likely to arise, could any war, even a war of defense, be fought justly with nuclear weapons. The late Hugh Gaitskell, who fought against the Campaign and in the end defeated it, drew most of his support, as one would expect, from "realists" who were not interested in legal and moral analysis; but a lot of support came from old pacifists who thought that the opponents of the bomb who were not pacifists were simply confused, so evident was it to them that war is hell and that therefore you either go in for it or you don't.

As Michael Walzer is able to show, in his powerful book *Just and Unjust Wars*, these are two strange doctrines. There really is and has been for some centuries now an agreement of mankind that war is, like any other human enterprise, subject to the judgments and restraints of morality and to the restraints of law. There is a mass of international conventions and agreements, and a body of precedents set out in the books of the international lawyers, all of which set limits to what may be done by the armed forces of powers at war. Not that such limits are always respected, any more than domestic laws against criminal conduct are always obeyed. But they are often respected, they have often made a difference to the ways in which war has been fought, they are often to be found in the manuals of military law in the hands of soldiers and have sometimes been effectively cited by conscientious soldiers pressed into illegalities by less scrupulous political leaders.

What is to count as murder is harder to establish in the flurry of war than in times of peace. But the proceedings against Lieutenant Calley showed that it can reasonably be maintained, against the Sherman doctrine, that soldiers who in combat cannot be censured for killing their enemies may properly be censured for the killing of innocent civilians, that is, for committing murder. We think Rommel acted rightly in burning Hitler's order that enemy troops found behind the German lines should be killed and not taken prisoner; he refused to be an accomplice in murder.

Sherman's confidence that in evacuating and burning Atlanta, an undoubted atrocity, though not a large one by the standards of our own time, he was acting legitimately came from his view that the cause of the North was just and that the war had been forced upon the Republic. This is not quite the same as the Clausewitz doctrine that "war is an act of force which theoretically can have no limits," for Clausewitz's view is connected with his belief that war is a natural activity of states and that acts of war may be imprudent but cannot be considered criminal. Sherman adheres firmly to one part of the theory of the just war, namely, that some wars are just on the part of some of the states who fight them, some unjust; and that in general a war of defense against aggression is just. Now, given that power A acts justly in fighting against B, the aggressor, it follows that the war is unjust on the part of B. On this theory there are only two possibilities in the case of a given war: that it is just on the part of one belligerent, unjust on the part of the other; or that it is unjust on the part of both. But a war that is for one belligerent just in its inception may become unjust in many ways. It may be fought by methods so unjust that the original justice is, so to speak, outweighed; or the original objective, to repel aggression and to seek recompense for damage, may be forgotten, swallowed up in newly conceived ambitions.

We have to distinguish, the theorist of the just war has always argued, between *jus ad bellum* and *jus in bello*. This means that there are criteria by which we can establish the justice of a particular belligerent's cause, those factors that entitle a state to go to war; and that there are also criteria for determining how far justice is observed in the conduct of a morally approvable war and how far the state concerned really sticks to its original good intentions. What begins well may be conducted badly and end in evil. Perhaps history leads us to expect this in any long war, and this is why the call for "unconditional surrender" is often so wicked, as it tends to prolong the war. We are too familiar with "the desire to injure, the cruelty of private vengeance... the arrogance of conquest, the appetite for power, and all such things, that are rightly condemned in war" (Augustine in *Contra Faustum*, cited by Thomas Aquinas, *Summa Theologiae* IIª IIae Q.xl art.1, *Utrum bellare sit semper peccatum*), and with all the good intentions along the road to hell, to have strong hopes for any war, no matter how just in its inception. The war that began in 1939 with the Nazi-Soviet partition of Poland was on the part of the Western powers as near a textbook example of the just war as we are likely to get; by 1945 we were still glad that the war had been won and that the powers of darkness in Central Europe had been destroyed. But a sad procession of names—Dresden, for instance, and Hiroshima—passed through our minds with a kind of rebuke, so that we felt relief but not joy, satisfaction of a sort but not the peacefulness of a good conscience. If we felt less than perfect satisfaction in victory, this could be traced in part to a consciousness of crimes committed in the course of a just struggle; we—or at least those who shared the feelings I have sketched—were not satisfied that in a just cause all things are permissible.

What I have said so far is substantially a part of Michael Walzer's argument, though he may not agree with the ways I have put certain things. He shows that most of us use the language of the just war theory, at least when it suits us, that we think certain wars right, others not, and that we praise or censure the ways in which wars are fought. Even those who hold theories of history or human nature that don't strictly allow for this kind of moral discourse (except as ideology) find it hard to be consistent. Writing to Engels, Marx expresses his hope for a Prussian victory in 1870, arguing that "if the Prussians are victorious, then the centralization of state power will be favorable to the centralization of the working class." But when he came to draft a resolution for the General Council of the International he wrote: "On the German side, the war is a war of defense." Later, he censured the decision of the Prussians to continue the war after Sedan, and spoke of "the crime of reviving, in the second half of the nineteenth century, the policy of conquest." Walzer rightly comments "that Marx has enlisted history not in the service of the proletarian revolution but in the service of conventional morality."

It is just a matter of fact that international laws and conventions exist and provide us with the principles of judgment that enable us to discriminate between just and unjust wars and between the just and unjust conduct of wars. Questions about how we know that such principles *really* bind us are, very properly, set aside by Walzer. Uniformed soldiers shooting at each other or bombing the supply routes of armies are engaged in an activity that is justifiable if the war itself is justifiable; the same soldiers lining up villagers not in the army, many of them women and children, and shooting them are engaged in a massacre, that is, they are killing the innocent, committing murder, just as are terrorists who set off bombs in public places or those (if there have been any such) who poison the public water supply.

But what about soldiers who are serving on the wrong side in an unjust war? It seems, at first glance, a part of the theory that they, unlike the soldiers serving on the right side, are committing murder when they kill their military enemies. For a number of reasons Walzer thinks this won't do. First, the laws of war, everything that makes up "the war convention," as he puts it, have been devised to guide the conduct of all the belligerents. It is a part of the convention that soldiers may be attacked and that most others may not, at least not intentionally. Then, it is not easy for ordinary men to sort out the rights

47

and wrongs of armed conflicts; they have really no choice about accepting the judgment of the public authorities, and of course they may be and often are compelled by law to serve in the armed forces. This is not the same thing as being compelled to commit murder, and only those who kill the innocent, and more especially military commanders who order this or are accomplices in it, ought to be held responsible for their actions. It is in the interest of all that war, quite apart from the attribution of guilt to one or other party, should be a limited activity.

All this seems a matter of common sense. All the same, I wish Walzer had gone into this question in more detail. One reason why the theory of the just war has often made people smile is that it seems (as distinct from the war convention) an idle theory, since it has to do only with the conduct of governments, and governments, as history shows us, are not morally scrupulous. The Spanish king asked the University of Salamanca if it was just to conquer the Indians of South America. Salamanca immortalized itself by saying it was unjust; but the Spaniards conquered the Indians all the same. Vitoria, one of the most important of the just war theorists, argues that the individual subjects of the ruler cannot be expected to sort out for themselves the moral issues of a particular war: "if the subjects cannot serve in the war except they are first satisfied of its justice, the state would fall into grave peril."

That this issue was more than academic comes out in the discussion between the disguised Henry V and the common soldiers on the eve of Agincourt, in Shakespeare's *Henry V*.

King Henry: . . . Methinks I could not die anywhere so contented as in the king's company, his cause being just and his quarrel honorable.

Williams: That's more than we know.

Bates: Ay, or more than we should seek after, for we know enough if we know we are the king's subjects. If his cause be wrong, our obedience to the king wipes the crime of it out of us.

Williams: But if the cause be not good, the king himself hath a heavy reckoning to make when all those legs and arms and heads, chopped off in a battle, shall join together at the latter day and cry all, "We died at such a place." . . . I am afeard there are few who die well that die in a battle; for how can they charitably dispose of anything, when blood is their argument?

Now it would seem unlikely that in a modern society, at least where there is a fair measure of freedom of speech and information, and where formally and in some degree actually governments are responsible to the electorate, we can be satisfied with what Bates says. We are in some degree morally implicated in the policies and decisions of government; and since the making of policy is a continuous thing, and new decisions are always being made, we may have a duty to bear witness for truth and justice where we think the government is mistaken or criminal. Walzer tells us he began to think strenuously about the problems discussed in his book when he found himself entangled in the political and moral questions raised by the American intervention in Vietnam. This is the period when there began to appear what is sometimes called "selective" conscientious objection, that is, conscientious objections to the war in Vietnam by men who were not pacifists but thought it morally unsafe to serve in what they took to be an unjust war.

This is not the first time conscientious objection by those who are not pacifists had appeared. There were a few cases in England in the Second World War, mostly Roman Catholics whose citing of the scholastic authorities greatly perplexed the tribunals set up to judge the validity of the conscientious objectors' arguments; the judges knew where they were with Quakers or Jehovah's Witnesses, but these others they found queer cattle. There were even a few cases in Hitler's *Reich*, perhaps more than we know about; that we know about one case, that of the Austrian martyr Franz Jägerstätter, in some detail is accidental, a piece of good fortune, as Gordon Zahn explains in the book he devoted to his life and death.[1]

We seem, then, to be moving away from the position that the justice of a particular war is a matter on which the good citizen is bound to take the advice of the public authorities. Indeed, if we take the just war theory seriously, we are bound, surely, to presume that any given war is more likely to be unjust than just. As we have seen, if one belligerent is in the right it follows that the other is in the wrong; and since there must be many cases where both parties are in the wrong the presumption against the justice of a particular war is always very strong. Aquinas's question, *Utrum bellare sit* semper *peccatum,* plainly assumes this. Under a despotism or an aristocracy it seems plain that the individual citizen is more a subject than a citizen; and under such a regime it probably makes no sense to impose on ordinary men duties they cannot comprehend. But this isn't the situation in North America or Western Europe. Here it is assumed that it is the right and may be the duty of the citizen to deliberate over matters of public policy. It may be said that it is also a part of the theory of democracy that majorities decide. In many matters this is true. But there seems to be an absurdity in applying the judgment of the majority to matters of deep principle—war and peace, slavery, racial oppression. And it isn't perhaps an accident that it is precisely in the democracies that those who have wanted to commend particular wars, knowing that the moral foundations were flimsy, have sometimes put out that most undiscussible of doctrines, "my country, right or wrong." This is a paralogism, for it implies that one may have a duty to act wrongly.

That we are better off if the war convention applies to all soldiers, quite apart from the justice of the cause they fight for, Walzer clearly establishes. It is a fact of modern society that most citizens if called upon by their governments will "wear weap-

1. *In Solitary Witness* (Holt, Rinehart and Winston, 1965).

ons, and serve in the wars," and will not make moral discrimina-
tions likely to imperil their own governments; but it may be
presumed that even in uniform and under arms they know that
certain kinds of killing are murder, that it is a crime to kill
prisoners, and so on. There is now an impressive body of case
law to support the doctrine that superior orders do not excuse
those who commit common crimes. Such a doctrine is in the
common interest and ought to be cherished, even if it tends to
blur the distinction between those who are fighting for the just
cause and those who are fighting against it.

All the same, it is conceivable, if conventional wars continue to be fought, that the selective conscientious objection that
became common in the United States in the course of the Vietnam war may represent the beginning of something, or rather
perhaps the extension of something that began in the civil rights
movement of the sixties. A conscientious refusal to observe Jim
Crow laws is not unlike the conscientious refusal to fight in an
unjust war. In both cases, it may be argued, the state is engaged
in destroying the moral foundations of society. Disobedience is
obedience to a law that stands above positive law. Many legal
theorists won't like this at all, for it seems to suggest that legal
positivists from Hobbes and Austin down to our own day have
blundered. I suspect the thought that Blackstone was in this fundamental matter in the right will be unwelcome in many law
schools and will be thought a confused inference from the
"morally tinted words," as Justice Holmes put it, that still haunt
legal discourse.

It has often been argued, by those who hold that the individual citizen has no choice but to accept the competence of
public authority to call on him to serve in a given war, that since
the justification of war is a complicated business, relying upon
information known only to the public authority, it is ridiculous
to suppose that the solitary man can competently judge in such
a matter. This is humbug. Even if the original occasion of the
war's being fought is hard to analyze, it is scarcely possible in a
modern society to conceal *how* the war is being fought. Franz

Jägerstätter was able to say in response to the socially superior
and better educated men who counseled him to obey the call-up
that *everyone* knew what National Socialism was and what its armies were doing in the occupied territories. That is, even within
a totalitarian society where the means of information were con-
trolled by the state a poor and not very well educated Austrian
farmer was perfectly informed about the character of the war he
was ordered to serve in.

It is hard, then, to suppose that in a democratic society the
actual conduct of a war (as distinct from the cause of its being
started) does not come under the judgment of ordinary people.
This is not to suggest that we ought to consider those who
engage, voluntarily or under legal compulsion, in a war that is
unjust in its origins or becomes unjust in its development to be
murderers. Presumably those who serve and are convinced that
the war is unjust, or take part in the killing of the innocent, are
murderers. But if we consider the manifold pressures to which
men are subject in modern society we shall be inclined to doubt
the culpability of most soldiers in respect, simply, of their serving in the armies. All the same, we may look upon the period of
selective conscientious objection to the Vietnam war as the
beginning of a quite new way of understanding the responsibility of the citizen under democracy.

It may be urged, and is sometimes urged by Walzer, that
we must distinguish between a man's doing his duty and his
being a hero. A man who acts unjustly under the threat of death
is not a hero—there are some who refuse and are killed, and these
are heroes—but he can scarcely be accused of having failed to do
his *duty*, and later prosecuted for the failure. This strikes me as a
doubtful position. A man who does what he ought to do has done
his duty, and when this duty is hard and dangerous one who
does his duty is certainly heroic. What we can quite properly urge
in the case of men who act wickedly under the severest compulsion (the immediate prospect of death or torture) is that the degree of culpability is small or perhaps not there at all. This is why
commanders are held peculiarly responsible in all proceedings

concerned with war crimes: it is they who exercise the compulsion. But it seems to me important not to waver on the question of what is properly required of a man, even in extreme circumstances. Many things excuse in whole or in part; but what is excused must *need* excuse.

For Walzer, as for perhaps all reflective men who examine the history of the world since the 1930s, National Socialism is, even more than Stalinism, the Great Beast, uncanny, evil in a unique way; it has all the marks of what medieval men would have called the Antichrist. (Recent arguments that Hitler was a ruler much like the others, not unlike a Napoleon or a Cromwell, that the full scope of the Final Solution was something that may never have come under his notice, *et patai et patata,* such arguments strike most men of my generation—those who were young adults in 1933—as merely laughable, or would do so if laughter were possible in such a connection.) It was and is for us, given the character of National Socialism, a strong temptation to suppose that in fighting horror without precedent some suspension of moral rules that would have been binding in a fight with an enemy less thoroughly malevolent was allowable.

Walzer's position on this issue is nuanced and intricately argued, and one can't do justice to it in a short account. But since it is in my view the crucial experiment, as it were, for his general theory, something must be said about it. He rejects altogether the crude position that rules don't bind those fighting in a just cause, and the scarcely less crude position that they have the right, especially if things are going badly, to bend the rules in their own favor (though he recognizes that this is probably what would happen).

He begins by noting that *Fiat justitia, ruat coelum,* let justice be done even though the heavens fall, "is not for most people a plausible moral doctrine." He then goes on to advance what he believes is a plausible doctrine.

There is an alternative doctrine that stops just short of absolutism. . . . It might be summed up in the maxim: do justice unless the heavens are (really) about to fall. This is *the utilitarianism of extremity* [my italics], for it concedes that in certain very special cases, though never as a matter of course even in just wars, the only restraints upon military action are those of usefulness and proportionality. Throughout my discussion of the rules of war, I have been resisting this view and denying its force. I have argued, for example, against the notion that civilians can be locked into a besieged city or reprisals taken against innocent people "in extreme cases." For the idea of extremity has no place in the making of the war convention. . . . The rules are adjusted to the everyday extremities of war; no further adjustment is possible if we are to have any rules at all, and if we are to attend to the rights of the innocent. But now the question is not one of rule-making, but of rule-breaking. We know the form and substance of the moral code; we must decide, at a moment of desperation and looming disaster, whether to live (and perhaps to die) by its rules.

This is certainly a doctrine that most people are likely to accept—after all, many are utilitarians on most issues and Protestants no longer argue that it is always wicked to use bad means to a good end—but it is not clear in what respect it is plausible, given the other positions Walzer wants to hang onto. After all, the test that establishes whether or not a man has a virtue, that of veracity or courage, for example, is always what he does in an extreme situation when it is very hard to do the right thing or where there seem to be extremely plausible arguments for abandoning the precepts of the virtue in question, arguments to show that some great good may be had or some great evil avoided. But we might want to say, without being censorious, that a man who abandons the precepts has failed the test; the whole point of the precepts is not that they should be guides for conduct when things are going reasonably well, but lights for our feet when the path is dark. In the biblical tradition there are odd cases where "bowing down in the house of Rimmon" (that is, idolatry) is sanctioned for a good end; but on the whole it seems to be believed that we ought not to worship false gods or to spill innocent blood even for the safety of Jerusalem.

Of course, Walzer is writing in and for a secularized world and he can't therefore raise the question: Doesn't abandoning the rules in an extremity show that we don't think God will sustain his servants if they obey him rather than the promptings of human wisdom? But something rather like this question has to be raised even in a secularized world. Why should we keep the rules in a situation that is *less* than extreme when keeping the rules is to our disadvantage? Walzer thinks we ought to keep the rules in any situation that is not extreme; this is why he is on the whole so hard on utilitarianism. But if utilitarianism is what gets us out of our moral difficulty in the hardest case we can conceive, then it may perhaps be a serviceable doctrine in cases that are not so extreme. I think Walzer will find himself forced into this position; and what he writes on the "case" most relevant to this discussion strengthens my conviction about this.

The "case" is that of British bombing policy in the Second World War. As late as June 1940 bomber pilots were instructed to aim only at military or industrial targets. Late in that year the decision was taken to remove this restriction and to bomb cities without discrimination. At first the decision was secret and the Cabinet put up Archibald Sinclair in the House of Commons to deny that any change of policy had been made. By 1942 residential areas of Germany had become primary targets; the Government was committed to the view that mass bombing would have decisive importance for victory in that it would destroy civilian morale and cripple Germany economically. When this change of policy took place Britain was alone and the world expected a German victory. But even toward the end of the war, when the German armies had been broken on the Russian front, when the enormous power of the United States had come into the war against the Third Reich, the policy was maintained, and came to its remarkable climax with the bombing of Dresden in the spring of 1945. "The destruction of Dresden remains a serious query against the conduct of Allied bombing." Thus Churchill himself. And it seems hard to doubt that the bombing of Germany was the precedent for the fire-bombing of Tokyo and the use of the atomic bomb in the destruction of Hiroshima and Nagasaki.

Briefly, Walzer's position is that 1940 was an extremity of the kind he has in mind. Britain was faced with the ultimate evil and the moral limits to be observed in all situations not extreme fell away. But the extreme situation passed and what had in 1940 been justifiable ceased to be so. The bombing of Hiroshima and Nagasaki is more plainly indefensible. Walzer writes:

> [people] have a right not to be forced to continue fighting beyond the point when the war might justly be concluded. Beyond that point, there can be no supreme emergencies, no arguments about military necessity, no cost-accounting in human lives. To press the war further than that is to re-commit the crime of aggression. In the summer of 1945, the victorious Americans owed the Japanese people an experiment in negotiation. To use the atomic bomb, to kill and terrorize civilians, without even attempting such an experiment, was a double crime.

Outside the limits of the rare and exceptional extreme situation (e.g., Britain in 1940) we are to respect those human rights that war is designed to protect, and "we are not to calculate consequences, or figure relative risks, or compute probable casualties, but simply to stop short and turn aside."

We may look back upon those situations in which "the utilitarianism of extremity" was invoked and wonder how we should now judge the situation. Walzer does this in connection with what he calls "the dishonoring of Arthur Harris." Harris directed the strategic bombing of Germany from February 1942 to the end of the war. He believed profoundly in the necessity of terror bombing and fought hard against all attempts to divert bombers from this to other and more defensible tasks. Of course, such responsibility must rest upon the government and above all on Churchill, though that Harris acted in obedience to the orders of his superiors does not, as the precedents show, free him of blame. But alone among the more important British commanders Harris was not given a peerage, and the names of bomber crews who were killed, a vast company, are not recorded alongside the names of the men of Fighter Command in Westminster Abbey. Walzer says of such men that it may be that "they had acted well and done what their office required [but that they] must nonetheless bear a burden of responsibility and guilt. They have killed unjustly . . . for the sake of justice itself, but justice itself requires that unjust killing be condemned."

It will be noticed that Walzer both condemns and justifies Harris and his fellows and seems thus to be involved in a paralogism like that we saw to be involved in the maxim: My country, right or wrong!

He is later uneasy about this and reaches out for a support that is in fact a confession that in the situation of extremity (e.g., Britain alone, faced with the menace of the German armies, her very existence as a free people in doubt) moral principles that are available in all other situations just won't do the job we ask of them. He takes from Professor Thomas Nagel the idea that there are situations within which there is a tragic conflict of absolutist with utilitarian moral principles, situations within which "we know that there are some outcomes that must be avoided at all costs, and we know that there are some costs that can never rightly be paid." In Nagel's words, "the world can present us with situations in which there is no honorable or moral course for a man to take, no course free of guilt and responsibility for evil." Walzer then says that he has "tried to avoid the stark indeterminacy of that description by suggesting that political leaders can hardly help but choose the utilitarian side of the dilemma. That is what they are there for. They must opt for collective survival and override those rights that have suddenly loomed as obstacles to survival." But, he continues,

> I don't want to say . . . that they are free of guilt when they do that. Were there no guilt involved, the decisions they

make would be less agonizing than they are. And they can only prove their honor by accepting responsibility for those decisions and by living out the agony. A moral theory that made their life easier, or that concealed their dilemma from the rest of us, might achieve greater coherence, but it would miss or it would repress the reality of war.

Surely this won't do. It is a rhetorical solution to a logical problem; the talk about agonizing decisions has been too cheapened of late to be serviceable in such a context. The thought that rulers may properly opt for the utilitarian side of the dilemma because "that is what they are there for" is obscure to me; in just that sense what they are there for is to drop nuclear bombs or defoliate the forests of Vietnam.

Earlier in his book Walzer argues against the style of argument he here uses, showing with great force the weakness of all those commentators on American policy who attack "moralizing" and commend "realism" and modest aspirations. Such commentators were influenced by the late Reinhold Niebuhr, who was a great practitioner of the kind of rhetoric Walzer here falls into. But I discern behind such arguments a greater ghost than that of Niebuhr: that of Max Weber. For Weber the essence of political leadership in dark times is a willingness on the part of the leader to imperil his salvation for the sake of the collectivity: "it is with reference to such situations that Machiavelli in a beautiful passage . . . of the *History of Florence* has one of his heroes praise those citizens who deemed the greatness of their native city higher than the salvation of their souls."[2] Antinomians in a good cause, Promethean figures bearing the wrath of the outraged gods for the sake of humanity, Byronic heroes, almost, savoring their tragic destinies: such, I fear, are our patterns of imitation if we invoke, in the hard cases, the utilitarianism of extremity. But this would be (keeping to the

2. "Politics as a Vocation," in *From Max Weber*, translated and edited by H. H. Gerth and C. Wright Mills (London, 1948), p. 126.

58

case of the war with the Nazis) to present Hitler with a post-humous victory. The hubristic picture of leaders who at nodal points in world history transcend the moral constraints of ordinary men and sin *greatly* for the sake of the collective—this is the romanticism, full of bad pathos, theatrical, self-pitying, out of which National Socialism came.

My interest in those matters on which Walzer writes in such a way as to provoke further discussion may have concealed the fact that I find *Just and Unjust Wars* a magnificent book, an honor to its writer and to the milieu out of which it comes, a book that makes for a return of civilized discussion of the question of the morality of warfare. It is a plea that we should look at history, rehearse and examine the moral principles on which there seems to be a consensus as reflected in traditional practice and in the corpus of international law, and not be afraid of inferences. He says of those who argue for terrorism as the only weapon that can liberate the oppressed that they "have lost their grip on the historical past; they suffer from a malign forgetfulness, erasing all moral distinctions along with the men and women who painfully worked them out." His book is a powerful remedy for the malign forgetfulness from which we suffer. What he writes on the moral problems of guerrilla warfare and on the balance of nuclear terror, to mention two questions I have not had the space to discuss, requires the thoughtful attention of all those (and this means all of us) who have special responsibilities in this field. Of course, if soldiers, politicians, and public officials were to read and note what he has to say, this would be the best response Walzer could hope for.

Nuclear Catholics ────────────────

Michael Novak proclaims himself a Democrat and is no doubt registered as one; but the policies he defends and advocates, in social and political matters, are largely those of the Reagan administration. One comes across his pieces in such doctrinaire conservative periodicals as *Commentary* and the *National Review.* His position is full of interest for those who want to understand the historic shift in the foundations of support for the two American parties; and what he writes as a Catholic may tell us something of what lies behind the recent explosion of anticlericalism among those Catholics the French call *les bien pensants*—the right-thinking, respectable people who were formerly supporters of the influence of the clergy in public life but have in recent years become increasingly anticlerical. Some things have brought these *bien pensants* to a pitch of frenzy, and the latest of these is the intervention of the American bishops in the debate over the morality of nuclear warfare.

Novak sees himself as having a public role as teacher and

From *The New York Review of Books* (December 22, 1983); reviews of Michael Novak, *Confession of a Catholic* (Harper and Row); Michael Novak, *Moral Clarity in the Nuclear Age* (Thomas Nelson).

stimulator. He thinks he owes his readers a candid account of his beliefs. In telling us *Confession of a Catholic* is his *Orthodoxy*, not his *Apologia pro Vita Sua*, he seems, with the implied references to Chesterton and Newman, to be putting himself intellectually and spiritually into the big leagues. I think this would be to mistake his intention. He is just carried away by the need to make it plain that his *Confession* is *confessio*, an avowal of where he stands, not the story of his soul. But he does make large claims for his message. He sits in his Resident Scholar's *cathedra* at the American Enterprise Institute in Washington and surveys the state of the republic and the condition of the Catholic Church, and makes many judgments.

Since I want to concentrate on examining *Moral Clarity in the Nuclear Age* I won't look at the *Confession* in detail. The plan of the book is to use the clauses of the Nicene Creed, recited on Sunday and on great feasts in the liturgy of the Roman Church, as material for reflection. His historical approach is out of focus. The custom of reciting the creed at Mass is not so venerable as he thinks it is; the creed as we now recite it is not the one approved at the Council of Nicaea; it was made a part of the Byzantine liturgy very early but was not adopted for liturgical use in Rome until the eleventh century. Novak gets very confused over one of the clauses in the creed as we now have it (in the West), the famous *Filioque* (that the Holy Spirit "proceeds from the Father *and the Son*"), twice saying that it was used by Nicaea, and then interjecting, without tidying up what he has said, that "the *Filioque* is a medieval Western insertion." In fact the *Filioque* became popular in the West long before the Middle Ages, after the fifth century, and its use was resisted in Rome until the ninth century. I don't note such things in the spirit of pedantry. Novak is in my view right in what he has to say about the low standards of theological argument and historical information among "progressive" Catholics. But he puts his right to say this in peril when he shows a lack of concern for accuracy in elementary matters.

There is a problem, one that spills over into *Moral Clarity*, about Novak's approach to the language of the creed. He begins

61

his reflections with a thesis about language and meaning. It is briefly expressed as follows: "The same Creed is assented to by all, yet each believer utters a different Creed." This is explained fragmentarily. "The Creed can only be appropriated by individual persons in personal ways." (This seems vacuous but should be handled with care.) "Words of the Creed . . . even when spoken, forming decipherable words and grammatical sequences, . . . are only as intelligible as each hearer makes them." This thesis on language and meaning is accompanied by a philosophical prejudice that pervades the book. It is represented by: "It is pointless to write about Catholicism without writing first about God. And that means to write about experience, of a sort."

Those familiar with philosophical discussion will recognize where Novak is. Meaning for him is something conferred on language by individuals, and it follows from this that each user or hearer of a sentence means something slightly different from every other user or hearer. But, of course, it *doesn't* follow. To the question: How do we know this?—and does *this* question have a slightly different meaning for each hearer?—Novak replies by asking how else sentences can be intelligible ("only as intelligible as each hearer makes them"). I won't go into detail on these points. It is enough to say that a language has to be something public and shareable. No doubt words and sentences set up in users and hearers idiosyncratic feelings and associations. But if "The cat is on the mat" reminds one of Tabitha and another of Tiger, this has nothing to do with what makes us able to use the sentence, that is, with what gives it its meaning. I don't know why Novak wants to tie his exposition to exploded theories, at least not in the *Confession*. He does have an interest in the theory of language in *Moral Clarity*, as we shall see.

Novak's characteristic approach is shown by his use of the clause about God's paternity ("I believe in one God, the Father almighty") to discuss questions about feminist theology. Against the drift of this theology he claims that: "The same words said by a woman and by a man often have quite different symbolic meanings." *Often* have? *Quite different?* What words can these be? The words for colors? Words expressing concepts of number and shape? Sentences ascribing emotions to subjects? All this is very cloudy, and we are from time to time given a lot of pious waffle. For example, just after telling us that we "are not privy to the purposes or ways of God," he writes: "The Creator sees all creation as a seamless garment made real in one act of life and love." It would perhaps be all right for Novak to tell us that this is how creation seems to him; but to say that this is how God sees creation seems to get us nowhere. What would it be to claim that God sees creation under a particular description? In any case, if we are to be poetic about creation, it is safer to repeat what the masters have said:

> I saw Eternity the other night
> Like a great Ring of pure and endless light,
>   All calm, as it was bright. . . .

Vaughan is too wise to attempt an account of how the world looks to God.

Most of the public issues that exercise Americans are ingeniously brought into Novak's meditations on the Creed. Some good points are made. In particular, I have to think well of his argument that Christianity is ravaged by a new Gnosticism which minimizes the importance of bodily life; for he repeats my own arguments, set out long ago in *The New York Review.*[1] But it is depressing to note how much the attitudes of the paranoid right have taken over. About the Vietnam War he writes:

> Good people were asked to choose between siding with the oppressors or siding with the oppressed. (Inexcusably too late, one learned that siding with North Vietnam might also be siding with an oppressor, less technically powerful but more politically ruthless, of whom the "boat people" were to be the victims.)

1. "Sex in the Head," pp. 3-26 above.

Novak should know better than to put the dilemma in this way, for he knows—he is a student, and says he is an adherent, of the doctrine of the "just war"—that refusing on the ground of conscience to join in a particular war has no necessary relation to the character of the enemy. It is as though an opponent of dropping the atom bomb on Hiroshima and Nagasaki were to be taxed with supporting the Mikado.

On two points Novak has something unexpected to say. He opposes the current Catholic teaching on contraception, though, perhaps out of deference to the Roman authorities, he doesn't deploy his arguments *con brio*. And he advances shrewd criticisms of what he calls "Latin" Catholicism, something expressed in many Roman documents in which there is criticism of liberal capitalism and an implied undervaluing of the American political tradition.

Moral Clarity in the Nuclear Age has made a stir in the world. It is a criticism, in the form of an open letter, of the second draft of the American bishops' pastoral letter on nuclear war. (In the present volume Novak has added further reflections.) It first appeared in a new periodical *Catholicism in Crisis* and was seized upon by William Buckley, who devoted an entire issue of the *National Review* to reprinting it. As an open letter it has subsequently been signed by a multitude of supporters. The list here printed is something of a curiosity. It includes nine Republican congressmen, three Jesuits, four Buckleys, and Mrs. Clare Boothe Luce. It seems to have been smiled upon by some people in Rome and in West Germany and it may have made a difference to the final revision of the bishops' letter. It uses very strong language about the positions taken by the bishops. It professes to be a reaffirmation, adapted to our time, of the "just war" doctrine. It is not this. It is an attack on the traditional principles of Catholic morality and its central argument, which applies the concept of intention to the analysis of deterrence, is either a confusion or a sophistry.

Novak gives a reasonable account of the "just war" doctrine as it was first roughed out by Augustine and developed by such later thinkers as Aquinas and Vittoria. Most of those who are not pacifists give at least lip service to the theory, certainly as it bears upon the limits within which war can properly be fought, sometimes—but more rarely—as it bears upon what justifies a country in going to war. It isn't often realized how stringent a doctrine it is. St. Thomas's presumption that war is more likely than not to be sinful is shown by the title of the first article in his chapter on the question, "Whether or not war is *always* sinful."[2] The answer is: not if it complies with certain conditions and not if in the course of waging the war the conditions continue to be respected.

According to Aquinas and the later commentators, for a war to be just it must comply with these conditions: it must be declared by a competent authority; there must be a just cause; there must be a right intention in waging the war (that is, the original just cause must be kept in mind—the desire for more territory or the desire to humiliate would corrupt a right intention); violence must always be a last resort after alternative means, e.g., negotiations, have been exhausted; there must be good reason to think a victory is possible; it must seem reasonable and probable that the good to be effected will outweigh the bad consequences of the war; and the means employed must be such as to distinguish between combatants and civilians and between combatants and those who yield to their opponents and stop fighting.

Very startling consequences follow if we take these conditions seriously. We can no doubt make a list of classic textbook cases of war that is justified; but the list of unjustified wars will be so much longer that we shall be inclined to think the "just war" doctrine an idle one, for it seems to have no influence even on those who are by reason of their religious profession bound by it. The German attack upon Poland and its partition of the country in partnership with the Soviet Union in 1939 were by the classic standards undoubtedly unjust; but no German

2. *Summa Theologica* IIa-IIae, Q.40.

Catholic bishop carried out the duty of enlightening the consciences of the faithful in this matter. It is as though what is written in the theology books is preceded by a rubric, legible only to the trained eye: No matter what may be stated in this book, it is to be understood that the maxim "My country, right or wrong" must always prevail.

The "just war" doctrine has had more effect on the conduct of war. It is still commonly accepted that prisoners may not be killed or tortured; that the direct killing of civilians is wrong; that "open towns" are not to be attacked; and so on. When the British government decided, in the Second World War, to pass from its proclaimed policy of bombing only military objectives to a policy of area bombing, Archibald Sinclair was sent to the House of Commons to lie about it, and he denied there had been any change of policy. I mention such matters only to suggest that sound, religious men and leaders of democracies are in the heat of war liable to deceive themselves, to become morally self-indulgent, and to lie.

Defense against enslavement by a foreign power seems a good reason for fighting a war, provided the other conditions can be met. If the foreign power be a brutal totalitarian state, as the Soviet Union is, then we have strong motives for defending ourselves. What complicates the question, and what caused the bishops to write "The Challenge of Peace: God's Promise and Our Response,"[3] their pastoral letter, is the likelihood that a war between the Soviet Union and NATO would be fought with nuclear weapons; and the belief that the nature of nuclear warfare makes it morally certain that the discrimination required by the "just war" doctrine cannot be made. It is theoretically possible to have a nuclear exchange aimed primarily at the weapons of the opposing powers, though even this would bring about civilian casualties and other horrid consequences on an inadmissible scale. In any case, the ultimate sanction required by the theory of deterrence is the obliteration of enemy cities; this is one reason why

3. Washington, D.C., 1983.

the powers have nuclear weapons in submarines, so much less vulnerable to attack than missiles on land.

The Soviet Union is a society poor and miserable and economically very unsuccessful; and yet, so Novak believes, it is a deadly threat to the rich Western societies. It resembles, he thinks, the Khomeini regime in thinking that American imperialism is the great Satan; whereas for him, of course, it is the Soviet Union that is the great Satan—Tolkien's Mordor, perhaps—inspired as it is with a fanatical belief in the ultimate victory of communism.

The existence and purposes of the Soviet Union have so altered the way in which we should think about war that, Novak argues, we have to think about intention in a new way; he even says, and I don't in the least understand what he means by it, "that the complexities of nuclear deterrence change the meaning of *intention* and *threat* as these words are usually used in moral discourse." To say that the meaning of these words is changed is so obscure that without some analysis of examples—and none is offered—it is impossible to know just what Novak has in mind. He certainly doesn't talk, as he should, about intention (2) in such a way as to distinguish it from mere intention.

In fact, everything he writes seems to require us to understand intention in its common use in the language. As we shall see he thinks we can have a wicked intention, that is, to use nuclear weapons without discrimination, in order to further another, *good* intention, never to have to fight a nuclear war. The latter of course isn't and can't be an intention. Indeed, what is startling is that Novak's argument falls to pieces, not through oversubtlety or through some slip in a complex logical chain, but through his failing to make an elementary distinction between what we intend to do and what we foresee as consequences of our doing what we intend to do. That such a distinction has to be made is evident. Unless we can make such a distinction the distinctive doctrine set out in all the Catholic moral theology books, the principle of "double effect," has no grip.

No doubt if Archbishop Romero of Salvador had kept his

mouth shut and stayed in the sacristy he wouldn't have been assassinated, just as Benigno Aquino wouldn't have been shot had he stayed in academic life in the United States. But it would be preposterous to argue that, because each of these men foresaw his death as a probable consequence of his action, each man intended his death. A pilot who uses skill and courage to place a bomb as nearly as he can on a military target may foresee that his bomb will kill some civilians; but he doesn't intend to kill them. But it would be an abuse of the principle of double effect to argue that it is all right to obliterate a great city with a million inhabitants because there are military installations in the city. Such an action has always been held, by Catholic moral theologians, to be wrong without qualification and always impermissible. Killing the innocent as a means to no matter what good end is always wrong.

The following passages illustrate the confusions into which Novak falls in the matter of intention. First:

> Those who intend to prevent the use of nuclear weapons by maintaining a system of deterrence in readiness for use do *intend* to use such weapons, but only in order *not* to use them, and do *threaten* to use them, but only in order to *deter* their use.

Later:

> The fundamental moral intention in nuclear deterrence is never to have to use the deterrent force. . . . Besides this fundamental intention, however, deterrence requires by its nature a secondary intention. For the physical, material weapon is by itself no deterrent without the engagement of intellect and will on the part of the entire public which called it into being. . . . A people which would be judged incapable of willing to use the deterrent would tempt an adversary to call its bluff. Thus, a secondary intention cannot be separated from deterrence. Without that secondary intention, distinct from the fundamental intention, a deter-

rent is no longer a deterrent but only an inert weapon backed up by a public lie.

Finally:

> A society which possesses a deterrent also has an organized objective intention [something which shows itself in a society's military organization]. In the case of the United States, individuals add to this objective intention subjective intentions which are both fundamental—that the deterrent succeed in never being used—and secondary—that the deterrent be held in readiness for use. To say that a nation may possess a deterrent but may not intend to use it is fulfilled by the fundamental intention. Not so by the objective intention and the secondary intention. To condemn weapons held in readiness (and the secondary intention to use them) is to frustrate deterrence and to invite a host of greater evils.

There is here no attempt to justify the contention that *intention* and *threat* have changed their meanings. The attribution of intention to a social and material system may be a fanciful Rousseauish kind of thing but doesn't give intention a new meaning; it is instead a claim that we may apply the predicate "intentional" to happenings that don't at first look like actions. If they have been given new and unexplained meanings the argument becomes inaccessible. What Novak seems to be saying is that we are involved in a pragmatic paradox. In order to make sure that a nuclear war doesn't break out we have to be prepared to fight one, and this entails, for example, that the commanders of submarines with nuclear weapons targeted on Russian cities must faithfully enter into a prior engagement to send the missiles on their way if ordered to do so. There is something to be said for the argument, put in this way, though it is not an argument a Catholic moralist can accept.

There cannot be an intention "never to have to use the deterrent force." Never to have to use this force may be the object of hope or desire, but not of intention. (Compare: I intend never to have to divorce my wife.) "I have no intention ever to use the deterrent" is intelligible as a statement about my *not* having the intention, and this because using the deterrent does indeed fall under the idea of an intentional action. The only version of the Novak doctrine we can hope to save is: We hope the deterrent will never be used; but this hope is vain unless we here and now have a strong and unwavering intention to use, in certain circumstances, nuclear weapons against the enemy.

The moral question then becomes: Is it right to have a present intention to use nuclear weapons in certain hypothetical circumstances? (I take it to be evident that to intend in hypothetical circumstances to perform an action we think to be wrong is itself wrong.)

Perhaps I should at this point make it plain that I am discussing Novak as one who claims to be a Catholic moralist; that is, I am not here and now discussing how far his position as I have reformulated it has merit or not. It has hitherto been an uncontested Catholic principle that there are some acts that are always wrong, even as means to some good end. One such act is the deliberate, intentional killing of the innocent. (Innocence has nothing to do here with moral innocence. The innocent are those who would be doing what they are doing even if the military-industrial complex were to evaporate.) This is an issue Novak simply will not confront, and his juggling argument about intention strikes me as an attempt to avoid the confrontation. For this there is no excuse for someone who writes as a Catholic moralist, for in one of the principal documents of Vatican II, the "Pastoral Constitution on the Church in the Modern World" (*Gaudium et Spes*), we find the following:

> Any act of war aimed indiscriminately at the destruction of entire cities or of extensive areas along with their population is a crime against God and man himself. It merits unequivocal and unhesitating condemnation.

Novak, who calls for "flinty intellectual integrity," quotes other parts of this document but avoids citing this crucial passage. This goes with his general approach, that of an advocate, not that of a disinterested and objective student. He cites such Protestant thinkers as C. S. Lewis and Reinhold Niebuhr (whose dark rhetoric, with its talk about tensions and contradictions and unavoidable ambiguities in applying moral principles to political life, is perhaps one of Novak's models), but not—this really is a reason for eye-rubbing—the contemporary Protestant who has done the most work on the morality of war, Paul Ramsey. Since 1961, with the appearance of *Nuclear Weapons and Christian Conscience*,[4] there has been an intense discussion among Catholics on questions of warfare. Novak shows no signs of having followed this discussion. It is extraordinary he shouldn't feel an obligation to examine the arguments in Professor Elizabeth Anscombe's papers, "War and Murder" and "Mr. Truman's Degree."[5] The best modern treatment of the problem of the just war, Michael Walzer's *Just and Unjust Wars*, is never mentioned.[6]

I hope it isn't true that Novak's pamphlet influenced the American bishops. The final version of their pastoral letter does make concessions to the doctrine of deterrence, though not all the concessions Novak would want. Bearing in mind the traditional doctrine about the direct and intentional killing of the innocent, the bishops interrogated government officials about US policy on targeting. They were told by Mr. William Clark, then national security adviser, that "the United States does not target the Soviet civilian population as such"; and he added: "There is no deliberately opaque meaning conveyed in the last two words." The bishops said they found this communication "particularly helpful." How far this remark may be ironical I don't know. But throughout the bishops' letter we are reminded

4. Walter Stein, ed., *Nuclear Weapons and Christian Conscience* (London: Merlin Press, 1961); published in the US as *Nuclear Weapons: A Catholic Response* (Sheed and Ward, 1962).

5. In G. E. M. Anscombe, *Collected Philosophical Papers, Volume 3: Ethics, Religion and Politics* (University of Minnesota Press, 1981).

6. See pp. 43-59 above.

71

that the deliberate killing of the innocent as a means to something else is always forbidden, that a refusal of all violence is an honorable option, that nuclear retaliation against enemy cities is immoral—no "secondary intentions" for them! An especially solemn reminder to all in authority is:

> . . . that their training and field manuals have long prohibited, and still do prohibit, certain actions in the conduct of war, especially those actions which inflict harm on innocent civilians. . . . To refuse to take such actions is not an act of cowardice or treason but one of courage and patriotism.

The final draft of the letter is weaker than the second draft in that it concedes more to the possible value of deterrence. Novak misconstrues this as saying that the bishops (and the Pope) support and approve of deterrence. What they say, following John Paul II's remarks on the subject, is that the present reliance on a posture of deterrence is tolerable if, and only if, it is used as a stage in serious negotiations for disarmament. This is understandable. Here is the actual state of the world and from this we must begin. The direction we try to take is a sign of our moral concern. Talk about "prevailing" in a nuclear exchange, discussion of how many million casualties would be "acceptable": these things just don't go with a serious attitude to the world's predicament. The bishops made this clear.

On November 8 the French bishops issued a statement on nuclear arms. It rests upon an argument that is in part like Novak's. It defends France's possession of nuclear arms and justifies the posture of deterrence. (It is worth noting that they are concerned only with the relatively modest French nuclear strike power.) They identify the "enemy" as the Soviet Union, and they portray it as a proselytizing power anxious to conquer the world. In a situation such as the present, with an enemy trying to "Finlandize" Western Europe, the state has a duty to defend its citizens and this means to threaten the use of even the most destructive weapons. So far, the argument is bound to please the

French government and Michael Novak. But there are passages in the document—I rely upon the long citations from the statement published in *Le Monde* of November 10, 1983—that suggest that there was some agonizing over the decision; and a part of the argument is different from and opposed to Novak's.

Novak argues that for the deterrent to be effective there must be a will to use nuclear weapons; if this will is lacking, there is no deterrent. The French bishops argue that there is a moral difference between threatening to use nuclear weapons and actually using them. Does it follow from the evident immorality of their use against cities (they recall the condemnation by the Council of the indiscriminate use of weapons against cities) that it is also immoral to threaten to use them? Their answer is that the immorality of the threat isn't obvious, even though to go from the threat to the act is hard to justify (*"la légitimité morale de ce passage à l'acte est plus problématique"*). Two other points testify to their moral uneasiness over the drift of the argument. They emphasize that they don't wish to strengthen a Manichaean view of the world in which the Soviet Union is evil and the West good; against the theoretical materialism of the East we have to set the practical materialism of the West; both kinds constitute *"une maladie mortelle pour l'humanité."* They also consider the question of the efficacy of nonviolent resistance as a technique more suitable for Christians than the use of arms. They admit that those who support this technique may be right in the long run and that it is important now to examine this alternative.

What the French bishops cannot quite bring themselves to do is to consider the question how far states in their relations are subject to the same moral rules as individuals. They seem at times to suggest the doctrine variously expressed by Machiavelli, by Hobbes, by Max Weber, that political leaders are, in virtue of the duties they carry, subject to a different and more elastic set of rules and are perhaps subject only to the rules of a worldly prudence. This is what most rulers have commonly assumed. It has never been the Catholic tradition, a tradition reaffirmed by John XXIII in *Pacem in Terris*: "The same law of nature [that is, moral law] which regulates the behavior of individual citizens must govern the relationships between states." He adds that rulers "cannot . . . abandon the law of nature which binds them personally and is the very rule of right conduct."

I fear *Moral Clarity in the Nuclear Age* deserves William Buckley's introduction. This is Buckley at his most offensive and most pompous. He writes that

> the suggestion that public policy should proceed on the understanding that no use of nuclear weapons is morally defensible, not even the threat of their use as a deterrent, is nothing less than an eructation in civilized thought, putting, as it does, the protraction of biological life as the fit goal of modern man.

The philistinism of the Catholic right, and its remoteness from the moral tradition of Catholicism, has rarely been so aptly illustrated, at least, not since the days of the *Action française*, when Maurras rejoiced that the musical settings of the *Magnificat* were so exquisite that they did something to temper the noxious Hebraism of its text.[7]

It is sad that a statement so gimcrack as *Moral Clarity in the Nuclear Age* should enjoy some reputation. It is incredible that among the signatures added to it there should be those of some philosophers; they must have known that Novak's stuff on intention is no good. But if Novak's work directs readers to the magnificent statement of the American bishops, this will be something.

7. Spiritual vulgarity is an invariable mark of the Catholic right. I choose two examples from Novak, the first from *Moral Clarity*, the second from *Confession of a Catholic*. He observes of Archbishop Philip Hannan of New Orleans, who was almost alone in opposing the general drift of the bishops' successive statements, from the first to the final draft, that he is a former paratrooper (p. 123). Monsignor Bruce Kent, formerly secretary of the British Campaign for Nuclear Disarmament, was a commander in the Tank Corps. So what?—in either case. Again, he writes: "Not only does one often see strong women in politics and war (from Golda Meir, Indira Gandhi, Margaret Thatcher, and Jeane Kirkpatrick to Elizabeth of Hungary and Mary Queen of Scots . . .)" (p. 37). This needs no comment.

The Idea of a Liberal Education ——

I suppose there can't be any doubt that the golden age of liberal education was in Western Europe in the nineteenth century. There, the adolescent members of the middle class, proceeding from families that were either bookish or thought it a defect in themselves that they weren't, went through the grammar school, or the *lycée*, or the *Gymnasium*, and then on to universities where the subjects having the highest prestige were the ancient classical languages, history, philosophy, literature, and mathematics. It was men educated in this tradition who founded some of the inquiries and the subjects of immense importance in the modern world. Comparative philology, that is, all intensive study of the vernacular languages, sociology, social anthropology, psychology, were all founded by men trained in this way, in what I shall call the tradition of humanism.

It is sobering to think that if Freud had been brought up in a contemporary school he might not have had enough mythology in his head to have characterized—or even noted—the Oedipus complex. And could one who was not already deeply read in history have seen as an intellectual challenge the palpable difference of social atmosphere between the Catholic and

From *Commonweal* (April 11, 1980).

Protestant parts of Europe, that is, could a man educated in the modern fashion have stumbled upon the hypothesis whence came *The Protestant Ethic and the Spirit of Capitalism?* These considerations show us that liberal education, the cultivation of the mind for the sake of the discourse itself, not for its utility (not that this is denied), came to its perfection in a society very different from our own and under conditions it would today be impossible to duplicate.

It strikes me that a difficulty in talking about liberal education—the education of those who are free so that they may exercise their freedom—is not so much that it isn't believed in as that many people have no idea what one is talking about. The ethic of self-realization, of life-fulfillment, the current view of the place of pleasure in a satisfactory life for the young (it is widely taken for granted that nonprocreative sexual activity is a natural right to be exercised from, at least, early adolescence), all these are, for so many, unquestioned presuppositions that anything that questions them is taken to be quaint, reactionary, even malicious. And yet it is quite plain that to be a liberally educated man, in the nineteenth-century sense, involves years of what seems to be unrewarding toil at subjects not always at the time very exciting, a limitation of choice springing from the authority of the older and wiser to shape the curriculum—the credit and elective system in high school or college-university seems to me incompatible with a liberal education—a life even at the undergraduate level very confined by today's standards.

The apprenticeship system was in the nineteenth century common to both the liberal and the useful arts and has in our time decayed in both cases for similar reasons: the system required the sacrifice of immediate gratification for the sake of possible future gratification; the life of the scholar or learned amateur or of the skilled artist was contemplated as a highly desirable state to be aimed at over a period of years, and the authority of the master craftsman was recognized if not always accepted in particular cases. Religion was no longer a supreme category of thought; but in at least Protestant countries vernacular culture, something shared by far more people than were liberally educated, was biblical—Luther's Bible or the King James Version provided a common measure of style, a source of illuminating stories—Abraham the man of faith, Moses the leader of the nation, David the King who combines heroism and depravity, the Gospel parables, the unforgettable exemplary story of the young man from Nazareth betrayed by his friends and executed by a foreign power, the rich thought of Paul, with his great opposition, Grace and the Law, his commendation of charity as the master virtue, and the thought that before God man is always in the wrong.

Such a culture, enriched in the English-speaking countries by the classics of the vernacular literature—e.g., Shakespeare and Bunyan—that were picked up in the home rather than at school, was the precondition for the valuing of liberal education. Through its molding effect upon the imagination it disposed men to look upon the world as a place for heroes and cowards, harsh suffering and transcendent joys; the world of the Bible was sober and real, and even what lent itself to romantic feeling and hinted at splendors lying beyond that world in which everything got old and decayed and died had this mutable world as its background and opposite. So that even if the ancient Greeks and Romans were closer to the center of the curriculum than the personages of the biblical record, they were nevertheless seen with Christian or biblical eyes and thus with irony. Saul was nearer the heart than Achilles; Socrates was a true martyr, but there was one greater than he.

The author of *Paradise Lost* is the great prototype of the liberally educated man, and he was certainly torn at times between the world of antiquity and the biblical world; but he saw in the biblical record the truth of the fables of the Greek world. In his description of Paradise (*Paradise Lost* iv.248-51) he speaks of

Groves whose rich Trees wept odorous Gumms and
  Balme,
Others whose fruit burnisht with Golden Rinde

Hung amiable, *Hesperian* Fables true,
If true, here onely. . . .

That is, the ancient story of the golden apples of the
Hesperides is true, not of the land of the fable, but of Eden.
And so he can use the story of the rape of Persephone to echo
the fall of Eve:

. . . that faire field
Of *Enna*, where *Proserpin* gathring flours
Her self a fairer Floure by gloomie *Dis*
Was gatherd, which cost *Ceres* all that pain
To seek her through the world. . . . (ibid. 268-72)

The forms and images of the biblical revelation haunt the
other great world of imagination, that of classical antiquity.
(Curiously, men only begin to look at the world of, say, Homer
realistically, that is, historically, in all its strangeness and otherness, when the scholars investigate and make available the almost forgotten epics of northern Europe.)

This mingling of the biblical account of man and the world
with the themes of antiquity represents the achievement of
humanistic education at its most elaborate. Perhaps we ought to
note that there is another tradition, that represented by Bunyan,
and before him by Langland, in which the biblical tradition is
seen in a different context, that of the ordinary life of men.
Vanity Fair, the Man with the Muck-Rake, Mr. Worldly, and Mr.
Pliable belong to the ordinary world of the tinker Bunyan; and
at the climactic moment of *Piers Plowman* the identification of
the poor plowman with Christ is obvious.

In the midst of Mass when men went to offering
I fell soon again to sleep, and suddenly was dreaming
That Piers the Plowman, painted bloodily,
Came in with the cross before the common people,
And like in all his limbs to our Lord Jesus.
Then I called Conscience to my counsel and asked him:
"Is this Jesus the jouster," I said, "whom the Jews
crucified?

Or is this Piers the Plowman! Who painted him so
   crimson?"
Then Conscience cried kneeling, "This is Piers' ensign,
His colours and his coat-armour, but he who comes so
   bloody
Is Christ with his Cross, the conqueror of Christians."[1]

You will notice here that the concepts and institutions of
chivalry are, with immense irony, used to present the Lordship
of Christ. The joust, the heraldic colors, the armor, are used to
portray Christ's heroic role; but this is turned upside down by
the identification of Christ not with the knight or the nobleman
but with Piers the Plowman. Langland and Bunyan have more
depth and delicacy—I think we have to say this in the end—
than men of elaborate education; neither, certainly, is a liberally educated man. The liberally educated man is Newman's
gentleman; and while the gentleman is as far as he goes a
remarkable artifact he is not the highest product of a Christian
culture. I note this that we may keep a sense of the limitations,
as well as the merits, of liberal education.

I want also to stress that whether we receive Christianity
as an ingredient of a culture dominated by a study of classical
antiquity or as an element in a culture more vernacular in style
and content, we necessarily receive it as an element in *some* culture. This is evident if we look at the ICEL translation of the liturgical texts or at such contemporary versions of the Scriptures as
the New English Bible or the New American Bible. The trivial
and jargon-ridden pop culture in which we live is reflected in
the poverty of such translations. I don't know how many have
noticed with a *frisson* of horror that the word "values" has come
into the Sunday collects.

So far I have maintained that liberal education in the
nineteenth-century sense, the sense explained by Newman in *The
Idea of a University*, occurred and could only have occurred in a

---

1. William Langland, *The Vision of Piers Plowman*, rendered into modern
English by Henry W. Wells (London, 1938 [1935]), Passus XIX, p. 225.

specific society in which the middle class reverenced such an education, not perhaps for what it was in itself but for its fruits, a certain grace and polish and flexibility of mind represented in an ideal form in the gentleman, a man distinguished not by birth but by qualities of mind and disposition, almost what the French call *comportement*. Such an education was a precondition for the rise of modern linguistic, historical, and social studies. And reflection shows us that while liberal humanistic education gives Christianity a distinctive cultural form, Christianity is not and could not be limited by any such form; the question for Christianity is not whether it could survive the disappearance of liberal education but whether it could survive the vanishing of a culture that is in some way biblical, that is, soaked in the narratives, the symbolism, and the moral attitudes conveyed in Scripture. (Perhaps I ought to insert here the remark that as a believer I am not concerned with whether or not Christianity will survive; but as a student of society I am bound to ask questions one might ask about any form of belief, about Buddhism, say, or Islam.)

I will put my question in another form. Could Christianity survive a *complete* break with the past of our culture? The answer to this question is plainly no: if the story of Israel and of the Crucified One were to drop out of human memory, then Christianity would obviously cease to exist; Christianity, and liberal culture, are essentially things mediated through time; total amnesia would produce in our society what it produces in individual persons, a loss of inner confidence and inability to take charge of one's own life. Even if an amnesiac does put together something of a new life for himself, the sense of a void in which all-important things had happened would always be there.

Now, the signs of a fraying of (if not of a break with) our link with the past are evident. There is the moral revolution of our time which I have already mentioned; this has the effect of making past morality not so much disliked or opposed as unintelligible. And there is what I can only call the collapse of literacy. Perhaps this isn't the right way to put it. I am not concerned with the decline in the practice of reading and writing or the growing inability, even in academic circles, to write in plain and intelligible English, free of gobbledygook, parasensical locutions, psychobabble, and other substitutes for the language, serious though all such things must seem to teachers in high schools, colleges, and universities. I am rather concerned with that of which such things are only the symptoms. I can best say what I mean by giving examples.

Take what is said in North America about "values." (This is why I thought it so alarming that the term had crept into the ICEL rendering of the Liturgy.) It is deeply impressed on the mind of the young, and they certainly get this from their teachers, who themselves got it from colleges, schools, and institutes of education, that there are many different sets of "values" to be picked out by the individual ("true for me," "right for me"), as from the counters of some vast moral cafeteria, and that growing up, becoming a mature person, is confecting one's own style and constellation of "values." Such a view is never—can never be—held consistently, in part for purely logical reasons, in part because it isn't arbitrary that certain dispositions—veracity and courage, for example—count as virtues, their opposites as vices; the notion that we can confect at will our moral stances, our value-systems, isn't intelligible. But many think it is, and it's therefore not surprising to find, e.g., supporters of abortion on demand rancorously opposed to capital punishment for murder, and prolife defenders of the human foetus in favor of threatening our enemies with nuclear weapons. It is amusing, in a macabre way, to find the confectors of value-systems exclaiming in tones of moral passion over the wickedness of censoring the books to be read by schoolchildren, and then, in almost the same breath, scrutinizing textbooks for traces of such heresies as racism and sexism. It is surely a very odd state of affairs that places on the library shelves *The Rainbow* and *Fear of Flying* and at the same time removes *Oliver Twist*, *Huckleberry Finn*, and *Little Women*.

Now, I call this illiteracy because I can't find a better word for it; and because it commonly goes with an incapacity to use the language with clarity. Those who defend the "values" nonsense will go in for the active use of "to relate" ("I don't relate to him/her"), and the jargon of input, parameters, meaningful relations, consciousness-raising, interface, and so on. They will commit pages of what I have elsewhere called "parasense." I invented a piece of parasense that would, I am convinced, scarcely raise an eyebrow in a document issued by a school of education or even by a university:

> The parameters of the problem can only be fully evaluated by those who are able to relate to the educational process in a meaningful way and thus interface-wise implement a viable solution in the ongoing future.

On this I commented as follows:

> It is totally parasensical. It differs from what may be taken as nonsense, in that there are no category blunders and no obvious logical foul-ups. It seems grammatical; its words are for the most part to be found in the standard dictionaries; the syntax conforms to standard models and thus our habitual expectations are fulfilled; above all, it is as though it were coated with a special kind of grease—it slips down (or past) easily.[2]

Such language would have been laughed out of existence in the nineteenth century or would have taken refuge in the inner life of some strange sect. (Chadband's discourse in *Bleak House* represents the religious parasense of the mid-nineteenth century.) That it is now common among the educated, that is, among those who have passed through the high schools and the universities and colleges, seems to me connected with deep confusions in politics, in theology, in thought about human life.

Most of us—I include myself—are not very good at using the techniques of logical analysis to sort out the wild and the plausible, the reasonable and the extravagant, from each other

2. J. M. Cameron, *On the Idea of a University* (Toronto, 1978), p. 49.

in discourse about men and the world. But so long as society retains a minimum of health certain sophistries and idiocies are recognized for what they are, men turn away from them as they turn away from what stinks or is liable to cause pain. Sometimes this kind of wisdom is expressed proverbially, as in "What is sauce for the goose, is sauce of the gander" or the Gospel saying about motes in eyes. Sometimes it shows itself in action and speech, when we show what we think is worth talking about and what not.

Nothing is to me more astonishing—and nothing is more frightening—than the eruption of astrology, talking to the flowers, doing things under pyramids, and so on, in our society. This is part of the same irrationalism that has been showing itself in mad racial doctrines. But whereas people are on their guard in relation to racial doctrines—after all, every "race" is an interest group—astrology and other kinds of nonsense seem to find believers among the educated. It was related of an English philosopher (I think G. E. Moore) that he used to say apropos of some problem and its proposed solution: I don't know what's true in this matter but I know *that* is not true. We may be puzzled by whatever the determinism/free will controversy is about; but offered astrology as a solution we can say: I don't know what's true but I know *that* is not true. It isn't a matter for discussion; it belongs to a great tract of territory that lies beyond profitable discussion. What I suppose puzzles me and frightens me is the large number of *lumpen* intellectuals we seem to be producing. What have the fathers done that the children's teeth should be so set on edge?

It is true that in every civilized society there is necessarily a gap between those who have received an elaborate education and have leisure in which to cultivate the arts, to speculate, to write, and those who give themselves to business and professional activity and to physical labor. But it isn't always true that this gap is such that there is no possibility of a common spiritual life. Shakespeare is an excellent example of one who belonged simultaneously to more worlds than one: to the court and the country, the laboring poor and their masters, the respectable and the debauched; and in this he represented the social reality of his time. But today the gap is *within* the educated classes of modern society; and while not everyone lies on one side of the gap or the other, there is plainly a great difference between most of those who come out of the institutions of higher education in our society—a very high proportion of the total age group—and the professional intellectuals. It would be hard, I think, to argue that they belong to the same spiritual world. Much that is valued by the latter is unintelligible to the former. The way of life of the former is not in general marked by strong intellectual or artistic interests.

I don't think it would make any sense to propose some scheme for the establishment of liberal education throughout the institutions of higher education in North America. These institutions are concerned with moving adolescents through the ever-increasing space between childhood and adult life. They can't all be imparters of liberal education in Newman's sense; it would be impossible seriously to propose they should be. And yet it seems to me necessary, to put it as strongly as possible, that liberal education should be available at the undergraduate level in a fair number of universities and colleges, even if this involves the existence, side by side, of two very different models of education, a college within a college or university.

We are faced with two sets of questions: about content—curriculum and syllabus—and about method—how the content, supposing our having agreed about it, is to be made available to the undergraduates.

In principle almost any subject may be studied liberally, that is, out of curiosity and for its own sake; indeed, what distinguishes a university from a technical school is that in a university even technological subjects are studied liberally at the graduate level. But I think there is a central core which has, historically, made university education a living and shaping element in our civilization. I think historical, literary and linguistic, and philosophical studies have to be a part of a core

84

curriculum, and this for a number of reasons, some of which I'll try to explain, sometimes in my own words, sometimes in Newman's.

"Literature stands related to Man as Science stands to Nature; it is his history."[3] "Literature is to man in some sort what autobiography is to the individual; it is his Life and Remains."[4]

Thus Newman in the ninth of the university Discourses. He is commending the study of literature not as an option, polish or decoration, but as a means of self-knowledge, knowledge about ourselves as a species and as individual members of a species. It is true, what he has in mind is the literature of antiquity; but he knows, and shows he knows by proposing the establishment of a Chair of English Literature at the new university in Dublin, that the vernacular literatures of Europe are classics in their own right; and I shall take it as something beyond dispute that Shakespeare, Milton, Pope, Wordsworth, Coleridge, Tennyson, Dickens, George Eliot, Hawthorne, and Melville, to pick out a few, can be in a curriculum what Homer and Virgil, Herodotus and Livy, were in the nineteenth century; and of course I would add to the English names those of French and German and Italian writers.

If we were to make such texts central in our curriculum, then it seems to follow that we must in some way enable students to pick up the historical sense. This is hard, in part because it is a not much questioned presupposition that the past is bad and the future good, that the record of the past is the record of the crimes and follies of mankind; this is peculiarly well established in the American tradition, in part by reason of the revolutionary ideology with which the United States begins, in part by the nature of its vernacular culture in the nineteenth century. I reverence Mark Twain as a great writer; but *A Connecticut Yankee in King Arthur's Court* strikes me as a representative and pain-

3. John Henry Newman, *The Idea of a University Defined and Illustrated*, edited by I. T. Ker (Oxford, 1976), p. 193.
4. Ibid., pp. 193-94.

fully philistine work, an attitude to the past of a man intolerably complacent about the present. "My, weren't they dumb?" he seems to be saying about the European Middle Ages. Now, I know very well that Twain wasn't at all complacent about his American present; all the same, the note of complacency is sounded in this book, and I hear behind it a lot of popular applause. And yet the United States has produced at least one historian of genius, Parkman (just as it produced a philosopher of genius, Peirce), and a mass of brilliant academic historians. The possibility of cultivating the historical sense must plainly be there.

To this central core of literary and historical studies I should like to add some philosophy. I don't mean that anyone without a taste for it should be made to attempt any technical philosophy. Philosophy is a very difficult subject and philosophical ability is rare—not logical ability: anyone who can do mathematics can do logic—and undergraduate students are on the young side for it, or perhaps they are neither old enough nor young enough. But I think they should know about philosophy.

One who has never read a Platonic dialogue or Descartes's *Meditations* or Berkeley's *Principles* is ill equipped to deal with critical problems in study or in life. This was forcibly brought home to me some time ago when I came across in something written by a scholar and published by a university press of great prestige the astonishing statement that the concept of the Unconscious would have been incomprehensible before Freud. Quite apart from Freud's distinguished nineteenth-century predecessors, there is the passage in Plato (*Republic* 571-72) in which he shows we have desires that we only know about through their expression in dreams, a passage with which Freud himself was of course familiar. I do a fair amount of general reviewing and I find that howlers of this kind are becoming more and more frequent in books put out by respectable publishers: a criticism of the editors as well as the authors.

A knowledge of literature; a sense of history; an acquaintance with some of the classics of philosophy: it seems reasonable that such things should be nourished as the core of a curriculum in the liberal arts. This is not primarily a matter of acquiring ease and polish in one's manners—we all know great and good men who are in this respect very deficient, and others who have such graces but are rogues—though such things are desirable. Such knowledge is fundamental to the health of society, for without it we have no criteria for picking out who we are or what we are. "Literature is [man's] history." It "is to man in some sort what autobiography is to the individual; it is his Life and Remains." With a deeper knowledge of literature, with a finer historical sense, with wider acquaintance with the many good and absurd things said by philosophers, much nonsense written and spoken in Western society wouldn't be expressed. Even if this be granted, we have still to think out a way to teach such a curriculum in our present circumstances.

First, I think the dominant method of teaching and study at the undergraduate level—in North America—has to go. By this I mean we have to get rid of the credit system, not necessarily for most students in universities and colleges, but for those who want a liberal education. Most degree courses, ending in the Bachelor's degree, are made up out of fifteen, or twenty, courses or their equivalent in half courses, in subjects more or less related to each other. Each course is a self-contained unit and is separately assessed and graded, the student's grade being recorded on his transcript. Sometimes requirements for "majoring" and "minoring," and the writing into the regulations of prerequisites of various kinds, impose some shape on this structure—the mosaic is given a pattern—but in other cases an elective system enables students to go in for very bizarre combinations.

I have a number of objections to this system.

First, where the undergraduate takes the system seriously he/she has no leisure. To carry five courses a year, with the reading and other assignments connected with the work—in a big university the sheer physical problem of getting from place to place on the campus—is not compatible with fruitful leisure, with rummaging through libraries, general reading, going to concerts and plays, extended conversation.

Second, the effect of the mode of teaching that commonly goes with this system is that the students become passive, giving back in examinations and term papers what they have received from their teachers. That so much regurgitating goes on is alarming, just as alarming as the widespread practice of plagiarism, though it isn't visited with the same penalties.

Third, the division of work into distinct courses, each course assigning a grade to the student, means that there is no continuity, no development in studies. I think this is true even where majors and minors do impose some pattern on the choice of courses. The course once completed, the grade once assigned, the substance of what has been learned may vanish from the student's mind, and will certainly not be revived if there are no final and comprehensive examinations, oral or written or both, on the work of the previous three or four years. It is a spasmodic system.

Fourth, it is a common though not a necessary part of the system that textbooks and anthologies rather than original works are studied; it is as though it is thought desirable to shield the young from the close embrace of the world's great minds.

Fifth, it seems to belong to the system that the writing of essays is not a prominent and sustained activity throughout a student's career; and where the pressure of numbers is great such essays as are written are often marked on content, not much attention being paid to questions of vocabulary, syntax, and style. I have noticed (in Toronto) that the written work of fourth-year undergraduates may be from a formal point of view just hopeless, of course not always but in a surprising number of cases. These are clever young men and women; their inability to express themselves in plain, intelligible, and reasonably correct English (in matters of correctness we are all of us liable to fall many times a day) wasn't their own fault; they hadn't been given any help; and they had been corrupted by bad models, sometimes bad models in the work put before them by their teachers. I know this is a very difficult problem with many causes: simply the decline of reading—even good students will only have read the works included in the high school syllabus—as a common leisure activity is a powerful negative influence (this is reflected by the wide use among the half-educated of the word "book" to mean a magazine, *Time* or *Reader's Digest*). Finally, I think the system as such militates against growing familiarity between teachers and taught. This is widely recognized and there are many attempts to remedy the evil by tutorial or counseling schemes, schemes that wouldn't be necessary if the system were changed.

These evils are not new and they arise under many different systems. I quote from Newman, who is maintaining that even self-education is to be preferred to certain kinds of university education. It is better, he argues, to be self-educated, with all its drawbacks and disadvantages, than to be one of

> those earnest but ill-used persons, who are forced to load their minds with a score of subjects against an examination, who have too much on their hands to indulge themselves in thinking or investigation, who devour premise and conclusion together with indiscriminate greediness, who hold whole sciences on faith, and commit demonstrations to memory, and who too often, as might be expected, when their period of education is passed, throw up all they have learned in disgust, having gained nothing really by their anxious labours, except, perhaps, the habit of application.[5]

This could today be used without alteration of undergraduate students working under the regime of many institutions in North America.

Again, higher education has a "natural" basis, in the following sense. In every enterprise concerned with finding things out and acquiring skills there is of necessity a partnership between older and younger persons. No doubt young persons left

5. *Idea of a University*, p. 132.

to themselves by some catastrophe would not be totally helpless: the young in Golding's novel *Lord of the Flies* even invented totemism and human sacrifice. But it seems reasonable to suppose that in schools, as in families and other collective enterprises, there is a necessary and desirable partnership between the younger and the older. Much will plainly depend upon the *quality* of that relationship. Where it is sour, achievement will be warped and limited. Newman saw this relationship as more important than systems and institutions.

> ... The personal influence of the teacher is able in some sort to dispense with an academical system, but that system cannot in any sort dispense with personal influence. With influence there is life, without it there is none; if influence is deprived of its due position, it will not by those means be got rid of, it will only break out irregularly, dangerously. An academical system without the personal influence of teachers upon pupils, is an arctic winter; it will create an ice-bound, petrified, cast-iron University and nothing else.[6]

A little later he continues:

> I have known a time in a great School of letters, when things went on for the most part by mere routine, and form took the place of earnestness. I have experienced a state of things, in which teachers were cut off from the taught as by an unsurmountable barrier; when neither part entered into the thoughts of the other, when each lived by and in itself.... I have known places where a stiff manner, a pompous voice, coldness and condescension, were the teacher's attributes.... This was the reign of Law without influence, System without personality.[7]

Teaching and learning are, then, two terms of a natural relation for satisfying the needs of civilization, and the college

6. John Henry Newman, *The Office and Work of Universities* (London, 1856), p. 112.

7. Ibid., pp. 112-13.

and university will be healthy where this relation is recognized and even celebrated. But in more specific terms what are the main features of the regime I would substitute for what prevails at present?

I think the first thing to do is to abolish all particular courses attendance at which is required for credit and in respect of which grades are awarded, at least in the second, third, and fourth years. (What to do in the first year, which ought to be a "sampling" year, is a special problem I neglect on this occasion.) Instead, students should opt for a major subject, with or without a minor, and the syllabus and book list covering the three years should be the main guide to the student.

There should be no lecture courses "covering the ground," no courses providing material to be regurgitated. Instead, the faculty members should lecture—if they do—on subjects that interest them or on which they are working. Since attendance at lectures would be entirely voluntary, only the charm and interest of the lectures would guarantee an audience. If some lectures didn't catch on it wouldn't matter. In any case, the main work of the faculty would be tutoring and conducting small seminars; for every student who put himself down for a major, or a major and a minor, would be brought within a network of tutorials of two or three students, and of small seminars, and these would be devoted to the discussion of the writing and reading of the students. Each student should be required to write at least one essay, perhaps more commonly two, each week, and to do recommended reading in connection with his writing.

The courses would be progressive. I can best illustrate this by examples. A good student in his final year in English might find himself studying in some depth the theology and politics of seventeenth-century England; a good student in French might find himself committed to a small research project on Pascal and Port-Royal. The program of study should be cumulative as well as progressive; and its cumulative character would be brought out by the setting of final examinations at the end of the fourth year, examinations the topics of which would range over the three years of work.

No grades would be awarded during the three years, though a careful record would be kept by tutors of the performances of their pupils; but there would be annual meetings of tutors to assess performances and these might issue in commendations or rebukes or, in some cases, judgments that the performance was so unsatisfactory that the student concerned should withdraw. Performance in final examinations should be graded, not in minute detail, and having regard to the students' performances during the three years, in such a way as to divide the finalists into three classes: those, presumably a small number, whose performances could be described as first-class or distinguished; those whose performances were in varying degrees satisfactory; and a small class of those who could be said to have "satisfied the examiners"—this meaning that on the whole they could receive the Bachelor's degree, but without glory.

Such, very crudely, are my proposals for reform. I don't think it is politically possible, nor, given the character of the students we receive, would it be desirable to attempt to universalize such a system. But I think it ought to be offered; and I think some of the best students would opt for it. Many students would be nervous at the prospect. Our present system provides ropes and banisters to hang on to, and some may be giddy without the reassurance of a frequent sprinkling of grades and the thought that if you give back to the instructor what he has given you can scarcely get less than a C. To operate such a program would in effect be to establish an elite college within the wider university or college.

I think opposition to this on the ground that it would be "undemocratic" is humbug. Elites are a part of social life, though it is possible to be a member of one elite and be excluded from another. There are very few—Wallace Stevens is the only one who comes readily to my mind—who belong simultaneously to a great many elites (in his case artistic, business, social, and conceivably political, if, that is, being a right-wing

Republican was to belong to a political elite in the Roosevelt years). In any case, education of the sort provided by public authorities inevitably involves a hierarchy of esteem: a university, a liberal arts college, a community college, are different institutions and their characteristic products are given a different formation, are in some relative sense elites as compared with contrasting groups. Where traditional elites are weak, it is even true that elites based upon competition are more powerful and more desperate, for the ground is never firm beneath their feet.

It seems to me plain enough that the products of such a scheme of liberal education as I have outlined—the best of them—would indeed be an elite. But I think we have good reason to think that they would be marginal in the present political and social scene. We might hope that as a minority, a remnant, they would make for sanity in the madness of the world. This would be a slow business; and it may be—this is one's three o'clock in the morning thought—there isn't much time.

The Bible Today ——————————

Evans-Pritchard once wrote, having in mind the fog in which, so he thought, the discussion of primitive religion had been plunged by Frazer, Durkheim, Marett, and others, that anyone who wanted to do fieldwork on this topic ought to have "a poetic mind which moves easily in images and symbols."[1] Such a prerequisite seems even more obviously needed for the study of the Bible. The materials in the biblical writings (the Bible, in what I have to say about Frye's book, is the Christian Bible, the so-called Old and New Testaments, with the apocryphal—deuterocanonical—books, Ecclesiasticus, Wisdom, I and II Maccabees, and others) include most of the traditional kinds of oral and written work: epic, chronicle, folk tale, myth of origin, epithalamion, songs of exile, collections of proverbs, letters, biographies, proclamations of salvation, apocalyptic visions.

Put together in the King James Version, they are the most widespread cult object in North America, for they rest on or near

---

1. E. E. Evans-Pritchard, *Theories of Primitive Religion* (Oxford University Press, 1965), p. 112.

From *The New York Review of Books* (April 15, 1982); reviews of Northrop Frye, *The Great Code: The Bible and Literature* (Harcourt Brace Jovanovich); Robert Alter, *The Art of Biblical Narrative* (Basic Books).

every bedside table in hotel and motel. New vernacular translations of the original Hebrew and Greek continually appear and are bought in great quantities. What it all amounts to is hard to determine. University teachers report (Professor Frye confirms the report) that their pupils—sometimes their younger colleagues—don't know the content of the Bible and don't know how to read the perplexing volume. Off-the-cuff references, in lectures, to Joseph and his wonderful coat, the deliverance from Egypt, the theophany of the burning bush, the suffering servant of Isaiah, the parable of the laborers of the eleventh hour, or the prodigal son, Paul's shipwreck on the shores of Malta, rarely produce a response. We know there are those who scrutinize the text for news of the coming of Antichrist and Armageddon; but we may think this has a lot in common with the hunger for fantasies (worlds in collision, flying saucers, babies possessed by demons) and the vogue of such follies as palmistry and astrology.

The ignorance of the highly intelligent seeking an advanced education in the humanities presents the universities with a technical problem, namely, how to make the body of literature in English intelligible, for Langland, Chaucer, Milton, Blake, Hardy, Henry James, Joyce, cannot be fully grasped and valued by readers who have no serious acquaintance with the Bible. (For example, *The Wings of the Dove* draws its pattern of feeling and not simply its title from Psalm 55: "For it is not an open enemy, that hath done me this dishonour: for then I could have borne it. . . . But it was even thou, my companion: my guide, and mine own familiar friend. . . . The words of his mouth were softer than butter . . . : his words were smoother than oil" [Book of Common Prayer version].)

Northrop Frye meets Evans-Pritchard's requirement. He has "a poetic mind" and is as well the most ingenious and comprehensive of the formal critics writing in English today. As a systematic thinker about the theory and practice of his own art he has no equal. His *Anatomy of Criticism*[2] tightened up the prac-

2. Princeton University Press, 1957.

95

tice and enriched the vocabulary of literary studies. We can say he completed what had been begun by Eliot in "Tradition and the Individual Talent": the exploration of the literatures of the past as composing an order to be circumnavigated, surveyed, and accounted for. Frye is not just a highly intelligent man of letters, as Trilling was, or Edmund Wilson. His mind is synoptic and orders—sometimes to excess—its material; so far these powers have been shown most impressively in *Fearful Symmetry*,[3] his book on Blake, and in the exposition of forms, categories, ways of proceeding, in the *Anatomy*.

Frye's notion of criticism, as it is set out and practiced in the *Anatomy*, is "the whole work of scholarship and taste concerned with literature which is a part of what is variously called liberal education, culture, or the study of the humanities." Such criticism has a variety of tasks; the most important is to give a voice to what is dumb, to make the verbal fiction itself deliver up its secrets. Imaginative literature is not (Frye argues) communication, but "a *disinterested* use of words"; "poems are as silent as statues."

We have to proceed inductively, rummaging through the great heap that is literature. There may be difficulties over what things are to count as data for the critic, what verbal structures are to count as parts of the heap. The difficulties are overcome— the move in argument is like Burke's in justifying the authority of traditional institutions—by prescription, not by a discussion of conflicting value judgments. We can then look at the material under four headings: a theory of Modes, of Symbols, of Myths, of Genres. These broad topics are then divided under headings: the theory of Modes, for example, treated historically, divides into the mode of fiction in general, then into the tragic and comic fictional modes, and into thematic modes. A particular topic, imagery (which comes under the theory of Myths), for example, divides up into apocalyptic, demonic, and analogical.

This doesn't do justice to the fineness of detail in the

3. Princeton University Press, 1947; Beacon, paperback, 1962.

analysis, but it indicates Frye's mode of procedure, which he keeps to in *The Great Code*. He sometimes argues that the persistence, over long periods, of similarities of structure in imaginative fictions means that underlying this unity of culture there "must" be "a common psychological inheritance." "Must" is a dire word in argument, suggesting a transcendental argument, as in Kant, from what is empirically given to what must be the case if this is given. The argument could be truistic, but then there would be no point in saying "must."

In the index of the *Anatomy* there are more references to the Bible than to any other set of books, except the poems and plays of Shakespeare. The Bible is followed closely by Aristotle, Plato, Dante, Milton, and Blake. Thus Frye is concerned with European literary culture in a broad sense; but his primary interest is in the imaginative, visionary expression of his way of taking the world, a way he believes belongs to the essence of humanity, not submerged in nature as are the other animals, but living in a universe of myth. The Bible is in the Christian era a principal contributor to our visionary account of the universe and of ourselves within it. If we are to move easily within our inherited culture, knowing how to read the Bible is not something we can do without.

The Bible, as a compilation of many books, as a sacred volume constituted by a canon or rule including this book, excluding that, and as a source of influence within literature, has plainly been squatting in Frye's path for a long time. Sensing in his pupils the lack of knowledge and competence we have already noticed, he has given a course on the Bible for many years, and some of *The Great Code* comes presumably from what was first roughed out for his fortunate students. The Bible is not, for him, just literature; it is *kerygma,* proclamation of a saving message, not, Frye is anxious to make clear, as expressing or being a foundation of a doctrine, but *kerygma* nonetheless; what this implies we must presently ask. Its suitability as material for commentary by the critic and the theorist of criticism lies in its use of so many literary modes, in its offering in rich confusion metaphor, metonymy, symbol, analogy, and other figures of language in its complete account, as it were, of human history and of human mind and self-reflection: "creation, exodus, law, wisdom, prophecy, gospel, and apocalypse."

The program of *The Great Code* is most conveniently stated in *Fearful Symmetry*.

> The basis of the Bible is, like that of the epic, religious and historical saga concerned with anthropomorphic gods and theomorphic men, part of it legendary history and part prophetic vision. But the Bible is neither a single work of art like the *Iliad,* nor an expanded one like *Mahabharata:* it is the historical product of a visionary tradition. It records a continuous reshaping of the earlier and more primitive visions, and as it goes on it becomes more explicitly prophetic, until the confused legends of an obscure people take the form of the full cyclic vision of fall, redemption and apocalypse. The Old Testament begins with an account of an escape from Egypt into Canaan led by Joshua, and ends with the prophetic allegorical recreation of this event: the escape of the imagination from a "furnace of iron" into a City of God through the power of a divine humanity or Messiah.
>
> The Gospels consolidate this vision of the Messiah into the vision of Jesus, who has the same name as Joshua, and the proof of the events in Jesus' life, as recorded in the Gospels, is referred not to contemporary evidence but to what the Old Testament prophets had said would be true of the Messiah. The imaginative recreation of Old Testament visions in the New Testament, reaching its climax in the dense mosaic of allusions and quotations in the Apocalypse, merely completes a process which goes on to a considerable extent within the Old Testament itself.[4]

Frye is able to take the Bible in English as an established fact that doesn't in practice raise severe problems for the critic whose Hebrew and Greek may not reach professional stan-

4. *Fearful Symmetry* (Beacon paperback), p. 317.

dards. Judaism and Christianity have always been hospitable to the idea of translation. In this they differ from Islam: the Koran is tied to Arabic in a way the Jewish and Christian Scriptures are not tied to Hebrew and Greek. There have been four great translations: the LXX (the Septuagint, for the Greek-speaking Jews of the pre-Christian diaspora), Jerome's Latin Vulgate, the King James Bible (Authorized Version), and Luther's Bible. (The best of the modern English translations, the Revised Standard Version, is closely tied to the King James.) We have to keep the original languages in mind, and profit from what the specialists tell us; but in practice it has to be assumed that a critical reading of the classic translations is sufficient for the study of the whole Bible. Specialized scholars don't go in for this; only theologians and exceptionally vigorous literary scholars have the courage to attempt synthetic and synoptic accounts.

The central idea of *The Great Code* is that of the many ways of reading to which the Bible invites us one is of capital importance: it has to be read typologically, not because this is an interesting pattern after we have given the kaleidoscope a shake, but because this is how the biblical authors, in the main, wrote.

To take the most majestic of the types, the "And God said, 'let there be light'" (Genesis 1:3) has as its antitype the prologue to the Fourth Gospel: "In the beginning was the Word. . . . All things were made through him. . . . In him was life, and the life was the light of men" (John 1:1-4). The Exodus is so much the dominant collection of types for the entire Bible that Frye can even write "that mythically the Exodus is the only thing that really happens in the Old Testament." Moses' organization of the Israelites into twelve tribes finds its antitype in the twelve apostles; the passage through the Red Sea signifies baptism; manna signifies the Eucharist; the Law is given from Sinai and thus the most celebrated collection of moral counsels in the New Testament is the "Sermon on the Mount." In all the Gospels the passion and death of Jesus are centered upon (despite the slight difference of timing between the Synoptics and the Fourth Gospel) the Passover; the Last Supper is a Passover meal, the

Crucifixion is the journey through the desert, the Resurrection is victory over Israel's enemies.

This is how the Bible has always been treated liturgically, in both the Jewish and the Christian traditions, though some of what is for the Christians realized antitype is for Jewish believers still to come (compare, for example, how Isaiah 53 would be read by the two sets of believers). The type-antitype relation is brought out plainly in the prayers and ritual actions of the Seder; among the Christian liturgies perhaps the most magnificent celebration of the relation is in the "Exsultet" of the Holy Saturday liturgy; this contains the famous "*O certe necessarium Adae peccatum. . . . O felix culpa. . . . O vere beata nox. . . .*" (O truly necessary sin of Adam. . . . O happy fault. . . . O night blessed indeed . . .).

Why the typological tradition should, despite its liturgical repetition, have for so many dropped out of mind is a many-sided question. Perhaps an important cause has been a presupposition, sometimes stated, sometimes taken for granted, of much liberal Protestant work on the Bible: that the Bible records a progressive change from the primitive and barbaric, if monolatrous, society reflected in the Pentateuch to the ethical monotheism of the Prophets, and then on to the pure ethical doctrine that can be extracted from the New Testament once it is purged of apocalyptic discourse and once it is separated (as by Matthew Arnold in *Literature and Dogma* and *St. Paul and Protestantism*) from its dead carapace of Hebraicisms.

In placing typology at the foundation of his reading of the Bible Frye has done much to rob the presupposition of its plausibility. And it is the types seeking, as it were, their antitypes, antitypes turning into types that have other antitypes, the whole to-and-fro movement of a searching reading of the Bible, that makes it proper to describe the volume as *The Great Code* (though there is a further implication that the Bible is a code for the deciphering of the secular literature into which it has entered in its text and through its spirit).

Typology gives us only the skeleton of Scripture. There are

many poetic devices that make up the density and richness of the Bible. Metaphor is picked out by Frye as one of the determining modes of biblical discourse. We have the imagery of Eden-Paradise, an oasis imagery of trees and water, Frye remarks, having a special charm for those who were originally desert nomads. The Bible moves between the images of pastoral life, shepherds, sheep, good shepherds, lost sheep, and those of the city, Jerusalem, the city of David, the place of the Temple, consigned to desecration and destruction, the place where God's wrath and justice are manifested in destruction and reconstruction; and finally "the Jerusalem above . . . , and she is our mother" (Galatians 4:26). The identification involved in metaphor is a curious, even a troublesome problem, and what Frye has to say deserves careful thought; he is certainly right in resisting moves to make metaphor no more than condensed simile or a mere metonymic reminder.

Frye's assembly of considerations and arguments, praisings and blamings, aphorisms, Chestertonian jokes, *obiter dicta*, needs and will receive thorough examination and criticism from scholars and critics. Here I confine myself to raising one question, a fundamental one, as I believe, that is forced upon us by Frye: what is the place of the Bible in human life? What is the Bible *about*? What is the connection of what is said by the biblical writers with the world of human history? These are simply ways of breaking down the question generated by the collision of Frye's view with the view of the believer. I don't assert that "the view of the believer" is something transparent and easily stated; but we have in some way to come to terms with it, precisely because Frye insists that the Bible is *kerygma*, the proclamation of a saving message, a collection of the oracles of God. This is not what the nineteenth-century liberal (Arnold is again the apposite figure) thought the Bible was; and it is not how students of "the Bible as literature" have taken it.

I understand Frye's argument in the following way. The Bible has the structure of two mirrors, each reflecting the other; and what the biblical writers say refers in a primary sense, even

101

where the intention of the writer seems historical, to other parts of the Bible. It is isolated from ordinary questions about truth and fact—to raise such questions is a solecism into which both fundamentalists and radical critics fall. Its function is not to point beyond itself, and to summon us to faith, with its conjoined virtues of humility and obedience, but to elevate us beyond faith to the higher life of vision. Our encounter with the Bible can induce in us a version of what Frye calls "upward metamorphosis," the making of all things new spoken about at the end of the Apocalypse.

> . . . the Bible deliberately blocks off the sense of the referential from itself: it is not a book pointing to a historical presence outside it, but a book that identifies itself with that presence. At the end the reader, also, is invited to identify himself with the book. Milton suggests that the ultimate authority in the Christian religion is what he calls the Word of God in the heart, which is superior even to the Bible itself, because for Milton this "heart" belongs not to the subjective reader but to the Holy Spirit. That is, the reader completes the visionary operation of the Bible by throwing out the subjective fallacy along with the objective one. The apocalypse is the way the world looks after the ego has disappeared.

As no one knows better than Frye, the questions that press upon us once we reflect on referential, descriptive, and other uses of language, on the logical status of fiction, the sense and testability of particular historical statements, on metaphor and metonymy, on the connections of sense with reference (to use Frege's standard example, "the evening star" and "the morning star" differ in sense but have the same reference), and other topics, are many and teasing. In most kinds of writing there is no need to be wary and to raise such questions, but here we must. We read, for example, that (Frye is following Aristotle) "History makes particular statements," whereas "Poetry expresses the universal in the event, the aspect of the event that makes it an example of the kind of thing that is always happening"; and later that "A myth is designed not to express a specific situation but to contain it in a way that does not restrict its significance to that one situation"; and then we come to the conclusion that "Its [the myth's] truth is inside its structure, not outside."

One can't read this without raising questions here about "inside" and "outside," and about how we get, as we surely must, from our knowledge of particular happenings to the kind of thing that is always happening. I think we are meant to think that Frye has clarified a set of problems whereas he has complicated very greatly these problems and added a quite unnecessary one, namely, how the truth of a myth, at least where it is to be considered "poetic"—and Frye thinks "the Biblical myths are closer to being poetic than to being history" (the truth I take it being the universal)—is *inside* the structure of the myth. Does this mean we mustn't fidget and ask silly questions about the archaeology of Ur of the Chaldees or Jericho or about whether or not there was an Exodus from Egypt? Plainly these are not the only questions, and perhaps not the most important questions, about the biblical stories; but they can't be proscribed.

Immediately after this excursus on myth and history, Frye stresses the impossibility of taking the Bible as through and through poetic; if we were to do this "we should have no criteria for distinguishing . . . Jesus from the prodigal son of his own parable." This seems right. But once we have allowed the distinction between fiction and fact, between poetry and history, to be made, then it seems inadequate to argue "that if anything historically true is in the Bible, it is there not because it is historically true but for different reasons." What can these be? Well, they "have something to do with spiritual profundity or significance." This seems weak, even when Frye elucidates spiritual profundity by referring to the admittedly poetic and unhistorical book of Job or to the heroic stories of enslavement and deliverance, stories in which "priority is given to the mythical structure or outline of the story," in Judges.

Frye's emphasis throughout is that if we want to understand the Bible, we can only do so by examining the intentions of the biblical writers themselves. If we do this, then we seem forced to conclude that the historical and, if we must use the phrase, the spiritually profound are conceived by them otherwise than Frye supposes. The catharsis, or whatever it is Frye thinks to be brought about by a faithful reading of the Bible, is connected in some cases with its reference to what lies outside the poetic myth or the literary aspect of the structure of typology. There are many instances of this. I choose only one: Paul's insistence on the nonmythical, historical, brutally factual character of the Crucifixion. When he writes (1 Corinthians 1:23) that "we preach Christ crucified, a stumbling block to Jews and folly to Gentiles," we may gloss what he says as follows. To the Gentiles the preaching is foolish; for the Greek world is full of stories about dying, suffering, and resurrected gods, but these things happen *in illo tempore* (as Mircea Eliade puts it), not "under Pontius Pilate." As to the Jews, here is the Messiah of promise, this scarecrow figure on a gibbet; and for this to be a stumbling block it has to be as historical as the Roman procurator under whom the Crucifixion happened.

I don't here want to dispute over Paul's claim, but simply to note it; for if we are to accept Frye's view that the Bible has a double-mirror structure, and that this structure represents the intentions of the authors, then we have also to note that here the intention is to use the structure and at the same time to go beyond it: to take the crucified one as the antitype of the figure in Isaiah 53 ("he was wounded for our transgressions, he was bruised for our iniquities," v. 5) and also to assert that the antitype is to be identified with a given man, Jesus of Nazareth, who belongs to history in the same way as do Paul and Gamaliel. What Frye a little contemptuously calls the scholar's "obsession with the Bible's historicity" is perfectly justified by the ethos and concerns of some of the biblical writers themselves. Whether or not there is good evidence for what the writers assert as historical is another, and logically independent, question. But they do make such assertions, and stress that their historicity is crucially significant.

There are many other difficulties in Frye's treatment of a number of questions. He falls too easily into persuasive definition: e.g., "there is no real evidence for the life of Jesus outside the New Testament"—a bullying way of saying that Frye doesn't think the evidence outside the New Testament is sufficient. There are several loose—too loose—generalizations about Marxism, of the kind that have been repeated from author to author during the past fifty years: e.g., "The burning bush contract introduces a revolutionary quality into the Biblical tradition, and its characteristics persist through Christianity, through Islam, and survive with little essential change [persuasive definition again] in Marxism."

But this is a magnificent book, a necessary recall to some fundamental principles of biblical interpretation, and a collection of problems and questions of the first importance for critics, biblical scholars, and the educated public in general. If I were asked to pick out the best thing in the book, I should choose the three pages (pp. 123-125) on Ecclesiastes, perhaps the most misunderstood and underappreciated book in the Bible. Frye shows that the weary cynicism often attributed to the author is a misreading. "Only when we realize that nothing is new can we live with an intensity in which everything becomes new." I ended my second reading of *The Great Code* with feelings of pleasure and envy: Frye's architectonic power is so astonishing.[5]

Professor Alter's approach is that of the literary critic, not that of the general theorist. He takes the Hebrew texts of the Jewish Bible and subjects them to the kind of critical analysis one might apply to Shakespeare or Proust. Of course, the stories of Ruth and of David the King, to choose two of his most loved subjects, have a character quite unlike anything else in literature.

5. It is a pleasure to handle a book so well printed and of such handsome appearance. I have noticed only two misprints, on pp. 36 and 213. There is what I assume to be an incomplete sentence ("The whole complex . . . witch-burning and the like") on p. 163.

The combination in the history of Israel of literary skill, moral passion, consciousness of mission, with low economic development and third-rate political status, is a marvel. We might well say that never has the world owed so much to so few.

The fundamental question is: "What role does literary art play in the shaping of biblical narrative?" To answer this question Alter has to move over some of the same ground as Frye, though he doesn't have to consider typology as having significance beyond the Hebrew Bible. But he necessarily stresses the quasi-symphonic character of the writings, the extent to which we are offered certain basic themes with a multitude of variations, "type-scenes"—the barren wife and the fertile concubine, the annunciation to the barren, the encounter at the well with the chosen maiden, and others—that provide "the grid of conventions upon which, and against which, the individual work operates." Again, he is also concerned with metaphor. He says very finely that the stones that seem to accompany Jacob's career are more than symbolic, though they are this: "there is something incipiently metaphorical about them: Jacob is a man who sleeps on stones, speaks in stones, wrestles with stones, contending with the hard unyielding nature of things." But such considerations are always urged with a view to a fuller analysis of the literary work.

Alter's work is in part an attack upon what he calls "the modern provincialism of assuming that ancient writers must be simple because they are ancient." He tries to show, on the whole with success, that the astonishing literary effects often achieved by the authors of the Bible and the "redactors" who wove together their material from different sources are the results of art and not of artlessness. Sometimes the argument seems a bit strained, as, for instance, when he argues that the conflict between Genesis 1:26, 27 and 2:18-24, the conflict between the creation of man as at once male and female and the separate creation of Eve from Adam's rib, "makes perfect sense as an account of the contradictory facts of woman's role in the post-edenic scheme of things"; we have side by side, in the milieu of the redactor, the conventions of a patriarchal society and the thin line of a contrary woman-centered tradition, that in which Rebekah, Tamar, Deborah, and Ruth stand. It is surely more plausible to argue, with Dr. E. A. Speiser, that the reverence of the redactor for the sources called "J" and "P" by scholars is such that he didn't feel free to eliminate what seem, at least on the surface, to be discrepancies between the two accounts, or difficulties within each account.[6] What Alter writes here seems to reflect the pressure of today's moral concerns.

We do not find in the Bible the mimetic techniques of Joyce or Proust, techniques which in a vulgarized form are now common in the novel at every level of art. In the narratives in which the subject matter is to us novelistic, an effect of great complexity, with strong emotional resonance, is achieved with means that seem very frugal. This is true of the stories of Joseph and his brethren, Joseph and Potiphar's wife, Joseph the interpreter of dreams. And it is true of the story of David, the youngest son of Jesse, keeping his flocks away from the world, his heroism in the battle with the Philistines, his ambiguous son-father relation, as it were, with Saul (Frye acutely calls Saul the only tragic hero in the Bible, surprising because the whole character of the Bible is that of divine comedy), his capture of the kingdom, the adultery with Bathsheba and the compassing of the death of Uriah, the death of the fruit of the adulterous relation between David and Bathsheba, the rape of Tamar, the career of Absalom and his death, the growing weariness of David, the haggling over the succession (Nathan the prophet and Bathsheba whispering over the bed of the failing king), the death of the king with Solomon already on the throne.

Alter shows what the basic features of narrative technique are. There is the initial statement (e.g., Ruth 1:1-5) which sets out the location of the story, or where it starts out from, the names of the characters, and their relationships (this is an enduring fea-

6. See The Anchor Bible, Vol. I: *Genesis*, introduction, translation, and notes by E. A. Speiser (Doubleday, 1964), p. xxix.

ture of narrative technique—*Robinson Crusoe* begins this way, as do all Jane Austen's novels except *Pride and Prejudice*, which begins with an apothegm). The main burden of the writer's task rests upon the account of what is done by the characters and by what they say to each other. Accounts of just *how* things are done make no attempt at detail (when, very occasionally, we are given such a detail as how Jacob disguised his hands the effect is powerfully felt), actions are named rather than described, and self-revelation is given over to a direct speech that is not egoistic or expressive in the ways familiar to us. Alter is able to show in detail how with such frugal means emotional tensions are depicted, complexity of motivation suggested, pathos achieved.

There are some particular ways in which the basic techniques are enriched; of these the leading one is the use of the *Leitwort*, the leading word which, with other forms of repetition, enables the biblical writers to impose a thematic unity on what we might suspect ought to have been a jerky, inconsequential narrative but nevertheless isn't so. For example, the Hebrew form of the verb "to see" and its related forms are shown to be thematically important in 1 Samuel, chapter 16. Naturally, a full response to the *Leitwort* is possible only to the reader of Hebrew. Martin Buber, whose account of the *Leitwort* phenomenon is in Alter's view definitive, and Franz Rosenzweig are commended for catching the *Leitwort* with some success in their German translation.

What underlies all the technical devices, and gives them their bite, is, in Alter's view, the conception of what it is to be human that is common to the biblical writers. Man is free, self-determined and this imposes on the writer a certain reticence, even ignorance. Curiously, it is this that gives a note of modernity to the Bible, as compared to other writings of antiquity (this is one of Auerbach's great topics in *Mimesis*).

> ... the underlying biblical conception of character as often unpredictable, in some ways impenetrable, constantly emerging from and slipping back into a penumbra of ambiguity, in fact has greater affinity with dominant modern

notions than do the habits of conceiving character typical of the Greek epics. The monotheistic revolution in consciousness profoundly altered the ways in which man as well as God was imagined, and the effects of that revolution probably still determine certain aspects of our conceptual world more than we suspect.

It is almost a cant phrase to say of a work that it is "seminal" and its use as commendation is sometimes mere puffery. But the works of Frye and Alter do seem to have within them much to be developed. Of course, this is to say that the Bible itself is seminal. In saying so, one can scarcely be thought to be going in for mere puffery.

PART II
ACADEMIC ESSAYS

History, Realism, and the
Work of Henry James ————————

It seems to follow from our knowing that imaginative literature consists of things that are made up, that questions about how far this or that fiction is "realistic" can have no sense. What is imitated or referred to or rendered by a fiction? What could be meant by claiming that an account of a battle or a love affair in a fiction is true (or untrue), faithful (or unfaithful), or "real" (or unreal)? It seems to follow from something's being a fiction, and not a report, that there is nothing of which it could be a true or false account. Tourists may be eager to see the place where Mr. Pickwick got into the wrong bedroom—after all, isn't the Great White Horse still there in Ipswich?—or where Sherlock Holmes had his duel with Professor Moriarty; but this we feel to be an amiable weakness of mind, a tribute to the bright hallucinations contrived by the expert framer of fictions. Someone once put as an epigraph to a novel: "I am not I; he is not he; she is not she." One could falsely claim that something was a fiction and use the claim as a cover for libel—a lying account is not the same kind of thing as a fictional account. Since World War II there have been some silly plays in which the recently dead are portrayed with gross malice as murderers or poltroons; it seems wrong for

From *English Studies in Canada* (September 1984).

the author to defend himself on the ground that what he has written is a fiction. This is like courting a woman and going through a marriage ceremony with her, and then at the end of it all saying *It was only a joke.* Such a claim wouldn't exempt a man from prosecution for bigamy. But these are borderline cases. Barsetshire, Hardy's Wessex, George Eliot's Loamshire, Scott's Louis XI, Trollope's Plantagenet Palliser, James's Isabel Archer, are all equally fictions no matter what geographical and historical references may exist in the intentions of the author and the mind of the reader.

But fictions have sense. If they don't involve, in the same way as do historical accounts and geographical descriptions, reference to the world, how do they appear to have such reference? The states of affairs the writer of fictions feigns to describe are *possible,* that is, we know what would be the case if this or that description were true. Plainly it is possible for a man to smother his wife out of jealousy, or for husband and wife to conspire to kill the king; and it is also possible for the hero to kiss the princess out of a hundred-year-old sleep and for the queen of the fairies to be infatuated with an ass. The case of the sleeping beauty, the case of Titania and the "translated" Bottom, these are possible in the Humeian sense: that whatever we can imagine is possible. What limits this sense of possible is a difficult question. We are inclined to think it is not a possible description if we say that the square roots of numbers are falling in love with the roses; but then we remember what Lewis Carroll is able to do in the two Alice books. Even what is in a more extreme sense than the fairy-story sense not possible may be treated as possible in a fiction. This we call nonsense. I mention it to bring out the broadness of the category of fiction.

We are still faced with this problem: all fictions have the form of accounts of states of affairs, but they are not accounts of states of affairs that exist independently of the fiction. Some are accounts of states of affairs we should be inclined to say are naturally impossible (the kind of thing we say *doesn't* happen); some are accounts of things that in some sense couldn't happen (nonsense). It is within this broad band of the category of fiction that we pick out fictions that are realistic—or naturalistic—as distinct from fictions that fall under other headings. But in what consists their realism, since they are fictions?

The possibility of talking, in the mode of possibility, about the world belongs to the nature of language. This is why fictions—fairy tales, epics, legends—long precede straight descriptions and historical narratives in the history of culture. Of course, fictional accounts presuppose genuine cognitive and practical dealings with the world. We can't talk unless there are semantic rules, that is, we make and acquire rules for the uses of such words as "red," "black," "light," "heavy," "good," "bad," "brave," "cowardly," "ascetic," "luxurious" . . . ; all these, with their metaphorical—impossible to list—possibilities. Plainly such rules, those that determine meaning, presuppose a shared practical and cognitive human life. We couldn't use the expression "The Princess is asleep" in a fiction unless we had first shared in a human life in which "is asleep" had applications. In this sense fictional discourse is parasitic upon discourse which applies to the world. But in the case of any given sentence its meaning is what it is quite apart from any application to the world it may have on this or that occasion, in this or that mouth. Thus anyone who knows the English language is in some degree capable of telling the truth, telling a lie, giving a command, asking a question . . . and telling a story. Telling a story, in whatever style, is not primarily a special use of language but a use of language for special purposes.

Now, the art of the novel is peculiar in that in the tradition of realism, and this is just as true of Richardson and Fielding as of the nineteenth-century novelists, there is an attempt to induce a state of rapture, in which from time to time we set aside our knowledge that we are dealing with a fiction.

As faithfully now as when it initially appeared, the novel has been dedicated to the trifling, trivial, minor and

> minute, to the first and second footstep, the half-smile, the sneeze, the skin-tight trouser, powdered bosom, little oddity of speech or dress. It has been and remains a realm where the passing of a thought is celebrated like a change of crowns, where a whim receives the solitude due to a desperate resolve.
>
> . . . [The novel] even wants to render in words the cake's moist taste, the crazed surface of the serving plate, a look which candle light has blown across the dinner table.[1]

Of course, such rapture, such dissolving of our consciousness of the here and now, of pangs of hunger and of social anxieties, isn't a peculiarity of fictions in the mode of realism. Fairy story or epic may achieve it. But the peculiarity of fictions in the mode of realism lies in the way its content dictates to us how we are to respond. Simple people have sometimes supposed that *Robinson Crusoe* is, as we say, a real-life story, just as simple people may think radio or television soap operas have a reality they don't in fact have (garments arrive for births and weddings, there is mourning for the dead).

We may ask what the point may be of realistic fiction. Why should we want something different from what is given in the *Odyssey* or *The Winter's Tale* or *Comus*?

Henry James expresses a part of the problem for us; and it is interesting to see how far James's practice helps to solve our problems and, perhaps, to raise others. The problem is set out in his 1884 essay on "The Art of Fiction." [2] I won't attempt to follow the entire sinuous movement of James's thought; it is a movement rather than, in any formal sense, a continuous argument. I pick out the following.

1. The novel's reason for existence is to "represent life." This is found disturbing (along with the other arts) in Protestant

1. William H. Gass, "Representation and the War for Reality," *Salmagundi*, No. 55 (Winter 1982), p. 75.
2. See *Henry James: Selected Literary Criticism*, ed. Morris Shapira, with a Note by F. R. Leavis (Harmondsworth: Penguin, 1968).

communities, where a deep suspicion of fictions as being "wicked" lingers.

2. The writer is looking for a "true" representation. The novel "is history," and thus it is a great betrayal of the novelist's "sacred office" to address the reader, as Trollope does, in such a way as to admit "that the events he narrates have not really happened, and that he can give his narrative any turn the reader may like best"—or, of course, a turn that may irritate the reader. If Johnny Eames doesn't in the end marry Lily Dale, this is because Trollope decides he shan't, just as, after overhearing a conversation in the Reform Club, he decided to kill off Mrs. Proudie. I don't think James is denying that the novel is made up and that what happens in the novel is within the power of the author. What he seems to suggest is that given the initial commitment of the novelist to his "story"—something like the Aristotelian myth, or plot—then something is imposed upon the novelist such that he can betray and falsify it.

3. The novel is the product of a peculiar subjectivity, what James calls "experience": "a kind of huge spider-web of the finest silken threads suspended in the chamber of consciousness, and catching every airborne particle in its tissue. It is the very atmosphere of the mind; and when the mind is imaginative . . . it takes to itself the faintest hints of life, it converts the very pulses of the air into revelations" (85-86). To be a novelist is to see commonplace incidents as expressive of character, as hints of destiny, as incidents in a drama which has an inside and an outside. "It is an incident for a woman to stand up with her hand resting on a table and look out at you in a certain way. . . . At the same time it is an expression of character" (88). With this sense of the large significance of "incidents" there must go "solidity of specification." This is a technical challenge: "It is here in very truth that he [the novelist] competes with life," in that he tries "to catch the colour, the relief, the expression, the surface, the substance of the human spectacle" (87).

4. "Art is essentially selection, but it is a selection whose main care is to be typical, to be inclusive" (91).

5. Advice to the young novelist: "Do not think too much about optimism and pessimism; try and catch the colour of life itself" (97). (That is, do not think too much about reaction and progress, or about "cultural identity," or about "what it is to be a Canadian.")

From these considerations I choose one as the key: "solidity of specification." This covers time, space, what is heard, seen, touched, smelled, and hearings, seeings, touchings, smellings, the life of feeling and of emotion, the moral life—attitudes, evaluations, guilt, remorse, the felt power of social institutions, events and actions, beheld, effected, undergone by the characters; above all, since it is necessary that a novel's characters should be articulate—or expressive in their inarticulateness—and show understanding and thought, calculative, reflective, whatever, there will be *words*, in direct speech and in reported speech, as acts of speech showing the interplay of the characters, and as reflective about what they do, suffer, remember, hope for, fear. . . . How this solidity of specification is effected is various without limit. Below I look at cases from *The Golden Bowl* and *The Wings of the Dove*.

The element of *time* ought to be looked at on its own. It is not simply a matter of what is included in the specification, one element among others that constitute the solidity of the specification—that B is seen to follow A and go before C. It is a matter of the novel's historical setting, and this is a datum of the novel, along with the myth or plot. "In these times of ours, though concerning the exact year there is no need to be precise . . ."; this is how *Our Mutual Friend* opens. Or at the beginning of *A Tale of Two Cities* we are given a more complex temporal indication: "It was the best of times, it was the worst of times, it was the age of wisdom, it was the age of foolishness . . . in short, the period was so far like the present period. . . . It was the year of Our Lord one thousand seven hundred and seventy-five" (that is, for the knowing reader, the American Revolution is just about to happen, the French Revolution is fourteen years ahead). The time indicated is often, even where we are inclined to call the novel in question realistic, the time of a generation back, a world the author knew in childhood or remembered as reflected, in his childhood, in the conversations of older people.

> With this drop of ink at the end of my pen, I will show you the roomy workshop of Mr Jonathan Burge, carpenter and builder, in the village of Hayslope, as it appeared on the eighteenth of June, in the year of our Lord 1799.

Thus begins *Adam Bede*, its fictional date being ten years earlier than the birth of Mary Anne Evans herself. The elegiac mood of Hardy's best fiction comes from its depicting a past that survives for the reader, and sometimes for the writer, only as an old story: plowmen, shepherds, furze-cutters, thatchers; men living in harsh poverty, buffeted by the weather, showing their humanity by humorous interchanges, sharing ceremonially in a cycle set by an archaic calendar, in part natural and pagan, in part religious and Christian; these men, this society, show us the end of something, the end of a form of life that in substance goes back for thousands of years. Hardy's rural society is closer to the previous three thousand years than it is to the encroaching society of industrialism. This makes the novels full and dense, and we find that in confronting Wessex we are confronting the human past. Of course, the leading characters rise above the peasant chorus and are touched with modernity; they are fascinated by the reflected glare of Christminster, or by other vanities. But it is the background against which they act that makes them serious; for they too belong, though not wholly, to that world, hard of access to most West Europeans and North Americans, where the barking of a dog breaks the silence of the night and a distant light relieves its darkness.

Time, historical time, personal time, this pervades Proust's novel. We begin with a recollection of the narrator's former ways of going to sleep; and the state of sleep; and the picture of time has the sleeping man at its centre. "When a man is asleep, he has in a circle round him the chain of the hours, the sequence of the years, and the order of the heavenly bodies. When he wakes up, he reads off, as by instinct, just where on the earth he is and how much time has gone by before his awakening."[3] This linking of the world of time with the unconscious and with dreaming gives to the encompassing world of the novel an extensiveness that goes beyond what is readily accessible. This consciousness is to be found before the rise of the novel, in Shakespeare, in Pascal, in Augustine. I add that Proust does not stay at this, as it were, metaphysical level. *La vieille France* is continually with us, through architecture, through heraldic conceits, through the particular locutions of Françoise and Charlus, and the Dreyfus affair is omnipresent; all social time is before Dreyfus, or after Dreyfus, or during the affair.

Solidity of specification in time is commonly effected by James in very subtle ways accessible only to the alert and well-informed reader. A most interesting example is that incident in *The Golden Bowl* when the Prince escorts Charlotte and Fanny to the ball, and "the greatest possible Personage" has "sent for" Charlotte. Who this Personage is one knows perfectly well, though James does not of course use names, and the Personage's being who he is lends wry humour to Charlotte's question: "What in the world does he want to do to me?"[4] The world of country houses with a faintly raffish tone, of aristocratic hostesses not too scrupulous, is the world within which the adultery of the Prince and Charlotte is committed, a world that is reflected in the *chroniques scandaleuses* of the period.

But in what sense could the novel be historical? James seems, in his criticism and in his practice as a novelist, to be feeling after something close to Aristotle's distinction between history and poetry, where the contrast is not one of verbal form— a history could be written in meter—but in the intention and, where the intention is realized, the effect: poetry is concerned with the universal. To take an example from his practice. In the

3. Marcel Proust, *A la recherche du temps perdu: Du côté de chez Swann* (Paris: Gallimard, 1954), p. 5.

4. Henry James, *The Golden Bowl* (New York Edition), I, 264-65.

later novels the dialogue, which bears so much of the burden of the novels, above all in *The Awkward Age,* is no closer to actual speech, not even the speech of such intensely conscious and wonderfully intelligent people as he posits, than is Shakespeare's blank verse. Yet it is intended, as he insists, to "represent life." What then is a "representation"? There is a betraying discussion in the preface to *The Golden Bowl.* James discusses what the point may be of drawings and photographs in illustrated editions of novels, in particular the photographs made by A. L. Coburn for the original edition. James and Coburn had looked for appropriate scenes in London; and one sought after, as a frontispiece, was

> a view of the small shop in which the Bowl is first encountered.
>
> The problem thus was thrilling, for although the small shop was but a shop of the mind, of the author's projected world, in which objects are primarily related to each other, and therefore not "taken from" a particular establishment anywhere, only an image distilled and intensified, as it were, from a drop of the essence of such establishments in general, our need (since the picture was . . . also completely to speak for itself) prescribed a concrete, independent, vivid instance, the instance that should oblige us by the marvel of an accidental rightness. (I, xii)

This is the search for what philosophers have sometimes called the concrete universal: that distinguishable entity which despite its particularity embodies in itself the features of a class. (I do not here raise the question how far the idea of the concrete universal is logically coherent.)

Many devices have been used to assist in producing and presenting the concrete universal, though I would emphasize that the final result—what distinguishes a James or a Proust from mere industrious practitioners—is not a matter of skill in the use of devices; if it were simply an acquired skill, there would be some justification for courses labelled "creative writing" in respectable universities. Among such devices is the use of an ancient fable long linked with the affective life of mankind. For instance, in *The Golden Bowl* we are given a patriarch who is Adam, a Princess and a Prince, a wicked step-mother, palaces, gardens, and a magical object, the golden bowl itself. But here the treatment, not simply the presence of the fable, is everything.

An example of James's attempted combination of the particular, the concrete, and the universal is the opening paragraph of *The Golden Bowl:*

> The Prince had always liked his London, when it had come to him; he was one of the Modern Romans who find by the Thames a more convincing image of the truth of the ancient state than any they have left by the Tiber. Brought up on the legend of the City to which the world paid tribute, he recognised in the present London much more than in contemporary Rome the real dimensions of such a case. If it was a question of an *Imperium,* he said to himself, and if one wished, as a Roman, to recover a little the sense of that, the place to do so was on London Bridge, or even, on a fine afternoon in May, at Hyde Park Corner. It was not indeed to either of those places that these grounds of his predilection, after all sufficiently vague, had, at the moment we are concerned with him, guided his steps; he had strayed simply enough into Bond Street, where his imagination, working at comparatively short range, caused him now and then to stop before a window in which objects massive and lumpish, in silver and gold, in the forms to which precious stones contribute, or in leather, steel, brass, applied to a hundred uses and abuses, were as tumbled together as if, in the insolence of the Empire, they had been the loot of far-off victories. The young man's movements, however, betrayed no consistency of attention—not even, for that matter, when one of his arrests had proceeded from possibilities in faces shaded, as they passed him on the pavement, by huge beribboned hats, or more delicately tinted still under the tense silk of parasols held at perverse angles

in waiting victorias. And the Prince's undirected thought
was not a little symptomatic, since, though the turn of the
season had come and the flush of the streets begun to fade,
the possibilities of faces, on the August afternoon, were
still one of the notes of the scene. He was too restless—that
was the fact—for any concentration, and the last idea that
would just now have occurred to him in any connexion
was the idea of pursuit. (I, 3-4)

If we consider, and this would not be altogether absurd,
this passage as the overture to a vast opera, as by Richard
Strauss, in which voices and instruments exist on the same
melodramatic plane, then we can say that it introduces virtually all the themes that are to be developed later.

Note the first sentence: "when it had come to him." The
picture is of Mohammed to whom mountains come; this suggests both attractive power and passivity; to *go* to London, as
distinct from having London presented to him on, as it were, a
silver tray, is something for which he lacks energy and will. He
is indeed effete, as Rome is; and yet, like Rome, he keeps the
power to attract. London is the new Rome in the afternoon of its
imperialism (we must link the picture of this successor empire
with the August afternoon, the flush of the streets fading). It is
not "a fine afternoon in May," the ideal moment for cultivating
a sense of the *Imperium;* the season is over, London is "empty";
but August does perhaps suggest an Augustan peace, something a little faded, post-climactic, after the supreme achievement under Caesar, the last great figure of the Republic. Bond
Street: this exhibits the energy and brutality of the imperial
achievement, its bounty, its touch of vulgarity: massive, lump-
ish objects in precious metal and all the natural substances that
when worked upon sustain the life of luxury. These are primarily the products of commerce and not of military victory, spoils
of peace and not of war. But there is nothing here to captivate
the Prince. Even sexuality has no present power, or rather no
consistent power. He does stop occasionally, in the indolence of

habit, and these stoppings, arrests, proceed from "possibilities in faces shaded, as they passed him on the pavement, by huge beribboned hats, or more delicately tinted still under the tense silk of parasols held at perverse angles in waiting victorias." The idea of pursuit—the activity of the hunter, the *coureur*—would not "just now" occur to him. He has something on his mind, attention to his accustomed pleasures has been deflected by something else; in fact, as we soon learn, by the ardors of a successful pursuit—he is, after all, capable of fits of energy—one that is now to present him with more anxieties than he had expected. He is proposing to replenish his depleted stores of wealth and energy, all that is left of the Roman inheritance, not from the British Empire in its late afternoon, but from farther West, from the new American Empire that is already despoiling Europe of its artistic treasures; and the Prince himself, proleptically christened Amerigo, is an old embossed coin coveted by the new imperialists.

The passage examined illustrates James's mastery of a certain method, one by which he presents something concrete—there is nothing wrong here with the required solidity of specification—and, at the same time, representative, something which goes far beyond what is in particular represented to bring before us great networks of human history. And what is here depicted, this moment of the Prince's progress, comes to a climax with the encounter between the Prince (Europe) and Maggie, Charlotte, Adam Verver, with the Assinghams as chorus (America and England respectively), in the setting of late Victorian society in England, an England that provides a moral medium as well as a setting—country house, cathedral city, gardens, streets with little antique shops.

Here is the Prince, at Lady Castledean's, on the eve of his first act of adultery with Charlotte. He becomes aware that Lady Castledean would be delighted if he and Charlotte were to go off together, leaving her with her lover, Mr. Blint. The Prince does not see how Lady Castledean can take Mr. Blint seriously, but "this question but sank for him again into the fathomless depths of English equivocation." The English preferred not to be clear in such matters.

> They didn't like *les situations nettes*. . . . They wouldn't have them at any price; it had been their national genius and their national success to avoid them at every point. They called it themselves, with complacency, their wonderful spirit of compromise—the very influence of which actually so hung about him here from moment to moment that the earth and the air, the light and the color, the fields and the hills and the sky, the blue-green counties and the cold cathedrals, owed to it every accent of their tone. (I, 354)

The Prince's bewilderment is then put in these terms:

> There were other marble terraces, sweeping more purple prospects, on which he would have known what to think, and would have enjoyed thereby at least the small intellectual fillip of a discerned relation between a given appearance and a taken meaning.

The real triumph of the whole passage is not so much—though it is very remarkable—the picture of the Prince's confusion, the account of the multiplicity of signals he is receiving but not wholly deciphering or separating out; it is rather the presenting of a composite object; and this is composed of personal feeling, social situation, the weight of history, and landscapes seen through the media of light and colour, and yet humanized and moralized: "the blue-green counties and the cold cathedrals." In his making of a composite in which landscape, history, a moral atmosphere, and the pressure of an impending choice, are so put together that their distinct meanings flow into a single complex meaning that cannot be stated outside the passage itself, in this James has predecessors, notably George Eliot, to whom he owes so much; but he is surely the master.

Another example will lead us into the problems of *The Wings of the Dove*: Milly Theale at Matcham:

The great historic house had, for Milly, beyond terrace and garden, as the centre of an almost extravagantly grand Watteau-composition, a tone as of old gold kept "down" by the quality of the air, summer full-flushed but attuned to the general perfect taste. Much, by her measure, for the previous hour, appeared, in connexion with this revelation of it, to have happened to her—a quantity expressed in introductions of charming new people, in walks through halls of armor, of pictures, of cabinets, of tapestry, of tea-tables, in an assault of reminders that this largeness of style was the sign of *appointed* felicity. The largeness of style was the great containing vessel, while everything else, the pleasant personal affluence, the easy murmurous welcome, the honoured age of illustrious host and hostess, all at once so distinguished and so plain, so public and so shy, became but this or that element of the infusion. The elements melted together and seasoned the draught, the essence of which might have struck the girl as distilled into the small cup of iced coffee she had vaguely accepted from somebody, while a fuller flood somehow kept bearing her up—all the freshness of response of her young life, the freshness of the first and only prime.[5]

Here we are given, not principally the narrator's consciousness, as in our first passage (the Prince in Bond Street), but that of the young American heiress Milly Theale. She is able to "place" Matcham through her acquaintances with Watteau . . . she goes through a compiled list of people, halls of armour, tea tables . . . the host and hostess are *illustrious,* at once distinguished and plain. . . . This is very much the response of the simple impressionable American girl she is. But intermingled with her consciousness is that of the narrator, for "the infusion," "the draught," and the *essence* of these, "*might* have struck the girl as distilled into the small cup of iced coffee." It would be a mistake to talk of synesthesia in the strict sense, but the effect of the ensemble of those things presented to us

5. Henry James, *The Wings of the Dove* (New York Edition), I, 208-9.

is to blend sensuous, moral, and intellectual acts and responses in such a way that there is a single composite object before us.

Of the three final novels *The Wings of the Dove* is the most ambitious. It is the closest James comes to doing through the form of the novel what is done by tragedy, as conceived by those who have interpreted Aristotle in a slightly romantic way, and as practised, realized, by Shakespeare.

In some ways James is very unlike Aristotle. Whereas for Aristotle character is depicted only for the sake of action, in James the life of consciousness is almost all, though there are decisive actions, often acts of speech, that spill over from a given consciousness; sometimes we are inclined to say that the acts of consciousness are the substance of the tragic action.[6] This is perhaps also true of Shakespeare, and this is why we sometimes find Aristotle's exemplary characters strange, like people in an anthropologist's account of an exotic tribe. But we can rescue from the Aristotelian formulations at least two things: the idea of a fatal, or bad, or mistaken choice, made by one who is neither outstandingly good nor outstandingly bad, but in the middle; and the idea of purgation by pity and terror induced by the spectacle, the concatenation of events that are set in motion by the bad choice. *The Wings of the Dove* is suffused by something else which is not at all Greek—a mood, a configuration of feeling, sounded, set, by the Scriptural passage alluded to in the title, Psalm LV:

3 The enemy crieth so, and the ungodly cometh on so fast: for they are minded to do me some mischief; so maliciously are they set against me.
4 My heart is disquieted within me: and the fear of death is fallen upon me.
5 Fearfulness and trembling are come upon me: and an horrible dread hath overcome me.

6. In the Preface to *The Portrait of a Lady* James tells us that he eschews such employments as "murders and battles and the great mutations of the world."

6 And I said, O that I had wings like a dove: for then would I flee away, and be at rest.

* * * * * * * * * *

9 ... and I have spied unrighteousness and strife in the city.

* * * * * * * * * *

11 Wickedness is therein: deceit and guile go not out of their streets.

12 For it is not an open enemy, that hath done me this dishonour: for then I could have borne it.

13 Neither was it mine adversary, that did magnify himself against me: for then peradventure I would have hid myself from him.

14 But it was even thou, my companion: my guide, and mine own familiar friend.

* * * * * * * * * *

22 The words of his mouth were softer than butter, having war in his heart: his words were smoother than oil, and yet be they very swords.

It is not by accident that James plucks his title from this psalm. It is plain that the psalm's central theme represents the central situation of the novel. It is true, the image of the dove gathers to itself other symbolic associations—the Holy Ghost, harmlessness, gentle purity. Even in its prophetic final verse—"And as for them [that is, the bloody and deceitful]; thou, O God, shalt bring them into the pit of destruction"—the psalm applies, for into this pit go Kate Croy and Merton Densher.

There is no doubt that *The Wings of the Dove* has a tragic plot and that it aims at the great catharsis through pity and terror. I summarize it as follows.

The immensely rich Milly Theale is presented to us as:

... the striking apparition ... the slim, constantly pale, delicately haggard, anomalously, agreeably angular young person, of not more than two-and-twenty summers, in spite of her marks, whose hair was somehow exceptionally red even for the real thing, which it innocently confessed to being, and whose clothes were remarkably black even for robes of mourning, which was the meaning they expressed. It was New York mourning, it was New York hair, it was a New York history, confused as yet, but multitudinous, of the loss of parents, brothers, sisters, almost every human appendage, all on a scale and with a sweep that had required the greater stage; it was a New York legend of affecting, of romantic isolation, and, beyond everything, it was by most accounts, in respect to the mass of money so piled on the girl's back, a set of New York possibilities. She was alone, she was stricken, she was rich, and in particular was strange. (I, 105-06)

This apparition in red, white, and black is launched into London society (of a minor sort); it becomes known that she is fatally ill; Kate Croy, with poor shabby relatives (by name Condrip—cp. Blint above!), and poor herself, is secretly engaged to an amiable, sufficiently intelligent for the burden the author lays upon him but not excessively talented, journalist Merton Densher—secretly, because Kate's patroness and aunt, Mrs. Lowder, has other plans for Kate—and Kate determines that Densher shall make Milly love him, marry the dying heiress so that, once she is dead, Kate and Densher may marry in a security guaranteed by riches. Half of this comes about. Milly does fall in love with Densher and he affects to love her. But she finds out, as she lies waiting for death in Venice, what her friend Kate and her would-be husband have in mind; turns her face to the wall; but has a final, unreported interview with Densher; all we know of it is "that something had happened to him too beautiful and too sacred to describe. He had been, to his recovered sense, forgiven, dedicated, blessed; but this he couldn't coherently express" (II, 343). Milly dies and leaves Densher a fortune. He tells Kate he will renounce the fortune and marry her, but will not marry her and accept the fortune. Kate believes he has fallen in love with Milly and her memory and has in effect been converted and has abandoned the Machiavellian gospel. Densher cries out: "We've played our dreadful game and we've lost." The end is in a sense "open." Whatever in particular may be thought to "happen," a correct stage direction would be: "Exeunt, pursued by the Furies."

Such a summary leaves out much richness, all the fine treatment of Mrs. Lowder's dining room and its guests, the magnificent landscapes and seascapes of Venice; but it brings out the plot's tragic structure and its aim at catharsis. The fatal choice is given to Densher, not to the more energetic Kate. Kate's will is fixed, on riches and social advancement and the enjoyment of Densher on Lowder-approved terms, from the beginning; the sign of her amiability is—along with her beauty and strength and intelligence—her unworldly choice of Densher as her lover; she wants to have *both* love of an uncalculating kind *and* the world, and the novel is a vast demonstration that she cannot have both, and that in choosing the latter she cancels her earlier choice. Densher is weaker and on the whole seems to drift into wickedness through Kate's pressure. But there is, nevertheless, the moment of choice, the moment when he might have done other than he did. There is a moment of which he says, retrospectively, "that something had at that moment hung for him by a hair" (II, 85).

As to whether or not the high tragic effect is realized, this strikes me as no more a matter for dispute than it would be in connexion with *Lear* or *Macbeth*. If tragedy is not *here*, "tragedy" is the name of a class without members. What I am more concerned about is its connexion with the "real" and the historical.

I assume that the point of the novel-tragedy is to do within a quite different set of conventions what the poetic tragedy did within its own set. With the development of the novel we are given the possibility of a treatment that has *density*—James's "solidity of specification"—the texture, the vibrancy, the color, the heat and the cold, of "real life." But it is necessary that through this solidity, not despite it, the tragedy should be deployed and the purgative end achieved. This is a "high" effect, an affair in which the leading characters and the issues must be undeniably "large," spiritually impressive through being visually impressive, and in which bodily actions and expressed thoughts must be striking. Small characters, humble actions, stumbling conversations, may achieve pathos, but not the tragic effect. Now, it would seem that in itself solidity of specification would distract us from large effects and a ready grasp of symbols, and the better it is done, the more, in general, distracting it is, as often in Dickens. James sometimes uses solidity of specification in such a way as to point to the larger structure of the fable; and to show how the use of a historical theme works with the symbolic, the tragic intention, not against it. It is true, any craftsman can do this kind of thing, and the world of the novel in English is marked by many examples. I put on one side, here, the question what it is that distinguishes the work of a James from that of those who have, merely, a craft at their command.

My example is taken from the sequel to Milly's visit to Sir Luke Strett (perhaps the "Luke" is a bit excessive), in which she learns indirectly—nothing plain is said—that she is doomed. She goes into the London streets. "She literally felt, in this first flush, that her only company must be the human race at large, present all round her, but inspiringly impersonal, and that her only field must be, then and there, the grey immensity of London" (I, 247). She is lost in the maze of shabby streets with their shabby inhabitants, but in the end discovers herself in Regent's Park.

> . . . Regent's Park, round which on two or three occasions with Kate Croy her public chariot had solemnly rolled. But she went into it further now; this was the real thing; the real thing was to be quite away from the pompous roads, well within the centre and on the stretches of shabby grass. Here were benches and smutty sheep; here were idle lads at games of ball, with their cries mild in the thick air; here were wanderers anxious and tired like herself; here doubtless were hundreds of others just in the same box. Their

> box, their great common anxiety, what was it, in this grim
> breathing-space, but the practical question of life? They
> could live if they would; that is, like herself, they had been
> told so. . . . All she thus shared with them made her wish
> to sit in their company; which she so far did that she looked
> for a bench that was empty, eschewing a still emptier chair
> that she saw hard by and for which she would have paid,
> with superiority, a fee. (I, 250)

She then tells herself that no one knows where she is, and this
produces in her a feeling of liberation and a judgment on her
past. "It was the first time in her life that this had happened;
somebody, everybody appeared to have known before, at every
instant of it, where she was; so that she was now suddenly able
to put it to herself that that hadn't been a life" (I, 250-51). In a
way, everything—her way of life, her wealth, her intrinsic interest and charm—is stripped from her. She is reduced "to her
ultimate state, which was that of a poor girl—with her rent to
pay for example—staring before her in a great city. Milly had
her rent to pay, her rent for her future; everything else but how
to meet it fell away from her in pieces, in tatters" (I, 253-54). Then
follows the moment of epiphany, in a way the equivalent of
Lear's "Poor naked wretches."

> She looked about her again, on her feet, at her scattered
> melancholy comrades—some of them so melancholy as to
> be down on their stomachs in the grass, turned away, ig-
> noring, burrowing; she saw once more, with them, those
> two faces of the question between which there was so lit-
> tle to choose for inspiration. It was perhaps superficially
> more striking that one could live if one would; but it was
> more appealing, insinuating, irresistible in short, that one
> would live if one could. (I, 254)

The word that stabs here is "burrowing": men strive to hide
themselves within the darkness of the earth, away from the glare
of day.

Here, then, is a case where within the convention of realistic fiction, that there should be solidity of specification, this solidity does not delay or distract us, does not trap us within the detail, but brings us under the combined influences of compassion and deadly fear into the heart of the tragedy. It also has the effect, characteristic of the finest tragedy, of showing us, not arguing us into it, that we are "all in the same boat."

In the age of the novel in which James is so splendid a late flourishing, romanticism and academic history have combined to influence the imagination in such a way that the novel requires historical markers and requires that the consciousness of the leading characters should be, not just reflectively, historical, as exemplifying or suggesting its historicity. It is plain that in the best work of James's middle and late periods historical themes are always present as confronting, no matter how enigmatically, the leading characters with issues that belong peculiarly to their own time. (The best example, or the easiest to analyze, would be *The Ambassadors;* but its fable is not tragic; it is rather James's dark comedy.)

James's historical themes are concerned with the relations of three cultures, the American, the English, and the European (on the whole Europe means France, Italy, and Switzerland) in the last quarter of the nineteenth century. The cultures are sketched with the broad, sure, and eloquent strokes of the great cartoonist; they come to a point of self-consciousness in certain figures. Innocence, ingenuousness, spontaneity, courage, beauty, are expressed primarily through a series of brilliant portraits of young women, from Daisy Miller—an early sketch—to Milly Theale. They offer a puzzle to the Europeans: they are unconventional, flighty, flirtatious, fiercely independent; they wander through Europe unprotected, or accompanied by chaperones who are negligent and uncomprehending to the point of absurdity; their initial approaches to anyone they find interesting, or like, are uncalculated and affectionate. This baffles the Europeans, for these young women conform in their outward behavior to the European stereotype of the unchaste adventuress; but they are virginal and innocent. Comparatively the English are cold, constrained, hypocritical, and greedy. The Europeans are baffled by the Americans and the English. The Europeans excel in finding their way through the intricacies of social life without getting lost or feeling embarrassed. They are clear where the English are, half deliberately, muddled: on the one side there is the fabric of conventional morals and manners, and this must be maintained in its external integrity; but behind this wall or shield intelligent people arrange their affairs as they please, as their desires run hither and thither. Thus we have comedies of misunderstanding; lives are wounded and wasted; white doves mangled and bloody. Early in James's career Daisy Miller dies of the vapors of the Roman night, but her true killer is a Europeanized American; in James's final phase Milly Theale dies with the great Venetian sky, and the city's decaying palaces, as her background—flames, rosy half-lights, glitters of gold and marble, and a blackness which now spreads from her garments to the dying world.

Of course, I am too schematic. There are not only the interchanges between the three great cultures; there is also a careful anatomizing of the American culture that first shaped James's imagination. Here the polarizing is between the deliquescent Protestant culture of New England—fine, rigorous, well-scrubbed, philanthropic (wonderfully described in *The Europeans*)—and the more relaxed, more "worldly," a little reaching-out-to-Europe culture commonly represented by "New York." Once again women are the more eloquent representatives: in *The Wings of the Dove* Susan Stringham is "from Burlington, Vermont, which she boldly upheld as the real heart of New England, Boston being 'too far south'" (I, 106), and, as we have seen, Milly is a New York romantic legend come to life, a bright flower nourished by an immense fortune and by the opulent many-layered soil of the population of her city. The handsome "Thackerayan" Kate Croy and Mrs. Lowder speak for England's disingenuous worldliness: concern with appearances rules them; and they are ruthless in action, cruel in pursuit.

Ian Watt's thesis about the rise of the novel is well-known

and—put in a general form—unassailable. The novel as an art form is connected with the tempo, the vicissitudes, the social concerns and agonies, the conceptions of the individual and of society, the views of the past and the future, of bourgeois society; of a society in which the commercial bourgeoisie overcame, through revolution or by absorption, the directing classes of the old regime. The transformation of social bonds from those of "status" to those of "contract," with its implication that the individual's substance is not shaped by his social role but is independent of it, is central to the bourgeois consciousness; the individual is an empty frame within which almost anything can be written. This goes with a certain kind of romanticism: here is Pamela, here is Julien Sorel, here is Philip Pirrip, here is Becky Sharpe, here is Emma Bovary; here perhaps is Kate Croy. The acrid truth is that the inviting empty frame is a delusion: these heroes/heroines (for obvious reasons setting Pamela aside) wound themselves or kill themselves, dashing themselves against the realities of social relations—I take the corruption of the heart, as with Becky Sharpe, to be a wound. In all this they answer to the expectations of their readers, who feel themselves swollen with freedom, on the verge of unrealized possibilities; but they also know themselves as bound by the forces of nature and of society. The programme of Naturalism is to stress that nature and society are one repressive force, shown by the natural sciences to be causally efficacious; this is why Zola, assuming this programme, can achieve pathos, never tragedy, for tragedy requires characters who, beleaguered as they may be by forces greater than themselves, can nevertheless choose and thus be the authors of their own fates. The hero/heroine of what I dare to call the "classical" novel (as distinct from the naturalistic or the romantic wish-fulfilling novel) is a center of possibility; but the effort to realize the dearest possibility brings either destruction or a sad accommodation to reality. Even those heroines so richly endowed with charm, beauty, and worldly power by James are destroyed (Milly Theale) or achieve a sad accommodation (Maggie Verver—I reject the interpretation of

Maggie as a triumphant and redeeming figure—and Isabel Archer).

The novel makes us more knowing about our own society and about ourselves; and since our society is one in which we are acutely aware of historical change—e.g., people still alive have passed from the horse as a common means of traction to the internal combustion engine and have known two world wars and a score of revolutions, have seen regimes and empires perish—the peculiar consciousness the novel presupposes and also informs is to be called historical. The novel displays before us an account of ourselves. But this is not to say anything about the novel as art. What I have so far said is as applicable to the work of C. P. Snow or J. B. Priestley, or of half-a-dozen novelists who use the great massacres of our time to give themselves and their readers a charge, so to speak, as to the work of serious novelists. What one gets from James, and this is one reason for his occupying the highest category, is what, apologizing for the jargon, I call the transcendence-effect. This occurs when we come to believe that in some way we are taken beyond the world of nature, and this includes the social world, into a life that lies beyond the world. We may differ over what the correct analysis of this belief may be. A great critic of an earlier generation, I. A. Richards, argued that "the joy which is so strangely the heart of the experience [of tragedy] . . . is an indication that all is right here and now in the nervous system." [7] But he did not doubt, even if he thought it a noble delusion, that characteristically tragedy produces the transcendence-effect.

A reference to what lies beyond the world is always in the western societies of our day enigmatic. Whereas the convention that lies behind *Lear* is the supposed fact that Fortune's wheel revolves in an impersonal way to determine the fates of men and kingdoms, the convention is shaken by—it may be no more than a tremor, but it is there—the kingdom of Grace, of freedom, something that cuts across the mundane categories and is rep-

---

7. I. A. Richards, *Principles of Literary Criticism* (New York: Harcourt Brace, 1950), p. 246.

resented by the figure of Cordelia. This does not, and cannot—this is the whole point—issue in the triumph of worldly power, the arrest of Fortune's wheel.

It is hard for the novelist in the nineteenth century and later to rely upon this delicately balanced set of considerations. This difficulty is certainly connected with the decline of religious belief and practice; and consequently the reference to the Transcendent can be taken as a reference to history, or to the Universe and its laws, or to a postulated great psychic reservoir, or, as with I. A. Richards, to the state of the nervous system. But none of these lies beyond nature. Where there is a direct reference to the Transcendent, as in the early and middle novels of Greene, or in those of Mauriac, there is a touch of the melodramatic. It is as though the presence of Grace may turn out to be no more than the noise of one's own heartbeats. (I should want to include as a special variety of the transcendence-effect the felt absence of the Transcendent, as in George Eliot and Hardy.)

I have suggested that in *The Wings of the Dove* James achieves the transcendence-effect. His attempt—I believe a perfectly conscious attempt—is conducted with enormous discretion. There are side-glances at religious themes, dropped hints, scarcely discernible suggestions of symbolic schemes, a preoccupation with certain words—in *The Wings of the Dove* "abyss" has crucial importance, though the reference to Augustine or to Pascal is not emphasized. But all these are nevertheless glimpses of a vast, hidden sustaining system without which the novel could not successfully carry the tragic theme and its purgative resolution. I do not doubt whence James drew his power to achieve the effect: it was from that remarkable childhood and youth so movingly depicted in *A Small Boy and Others* and *Notes of a Son and Brother*, a childhood in which he breathed "the air of that reference to an order of goodness and power greater than any this world by itself can show which we understand as the religious spirit." [8]

8. Henry James, *Notes of a Son and Brother,* in *Henry James: Autobiography,* ed. with introduction by Frederick W. Dupee (New York: Criterion Books, 1956), p. 335.

Dickens and the Angels ————————

"Do be an angel and fetch my spectacles / slippers / newspaper. . . ." This is a characteristic use of "angel" in modern
demotic English. It trails wisps of meaning from the theological
past of the term: the work of an angel seems a work of supereroga-
tion (Fido isn't an angel if he brings the newspaper in his mouth,
nor is the newsboy who delivers the paper), a free manifestation
of goodness, not constrained or dutiful, and what is thus free is
celestial, not earthly, or, if earthly, reminds us of the celestial. She
(it is commonly "she," though the nineteenth-century angel is
often represented as epicene) may be "A Creature not too bright
or good / For human nature's daily food" and "A Traveller be-
twixt life and death." And yet she is "a Spirit still, and bright /
With something of angelic light." We are also reminded by our
locution of what is traditionally one of the functions of the angels:
they are messengers, fetchers and carriers of the heavenly courts.

    The great clouds of glory that once accompanied the idea

From *University of Toronto Quarterly* (Winter 1980-81).

of the angels have in such a locution been lost; this is why I spoke of wisps of meaning. The concept has been domesticated. This seems to have happened after the seventeenth century, perhaps after the Restoration (in England). Milton's angels are an immense problem in themselves. The fallen among them display grandeur and heroism, and they delight in their "intellectual being, / Those thoughts that wander through eternity" (*Paradise Lost*, II, 147-48), and these qualities can be traced back to Christian and Jewish speculation about the nature of the angels, as well as to classical mythology—Hercules, Prometheus, Mulciber (the celestial architect). But the unfallen angels are relatively uninteresting; they prose and declaim, and suffer under the immense disadvantage of being the allies of omnipotence. They even go into quasi-anatomical detail in discussing the quasi-sexuality of angels and they blush as they do so, and although the blushing goes with their sensible appearance, not their real nature, it seems that being a spirit involves having a very subtle kind of body, a kind of undetectable and unenclosable gas. At any rate, my belief is that *Paradise Lost* is, for these and many other reasons, a stage on the journey towards the domestication and degradation of the angels. With Pope the angels have become theatrical properties. They are necessary parts of the picture of cosmic order he gives us in the *Essay on Man*—they rule the spheres (*Essays on Man*, Epistle I)—but since no one in Pope's day any longer takes this picture seriously, as an account of how things are, angels have in effect been given the same ontological status as the dragon or the phoenix.

And yet, and yet . . . the Bible and the Book of Common Prayer, never, surely, more closely studied by the general reader than in the eighteenth and nineteenth centuries, are full of angels, in various settings and in various imaginative guises. One of the books to be found in any house, palatial or humble, that possessed any books at all, was *The Pilgrim's Progress*, and it contained some of the last genuine angels in English letters: Apollyon, a fallen angel, and those who sounded their trumpets on the other side of the river. Again, Shakespeare was widely read and had recovered from the period of neglect, embarrassment, and misunderstanding in which neoclassical criticism seemed for a time to have plunged him; romanticism was a great victory for Shakespeare. And a notion of the angels as splendid and powerful beings who play a necessary part in the economy of earth and heaven is alive in his work. After the exit of the Ghost Hamlet cries out: "O all you host of heaven!"—an appeal to the celestial armies to witness and perhaps to aid. Again: "Angels and ministers of grace, defend us!" And in the soliloquy on the nature of man he takes as established the medieval notion of the angel as a creature of immense intuitive intellectual power. "How like an angel in apprehension" is said (II.ii) of man at his highest. Also in *The Merchant of Venice*, V.i:

> There's not the smallest orb which thou behold'st
> But in his motion like an angel sings,
> Still quiring to the young-ey'd cherubins;
> Such harmony is in immortal souls,
> But whilst this muddy vesture of decay
> Doth grossly close it in, we cannot hear it.

For the biblical account we may go to Isaiah 6:

> In the year that king Uzziah died I saw also the Lord sitting upon a throne, high and lifted up, and his train filled the temple. Above it stood the seraphims: each one had six wings; with twain he covered his face, and with twain he covered his feet, and with twain he did fly. And one cried unto another, and said, Holy, holy, holy, is the Lord of hosts: the whole earth is full of his glory. And the posts of the door moved at the voice of him that cried, and the house was filled with smoke. Then said I, Woe is me! for I am undone; because I am a man of unclean lips, and I dwell in the midst of a people of unclean lips: for mine eyes have seen the King, the Lord of hosts.

In the Book of Common Prayer the feast of Saint Michael and All Angels survived the vicissitudes of the Reformation and kept its place in the calendar and had its own proper. The Collect:

> O everlasting God, who hast ordained and constituted the services of Angels and men in a wonderful order; Mercifully grant that as thy holy Angels always do thee service in heaven, so by thy appointment they may succour and defend us on earth. . . .

And in the office for the Holy Communion the Preface to the prayer of consecration invariably ends:

> Therefore with Angels and Archangels, and with all the company of heaven, we laud and magnify thy glorious Name; evermore praising thee, and saying, Holy, holy, holy, Lord God of Hosts, heaven and earth are full of thy glory. . . .

This of course sends us back to Isaiah 6.

I need not argue that in the nineteenth century the imaginative force of the biblical imagery and of the theological concepts presupposed by the compilers of the Book of Common Prayer had greatly diminished, as compared with the age of Shakespeare and George Herbert. In part this is a consequence of the collapse of the old cosmology. It is the *silence* of the infinite spaces—the silencing of the music of the spheres—that bothers and terrifies Pascal, one of the first to feel deeply the loss of the medieval cosmos. In part, perhaps, it is a consequence of the dwindling of the popular culture reflected in old songs and ballads, the culture of fairies and witchcraft, something that was much older than Christianity.

As early as 1647 we find Richard Corbet (the strange Anglican bishop about whom Aubrey writes so affectingly) writing

> Farewell rewards and fairies
>   Good housewives now may say,
> For now foul sluts in dairies
>   Doe fare as well as they . . .

> Wittness those rings and roundelayes
>> Of theirs, which yet remaine,
> Were footed in Queene *Maries* dayes
>> On many a grassy playne

* * * * * * * * * *

> By which we note the Fairies
>> Were of the old profession;
> Their songs were Ave Maryes,
>> Their daunces were procession:
> But now, alas! they all are dead
>> Or gone beyond the Seas,
> Or farther for Religion fled,
>> Or else they take their ease.

I can't refrain from one final citation before we come to Dickens. Few philosophers did more than Thomas Hobbes of Malmesbury to kill the pagan-medieval cosmos stone dead (though he maintained the existence and indeed the corporeal existence of angels, *Leviathan*, ch. xxxiv); and yet we feel his sense of melancholy that great Pan and all his train really are stone dead. The Gentiles, he writes,

> filled almost all places, with spirits called *Daemons;* the plains, with *Pan* and *Panises,* or Satyres; the Woods, with Fawnes, and Nymphs; the Sea, with Tritons, and other Nymphs; every River, and Fountayn, with a Ghost of his name, and with Nymphs; every house, with its *Lares,* or Familiars; every man, with his *Genius;* Hell, with Ghosts, and spirituall Officers, as *Charon, Cerberus,* and the *Furies;* and in the night time, all places with *Larvae, Lemures,* Ghosts of men deceased, and a whole kingdom of Fayries, and Bugbears. (*Leviathan,* ch. xii)

The angels, then, insofar as they belonged imaginatively to a whole complex of beliefs about the world that had by the nineteenth century ceased to be entertained, or even understood or appreciated, by educated people, or by a majority of them, belonged to a past era, with all the advantages and disadvantages such belonging carries with it. The disadvantages are that speech referring to the angels doesn't belong to the *real* world of power and money, disease and sanitation, violence and the police, useful education and electoral reform. But since the real world comes under unfavorable judgment by men of refined sensibility, the angels have the charm precisely of the unreal, of the far away and long ago. They console men for their having been despoiled of the twopence-colored past. But since they don't belong to the real world, since they are now locked up in the Bible and the Book of Common Prayer, since their only remaining known function is to guard the young, especially at night when they are asleep, they are taken as ways of talking that have sense and emotional force but no reference, or only a vague one. And few any longer, certainly not Dickens, feel in any way constricted by tradition or by theological definition.

II

The attempt by the Tractarians to put flesh on the bones of tradition angered Dickens, as did any attempt at theological definition in Christianity. Dogmatic religion disturbed him so much that he was for a time a Unitarian; and as an Anglican he was a fervent sustainer of Broad Church divinity. In 1844 he wrote to John Forster, concerning some extracts Forster had sent him from the newly published life of Thomas Arnold: "I must have that book. Every sentence that you quote from it is the textbook of my faith" (John Forster, *Life,* II.v). Arnold himself lacked the complacency of some other Broad Church divines (see, for example, the final lecture of his *Introductory Lectures on Modern History*), but Arnold's theology, when it had passed through the undiscriminating mind of Charles Dickens, became the unintellectual moralism that seems Dickens's central religious position. He adhered to "the teaching of the New Testament in its broad spirit [and] put no faith in any man's narrow construction of its letter here or there" (his will of 1869, in Forster, Appendix II).

This enabled him with a good conscience to lambaste and caricature dissenting preachers (Stiggins, Chadband) and to feel superior to those who attached importance to dogma and ritual, such
as the curate in *Sketches by Boz* who "got out of bed at half-past
twelve o'clock one winter's night, to half-baptize a washer-
woman's child in a slop-basin."

Perhaps I do less than justice to Dickens's originality. He
did in fact expound one dogma, express one belief, the belief,
never so far as I know entertained by any Christian body,
though it may have been held by some obscure Gnostic sect in
the fourth century, the belief, namely, that children when they
die are turned into angels ("they say . . . that you will be an
Angel, before the birds sing again," *The Old Curiosity Shop*, ch.
lv). It isn't clear that *all* children are turned into angels; and it
could be argued that some of the children portrayed on the pattern of Oliver Twist, those who carry uncorrupted hearts and a
pure diction through the filth of the world, are as near being angels already as makes no matter, as are virginal young women
such as Rose Maylie *(Oliver Twist)* and Agnes *(David Copperfield)*.
Adults don't seem to look forward to such a metamorphosis. I
can think of only one adult man who is portrayed as angelic in
nature and that is Mr. Pickwick, who is, says Sam Weller, an
angel "in tights and gaiters" and "a reg'lar thoroughbred angel"
(The Pickwick Papers, ch. xlv). The brothers Cheeryble are too unreal to count even as angels.

The notion that some human beings at any rate become angels when they die seems to be implied in Oliver Twist's appeal
to Bill Sikes:

> Oh pray have mercy on me, and do not make me steal.
> For the love of all the bright Angels that rest in Heaven,
> have mercy upon me! (Ch. xxii)

Rest is scarcely to be attributed to angels as traditionally conceived; they are thought to be in a state of constant activity, intellectual and practical; but *rest* is commonly attributed to the
dead. We pray that they may rest in peace, that they may have

a place of light, refreshment, and peace. I conclude, then, that the "Angels that rest in Heaven" are the dead. Of course, the expression may simply be a bit of Chadband-style talk, without serious content or implication. There is another ambiguous passage in *Oliver Twist*. It is the one describing the death of the old woman in the workhouse.

> Alas! how few of Nature's faces are left alone to gladden us with their beauty! The cares, and sorrows, and hungerings of the world, change them as they change hearts; and it is only when those passions sleep, and have lost their hold for ever, that the troubled clouds pass off, and leave Heaven's surface clear. It is a common thing for the countenances of the dead, even in that fixed and rigid state, to subside into the long-forgotten expression of sleeping infancy, and settle into the very look of earlier life; so calm, so peaceful, do they grow again, that those who knew them in their happy childhood, kneel by the coffin's side in awe, and see the Angel even upon earth. (Ch. xxiv)

I suppose it is just possible that there is a confusion, or a blurring, between the look of earlier life, of infancy, that is the appearance of the Angel, and the notion of the child's guardian angel; but I think that there can't really be any doubt that when we look at sleeping infancy we are said to perceive, with almost no disguise intervening, the countenance of the angel. The theme had already been stated earlier, in the picture of the sleeping Oliver that causes even Fagin to turn away for a moment and postpone Oliver's instruction by Sikes until the next morning.

> The boy was lying, fast asleep, in a rude bed upon the floor; so pale with anxiety, and sadness, and the closeness of his prison, that he looked like death; not death as it shows in shroud and coffin, but in the guise it wears when life has just departed; when a young and gentle spirit has, but an instant, fled to Heaven, and the gross air of the world has not had time to breathe upon the changing dust it hallowed. (Ch. xix)

145

It is in *Oliver Twist,* too, that we first come across an idea that has a big future in Dickens: that the approaching death of children is made plain to the dying child by visions of angels. Little Dick, when Oliver calls to say good-bye before running away to London, tells him he knows that the doctor who says he is dying is right, for "I dream so much of Heaven, and Angels, and kind faces that I never see when I am awake" (ch. vii). (An interesting variation on this, one that almost comes off, is in *Dombey and Son,* chapter xvi—the death of Paul Dombey.) And in *Oliver Twist* we find that identification of the virginal girl with the angel that is a motif, on the surface in the earlier novels, disguised in the later, absent only from the remarkable *Great Expectations,* in almost all Dickens's work:

> The younger lady [Rose Maylie] was in the lovely bloom and spring-time of womanhood; at that age, when, if ever angels be for God's good purposes enthroned in mortal forms, they may be, without impiety, supposed to abide in such as hers.
> She was not past seventeen. . . . (Ch. xxix)

This makes us uneasy; and we surely have good reason to be so. The more we read Dickens the more it is brought home to us that much of the charm of the Rose Maylies is that they are on the edge of turning into Dolly Vardens, as at that climactic moment when Dolly and Emma Haredale appear to be menaced by rape.

> Do what she would, she only looked the better for it, and tempted them the more. When her eyes flashed angrily, and her ripe lips slightly parted, to give her rapid breathing vent, who could resist it? When she wept and sobbed as though her heart would break . . . who could be insensible to the little winning pettishness which now and then displayed itself, even in the sincerity and the earnestness of her grief? When, forgetful for a moment of herself, as she was now, she fell on her knees beside her friend, and bent over her, and laid her cheek to hers, and put her arms about her, what mortal eyes could have avoided wander-

ing to the delicate bodice, the streaming hair, the neglected dress, the perfect abandonment and unconsciousness of the blooming little beauty? Who could look on and see her lavish caresses and endearments, and not desire to be in Emma Haredale's place; to be either she or Dolly; either the hugging or the hugged? (*Barnaby Rudge*, ch. lix)

Dickens rarely drives so hard without putting on the brakes at an earlier point than this; but we feel such contemplations are always, as it were, round the corner, and tend to be openly indulged, where the social status of the young woman concerned (for example, in *The Pickwick Papers* Mary, Mr. Nupkins's parlor maid, later to marry Sam Weller, is treated with more familiarity than Mr. Wardle's daughters) is low; but these contemplations are present, giving the reader, as presumably they gave the writer, a slight *frisson*, even in the descriptions of Rose Maylie and Little Nell. (". . . such a chubby, rosy, cosy, little Nell. . . . She's so . . . small, so compact, so beautifully modelled, so fair, with such blue veins and such a transparent skin, and such little feet . . . ," *The Old Curiosity Shop*, ch. iv; but of course this is Quilp speaking.)

III

What is the religious setting in which the talk about angels, and young women who resemble the angelic chrysalis, and death, and going off both to be with angels and to be angels, goes on? It is purely sentimental and picturesque, religiously vacuous. Whereas we learn from the work of the sceptical, Feuerbachian George Eliot a great deal about English religion, notably in the *Scenes of Clerical Life, Adam Bede, Silas Marner,* and *Felix Holt,* from Dickens we learn nothing, though of course we may pick up an implied moral and political attitude. Take, for example, the rural parish in *Oliver Twist:*

And when Sunday came, how differently the day was spent from any way in which he had ever spent it yet! . . .

There was the little church, in the morning, with the green leaves fluttering at the windows: the birds singing without: and the sweet-smelling air stealing in at the low porch, and filling the homely building with its fragrance. The poor people were so neat and clean, and knelt so reverently in prayer, that it seemed a pleasure, not a tedious duty, their assembling there together. . . . Then, there were the walks as usual, and many calls at the clean houses of the labouring men; and at night, Oliver read a chapter or two from the Bible, which he had been studying all the week, and in the performance of which duty he felt more proud and pleased, than if he had been the clergyman himself. (Ch. xxxii)

The generality of this evocation of the church and rural society is common in the earlier Dickens; I refrain from citing other examples. There is none of that wonderful precision which marks his observation of the urban scene (for example, *Martin Chuzzlewit*, ch. ix: "Town and Todgers's"); there is no suggestion of strong emotion in the observer through whose eyes the fictive description is perceived; and there is no moral comment such as there is in the accounts of city churches with the slime oozing from the overcrowded graveyards into the streets and the water conduits. The light that bathes these generalized landscapes of the early Dickens is like that we encounter in the weakest kind of Victorian landscape-painting, with the ivy-covered church, the grazing cattle of indeterminate breed, the ploughman going home as the sun sets. The pleasure such passages may give is that of a weakly entertained fantasy that has no relation to the deeply felt issues of personal and social life or to the deepest themes of religion, God, conscience, sin, death, forgiveness, resurrection, grace, and glory. . . . Such descriptions are opiates to make us spiritually drowsy.

Contrast a passage in *Adam Bede* in which the author is aware of the Dickensian-style rural landscape as a temptation, and so puts it aside. Further, the passage gives us the setting of the first stage of Hetty's flight; it has a function in a narrative we

148

are bound to take seriously as a genuine piece of human history—quite unlike the journey, for example, of Nell and her grandfather, something which of course may have a virtue of another kind, as symbolism or allegory.

> Bright February days have a stronger charm of hope about them than any other days in the year. One likes to pause in the mild rays of the sun, and look over the gates at the patient plough-horses turning at the end of the furrow, and think that the beautiful year is all before one. . . . There are no leaves on the trees and hedgerows, but how green all the grassy fields are! and the dark purplish brown of the ploughed earth and of the bare branches is beautiful too. What a glad world this looks like, as one drives or rides along the valleys and over the hills! I have often thought so when, in foreign countries, where the fields and woods have looked to me like our English Loamshire—the rich land tilled with just as much care, the woods rolling down the gentle slopes to the green meadows—I have come on something by the roadside which has reminded me that I am not in Loamshire: an image of a great agony—the agony of the Cross.

And then, after speaking of the appropriateness of this image of torture and degradation in the beautiful and fertile human world that is nevertheless full of bitterness for so many men and women, Eliot adds: "No wonder man's religion has much sorrow in it: no wonder he needs a suffering God" (*Adam Bede*, ch. xxxv). When we go from Dickens's generalized rural landscapes to such a passage it is as though we pass from a sentimental literature written (and how mistakenly) for children, those centers of appetite, fear, and rage, to a literature for adults. Apart from the sureness of touch with which Eliot places this in the narrative of Hetty's wanderings, we note many felicities: the description is general but it contains just enough observation to give it bite: the noting, for instance, that at just this season the color of the newly plowed earth answers to that of the branches and twigs. And there is the fine suggested contrast between the

149

sentiment of the confident observer ("the beautiful year is all before one") who is *not* on foot—"as one drives or rides along the valleys and over the hills"—and what even at first reading we conjecture to be the actual situation of Hetty.

Now, Dickens can do all this—indeed, can do it quite as well and perhaps with more demonic power—with the city scene or with what he reconstructs from his gazings upon and dreams about this scene: the moldering chambers of the Inns of Court, the tumbledown wooden huts covered with fungi and mold, the shores of the Thames strewn with the debris left behind by the industrious and idle lives of men, the great river itself flowing "between Southwark Bridge which is of iron, and London Bridge which is of stone" (*Our Mutual Friend*, ch. 1) and carrying its dreadful cargo of the dead, those who are killed by their own hands or by those of others. The reverberations of "iron" and "stone," of ooze and slime, of the bodies of the dead drifting with the current, of all that assails the eye and ear and nose of the nocturnal prowler (the novelist himself in a strange half-partnership with the criminal and the outcast), all this feeds the most powerful imagination of all the novelists writing in English. No doubt this is in part an unanalyzable idiosyncrasy of the man Dickens; but in part it represents something characteristic of Dickens's attitude to the world of religion. It is as though he had to keep the beliefs and attitudes of religion in solution—in some way he found it threatening when they began to crystallize out, with sharp edges and definite shapes. Even when he wants to make religion a matter of significance in the action of the novel, as with the religion of the Murdstones or of Mrs. Clennam, we are shown only the attitudes, never the doctrines. We assume an austere Calvinism in the background, but we are never told anything, just as we are never told anything about the content of sermons or what it is Tom Pinch plays on the organ. Notice how the attitude changes when Tom Pinch goes into Salisbury and gazes into the window of the bookseller: we are given the titles of the books and their physical appearance. But when he gets into the cathedral and sits at the organ: "Great thoughts and hopes came crowding on his mind as the rich music rolled upon the air" (*Martin Chuzzlewit*, ch. v).

It seems to me that Dickens is frightened of any suggestion of reality (over and above, that is, the expression of a rather vague moral attitude) in religion. This, surely, is what underlies his famous attack upon Millais's picture "Christ in the Carpenter's Shop"; we can't mistake the presence of a genuine panic, a deeply founded hysteria: "a hideous, wry-necked, blubbering, red-headed boy in a bed-gown; who appears to have received a poke in the hand, from the stick of another boy with whom he has been playing in an adjacent gutter, and to be holding it up for the contemplation of a kneeling woman, so horrible in her ugliness, that . . . she would stand out from the rest of the company as a Monster, in the vilest cabaret in France, or the lowest gin-shop in England. . . . Such men as the carpenters might be undressed in any hospital where dirty drunkards, in a high state of varicose veins, are received" (in House, *The Dickens World* [London 1960], pp. 126-27). We commonly suppose that one of the things Dickens stressed and held dear was the humanity of Jesus and that this explains his Socinian excursion; but here a realistic, naturalistic depiction of Jesus, Mary, and Joseph as human beings going about their business draws from him this strange, unnerving, high scream of agony. We guess he would have been quite untroubled by religious *Kitsch*, by a blue-eyed, golden-haired young person of indeterminate sex attended by a blue-eyed, golden-haired young matron; of course, such a youth, no doubt clothed in white garments—of what cloth one wouldn't know (perhaps "samite, mystic, wonderful")—and no doubt treading upon flowers and grasses known to no botanist, is precisely a Dickensian angel: a representative of Christianity as a tone, a flavor, a not too bad-tasting moral tonic; but with the heart and bowels torn out of it and the brains scooped out of the skull.

I want now to pass from the Broad Church Dickens of faintings and screamings before the spectacle of a dogmatic and historical religion to another Dickens in which what is rejected at the level of intellect is restored by the poetic imagination. This can happen even in *The Old Curiosity Shop* and even with little Nell:

> The sisters had gone home and she was alone. She raised her eyes to the bright stars, looking down so mildly from the wide worlds of air, and, gazing on them, found new stars burst upon her view, and more beyond, and more beyond again, until the whole great expanse sparkled with shining spheres, rising higher and higher in immeasurable space, eternal *[sic]* in their numbers as in their changeless and incorruptible existence. She bent over the calm river, and saw them shining in the same majestic order as when the dove beheld them gleaming through the swollen waters, upon the mountain-tops down far below, and dead mankind, a million fathoms deep. (Ch. xlii)

I won't pause to analyze this passage. The sudden change in literary quality is evident; from the point of view of this essay, the striking thing is its use of the story of the Flood as a motif or organizing principle. There is the explicit reference to the biblical story; but perhaps we should note that this story presents no kind of dogmatic challenge to Dickens; it belongs to the world of the Noah's ark, a world of toys and childhood and offering no challenge to the mature man, and the biblical theme can thus be put into the text without disguise, and in this, as we shall see, the attitude is different from that towards other themes of a biblical kind, such as death and resurrection. Here the imagination transforms the themes so that they cease to be religiously disturbing. They belong to the world of consciousness, dream and reverie, fear and desire, but not to the sentimental world of ivy-covered churches, poor people who are neat and clean, and angels enthroned in the forms of seventeen-year-old girls belonging to the genteel classes.

Resurrection. My first example is the one, often remarked on, at the beginning of *Great Expectations*. Little Pip finds himself in the churchyard in which his father, mother, and five brothers are all buried. But this is not the churchyard of Little Nell, picturesque, tinged with sunset hues, and deliciously sad.

152

The graves are "five little stone lozenges, each about a foot and a half long"—how different from the venerable graves of *The Old Curiosity Shop,* where "there was music in the air, and a sound of angel's wings" (ch. lii)—and it is a "bleak place overgrown with nettles," and it is here that Pip first finds out for certain that it is the churchyard,

> and that Philip Pirrip, late of this parish, and also Georgiana, wife of the above, were dead and buried; and that Alexander, Bartholomew, Abraham, Tobias, and Roger, infant children of the aforesaid, were also dead and buried; and that the dark flat wilderness beyond the church yard, intersected with dikes and mounds and gates, with scattered cattle feeding on it, was the marshes; and that the low leaden line beyond was the river; and that the distant savage lair from which the wind was rushing was the sea; and that the small bundle of shivers growing afraid of it all and beginning to cry was Pip.

And it is at this moment that the unexpected resurrection of one who will in the course of the novel's action turn out to be the father and the tyrant, the murderer and the savior, comes upon little Pip with a great shout:

> a man started up from among the graves. . . . A fearful man, all in coarse gray, with a great iron on his leg. A man with no hat, and with broken shoes, and with an old rag tied round his head. A man who had been soaked in water, and smothered in mud, and lamed by stone, and cut by flints, and stung by nettles, and torn by briars; who limped, and shivered, and glared and growled; and whose teeth chattered in his head as he seized me by the chin.

This is indeed, as well as a father in deep disguise, a man of sorrows, acquainted with grief, a man who has struggled up from a grave and bears upon him the signs of water and earth, and who dreadfully resembles the risen Lazarus wearing the grave clothes: the "old rag tied round his head" echoes the cloth used to tie up the jaw of the dead. He can scarcely escape from the kingdom of the dead, for after he has given Pip his instructions, Pip tells us:

> As I saw him go, picking his way among the nettles, and among the brambles that bound the green mounds, he looked in my young eyes as if he were eluding the hands of the dead people stretching up cautiously out of their graves to get a twist upon his ankle, and pull him in. (Ch. i)

(On the many parental roles in *Great Expectations* see Professor R. D. McMaster's fine introduction to the Macmillan College Classics edition of the novel.)

The other—and earlier—example of the appearance of a death-and-resurrection theme is in *David Copperfield*:

> My father's eyes had closed upon the light of this world six months, when mine opened on it. There is something strange to me, even now, in the reflection that he never saw me; and something stranger yet in the shadowy remembrance that I have of my first childish associations with his white gravestone in the churchyard, and of the indefinable compassion I used to feel for it lying out alone there in the dark night, when our little parlour was warm and bright with fire and candle, and the doors of our house were—almost cruelly, it seemed to me sometimes—bolted and locked against it. (Ch. i)

Again:

> One Sunday night my mother reads to Peggotty and me ... how Lazarus was raised up from the dead. And I am so frightened that they are afterwards obliged to take me out of bed, and show me the quiet churchyard out of the bedroom window, with the dead all lying in their graves at rest, below the solemn moon. (Ch. ii)

Here the connection with the resurrection of Christ and with the New Testament is made through the reference to Lazarus; but it brings terror, not consolation, it inspires pity—the dead can't get through the bolted door and share the light and warmth of the parlor—and a sense of the uncanny. But the dead are indeed the dead, "all lying in their graves at rest, below the solemn moon." And this, it seems to be suggested, is just as well. Of course, here everything is subordinated to the central aim of giving us the sense of the child's imagination; but we are made aware that the doctrine of the resurrection is no more an operative belief in the minds of David's mother and Peggotty than the virtues of charity and humility are formative in the dead lives of the Murdstones. That the dead will never stir any more is consoling.

IV

So far we have seen that biblical and Christian dogmatic themes are used by Dickens in those situations in which they don't have the force and therefore the menacing claim of something that has reference to everyday life. In part, this is because they have descended into the depths of Dickens's imagination, so that when they come to the surface again we are not clear how far Dickens recognizes the theme; in part because, as with the Flood story, they belong to the childhood world of wooden toys as much as the figures in a Punch and Judy show.

Taking over from other writers what is nourishing and producing something touched with their spirit and yet something that is unique in its individuality—this is what Dickens can do wonderfully. In a large way this is what he does with Fielding and Smollett and Cervantes and Goldsmith and Defoe in the earlier novels, until the shadows begin to fall round about *Dombey and Son* and he goes on to become a less happy and inviting writer, but the great imaginative writer of *Bleak House, Little Dorrit,* and *Great Expectations.* Even when, as in *Edwin Drood,* he returns to graves and crumbling ruins and the music of the organ, all is now treated with irony and the observation is sharp and not evasively generalized; and in Mr. Crisparkle we are given a genuine cleric (Mr. Milvey in the late *Our Mutual Friend* is also well done). Dickens's invention may have lost its earlier preternatural energy; but he can look steadily and with a cold eye at what formerly he glanced at evasively and sometimes ignored for the sake of a compensatory fantasy. But here he is establishing a new tradition, not extending an old one.

One of the most striking examples of Dickens's ability to nourish himself upon another writer (as he nourishes himself on biblical themes and Christian dogma where these are not perceived as threatening) is in *The Old Curiosity Shop*. It has often been noticed that the influence of Bunyan is heavy in this novel, as regards theme and imagery, the journey of the old man and maiden from Babylon-London to the heavenly city. The journey is conceived both as a panorama, as in

> . . . the child looked back upon the sleeping town, deep in the valley's shade: and on the far-off river with its winding track of light: and on the distant hills. . . . (Ch. xlii)

and as a pilgrimage to be endured, as in the journey through the dark, demonic landscape of midland (northern?) industry, with its many incidents, recalling Christian's journey through the valley of the shadow of death, above all the incident of the Man of the Fire. Notice the echoes of Bunyan, the voice more than the theme, in the following:

> They had long since got clear of the smoke and furnaces, except in one or two solitary instances, where a factory planted among fields withered the space about it, like a burning mountain. When they had passed through this town, they entered again upon the country, and began to draw near their place of destination. (Ch. xlvi)

The cadences of Bunyan are unmistakable, even though we have to say that it reminds us of a plainsong theme harmonized by a nineteenth-century composer. But I don't count this against Dickens: it would be absurd to criticize him for not writing pastiche of Bunyan.

What doesn't enter Dickens's mind, at least at the level of

conscious thought and deliberation, is Bunyan's theology of grace and glory. Little Nell and her grandfather do leave the city of destruction, and pass through perils, threatened by men and demons, to the celestial city; but Dickens's enterprise in setting out his parallel allegory is vaguer than Bunyan's: Bunyan thinks out his moral and religious scheme in accordance with a dogmatic picture which he takes realistically, whereas Dickens is intuitive rather than discursive in his approach to his material. Whereas Bunyan's allegory is given a hard skeleton of signs that can be read off without difficulty, the symbolic reverberations of the allegory being left to take care of themselves, Dickens offers no unambiguous signs; his story is allegorical only derivatively; the life of symbols, as distinct from signs, is strong, and this is why we often find Dickens's most powerful effects come from material that is, as I put it earlier, held in solution, not crystallized out. It would be too strong to say that we know more about Bunyan than Bunyan himself did; but the same remark wouldn't be in the least too strong made about Dickens. Bunyan, in his acceptance of a dogmatic scheme, is, despite his strong Protestantism, close to the man who also saw visions in a dream when, "In a summer season when the sun was soft," he fell asleep on a hillside near Malvern and had visions even more wonderful than those of John Bunyan; Bunyan is much closer to Langland than he is to Dickens. Dickens retains here, in Renan's unforgettable phrase, "the perfume of an empty vase." He looks out on the wilderness of this world, sees the tower on the hill and the great gulf with its pits and dungeons and the fair field full of folk, some of them weary with toil, others consumed with vanity, and, so long as he stays in a state of negative capability, he has few equals in depicting all this. It is from this Dickens that the haunting first paragraph of *Our Mutual Friend* comes, a paragraph in which he marries, so that they become one indissoluble unity, ontology, and symbolism: "the Thames [flowing] between Southwark Bridge which is of iron, and London Bridge which is of stone, as an autumn evening was closing in" (ch. i).

Dickens is, in his tone and chosen subject-matter, in his manipulation of themes and symbols, in his sudden transitions from the sublime to the bathetic, in his low tastes and his self-indulgent sentimentalities, in his passion for justice so curiously combined with the petty snobberies of an aspirant to gentility, in his secure possession of moral seriousness at one moment and his sudden drop into moral triviality at another, the hardest of English novelists to deal justly with. Nothing, we think, lies beyond him except to give us a credible pretty young woman as heroine; he can give us dwarfs and grotesques, such savage portraits of female silliness as Mrs. Nickleby and Flora Finching, for once a woman is no longer young everything is allowable, even if she remain a maiden (for example, Miss Tox in *Dombey and Son*), and then he gives us his splendid Bella Wilfer in *Our Mutual Friend*, splendid despite her alarming tendency to turn into Ruth Pinch towards the novel's end. Indeed, we are sometimes tempted to generalize about Dickens only to be brought up short by some enormous exception. We think of Edith Dombey and conclude that Dickens makes a hash of portraying a passionate woman; and then we remember the darkness and excitement of his portraits of Rosa Dartle and of Estella, where what is cruel and perverse gives such an edge to the writing. We can't of course find in Dickens that unity of tone and sense of formal considerations and feeling for decorum we find in such novelists as James and even Thackeray; but Dickens illustrates more vividly the wildness of the human mind, the gratuitous and uncontrived production of romantic genius. He lacks the virtue of civility but he has some of the uncontrived virtues of the barbarian, generosity and gusto and a strong desire that his own side should win, and an uncritical passionate belief in the justice of his own cause. Hence his philistinism in religious matters and his failure to discriminate intellectually between the weighty and the trivial.

One dogma strongly rejected at the level of full consciousness returns as a categorical requirement of the imagination: the doctrine of election, of predestination to glory and to damnation. We are given to understand, though the language is always vague, that such characters as the Murdstones, Esther Summerson's godmother, and Arthur Clennam's mother are Calvinists of the strictest sort, strong believers in the effects of original sin and in God's inscrutable decrees by which some are saved and some damned without regard to merit. At the conscious level nothing is more hateful to Dickens than this form of dogmatic Christianity. Nevertheless, it is also noticeable that the men and women of the Dickensian cosmos divide for the most part into the saved and the damned. We have very little sense of the possibility that one who is mired in evil may be converted and live; or that one who is truly amiable may be lost. The idea that Newman presses upon us, that of the gentleman with "a cultivated intellect, a delicate taste, a candid, equitable, dispassionate mind, a noble and courteous bearing in the conduct of life" who may also be a heartless profligate, would have seemed repugnant to Dickens. For the most part his characters are walking and talking examples of virtue and vice, with appropriate physical attributes, unless they transcend moral categories altogether, as perhaps Micawber does and such cheerful rogues as Alfred Jingle and Mr. Mantalini. But Squeers and Uriah Heep (but why did Dickens give him as a first name that of the Bible's most notable cuckold?) and Quilp and Mr. Vholes and Tulkinghorn are singled out for damnation and breathe out upon us the fetid odor of the pit. Curiously, the overt model of salvation that pervades the novels is Pelagian—salvation is to be achieved through work—but the deep structure is Jansenist or Calvinist. I think Dickens came to some insight into this, for in *Little Dorrit* and *Great Expectations* he handles the problem of change and development of character, he faces the fact of irredeemable mediocrity among the mass of human beings. His success is, I think, complete only in *Great Expectations*; but little Dorrit genuinely embodies the supernatural virtue of charity: there is only the slightest trace in her of Rose Maylie. She is born in a prison, and christened, sheltered, and married in one of those churches of the city that never failed to excite the imagination of Dickens. As she and Arthur Clennam go down into the roaring streets of the city, Dickens is now too wise to call up as a special effect factitious choirs of angels to mark their union; like their first parents, they make their way unaccompanied through the corrupted Eden of the world.

Note

This paper was originally given in April 1979 at the annual meeting of the Victorian Studies Association of Ontario.

I am of course indebted to much writing on Dickens's use of symbolic and allegorical forms. Two books strike me as very valuable: Bert G. Hornback's *"Noah's Arkitecture": A Study of Dickens's Mythology* (University of Ohio Press, 1972) and Alexander Welsh's *The City of Dickens* (Oxford, 1971); John Carey's *The Violent Effigy* (London, 1973) I find stimulating but perverse and unbalanced. The great difficulty with this kind of criticism is to know when and how to place limits on it. (In this it resembles Freudian interpretations of speech and dream materials.) Given that any large account of the world must necessarily refer to fire and flood, rivers and mountains, all the forms of time and space; given that all natural and artificial objects are in whole and in part concave or convex; given that, whenever men and women of different ages are brought together, sexual, paternal, maternal, and filial relationships may be supposed to subsist; given that our language, its vocabulary, its syntactical forms, its styles of rhetoric are, as it were, a partially decipherable register of the past; given that Homer and Virgil and the Greek dramatists and Dante and Shakespeare and Milton . . . *et al.* are just visible in the wings of any entertainment we put on, then it would be strange not to find symbolic patterns in every kind of writing from the highbrow novel to the comic strip. Indeed, I dare say there are doctoral theses on Rex Morgan as the Great Physician and Dagwood Bumstead as the Scapegoat (though not, I am confident, at the University of

Toronto). This means that we ought to be cautious in our approach to the possibility of symbolic themes in a given novel. Sometimes there can't be any doubt, as in the use of gold, and rose, and bronze, and the chosen names of characters and places, in a novelist so plainly fertile in contrivances as Henry James. Sometimes it is a matter of explicit reference, as in the passage in *The Old Curiosity Shop* that refers to the Flood. Sometimes it is a matter of critical judgment, as in the resurrection theme in *Great Expectations*, where the force of the passage exceeds what can be accounted for by the surface meaning. But I think we ought to be aware that there are logical difficulties in the way of too easy a resort to symbolism and allegory in the work of Dickens or any other novelist. Any narrative set in the changing world of human beings and natural objects cannot fail to be interpretable in accordance with an indefinite number of symbolic schemes; but it remains that some interpretations are critically fruitful, others are idle and a distraction.

Colleagues have drawn my attention to an apparent exception to my general position that in the novels of Dickens's earlier and middle period the author has no sense "that one who is truly amiable may be lost." This exception is Steerforth in *David Copperfield*. I think it is true that in David's eyes Steerforth is amiable and that we have a sense of the coexistence in him of contrary impulses. But the Steerforth who seduces little Emily is exactly the same as the cruel youth whose conduct to the poor usher, Mr. Mell, is so abominable, and who manipulates and exploits the young Copperfield in such a way that here, too, we may speak of a seduction; and who delights in a sado-masochistic relationship with Rosa Dartle. Steerforth has charm for David but not for the reader. He is relevant to the theme of the angels in that he is portrayed as a fallen angel, even archangel, but one who is fallen from the beginning, who has set his brand on Rosa Dartle, and who has, as befits a ruined archangel, an infernal attendant, Littimer.

Mr. John Baird has pointed out to me the following passage from *Silas Marner*:

In old days there were angels who came and took men by the hand and led them away from the city of destruction. We see no white-winged angels now. But yet men are led away from threatening destruction; a hand is put into theirs, which leads them forth gently towards a calm and bright land, so that they look no more backward; and the hand may be a little child's. (Ch. xiv)

This sounds a bit like Dickens, but what George Eliot writes has a more self-consciously constructed intellectual foundation. On a matter about which Dickens is fuzzy, namely, the present existence of angels, Eliot is firm; they belong, with their iconography, to a past epoch; now they are signs of an alienation, necessary and beneficent in the past, that has been overcome by the educated. But the Feuerbachian reduction guarantees that the substance of what was nourished by the alienated consciousness—guidance and protection by other members of the human family—remains with us; the white-winged angel is a surrogate for the child. We sometimes think that is what Dickens would mean if he had the mind and inclination to work the matter out for himself. The cadences of the passage are Victorian but they echo, as do some passages in Dickens, the New Testament in the Authorized Version and, especially, Bunyan.

The Description of Feeling ————

That we feel as well as reason, have qualms and inner delights
as well as calculate, seems to be as well established as anything
can be. Much of the conduct we praise and censure would be
impossible if we didn't feel; it is possible to construct amusing
stories about relations between computers because in them we
find the analogue of reasoning; but the analogue of feeling is in
them hard to discover and it is therefore hard to give such stories
moral weight. The definition of the gentleman includes unwillingness to hurt the feelings of others; people often say today, in
discussing some particular action or practice: "It's all right so
long as he/she/they isn't/aren't *hurt*"; and this doesn't usually mean *hurt* in the physical or sensational sense, and even if it
does the physical hurt is resented on account of its bringing
about or representing some psychic hurt. The headmaster's
famous "This hurts me more than it hurts you" may be humbug but it makes perfect sense. That in the world we feel jealous
or angry or resentful or happy, or that we have feelings, strange,
familiar, curious, hateful, desirable, seems beyond question, and
of course it is. If claims and statements about feelings are not
clear, nothing in our language is clear.

From *University of Toronto Quarterly* (Spring 1978).

There are, all the same, a number of puzzles, just as there are puzzles about "mind" and "thinking." We are tempted to assimilate the concept of feeling to that of sensation, and there are many cases where this can scarcely be wrong, for I certainly feel pains and tickles; but there are other cases (quite apart from the cognitive uses of feel—I feel certain, I feel you may be right, and so on) where it is plain this won't work, as in I feel happy / I feel depressed, etc. These claims don't entail that I have any sensations, certainly not any particular sensations, even in those cases where it might be a plausible hypothesis that there are connections between feeling happy / depressed and the sensations I happen to have. I might *suspect* that I am depressed on account of my arthritic pains but of course I might be wrong; even when people claim to be certain in such matters such claims may in principle turn out to be ungrounded, as when people say: I should be perfectly happy if X, and then X and they're not happy.

I ────────────────────────────────────

I begin by distinguishing, so far as this can be done, between naming and describing, and again, so far as this can be done, between describing and reporting. These distinctions are necessarily imprecise, and what is to count as one or another is often a matter of the context and even of the particular natural language one is using. In some languages what are descriptive phrases containing names are, in English, just names. I understand there are some primitive languages that don't contain a name for water; there are various names we should have to translate as water in the pot, water from the sky, water in the river, and so on. While I don't rely upon English usage I shall suppose that it has sufficient authority for most of the problems I want to discuss. I shall assume what in some philosophical contexts would be absurd—that naming doesn't pose special problems. Pain is a name, happiness, depression, nausea, jealousy, anger are names. Names commonly require verbs, adjectives, and other parts of speech to convey thoughts, though there are many exceptions, as, e.g., Water! "The troops are ready for embarkation" is a report; "The men in khaki, each leaning on his rifle, were formed up in groups of eight all along the quay" is a description. Of course, descriptions can also be reports; in the case just cited the man listening could say: Why are you giving me such an elaborate report? I just wanted to know if the troops were ready. Now, is "Suddenly, I feel so happy!" a description or a report? I think we should hesitate to call it a description. It is a report but one quite unlike the instance just given. I could be mistaken in thinking the troops were ready; I might well have mistaken a fortuitous congregation of policemen for the troops in question. But "Suddenly, I feel so happy!" is incorrigible. We might at first think that the only difference between the cases is that in the latter case I am introspecting and that I could just as much make a mistake about what is within as about what is without. This rests upon a misunderstanding of introspection. Feeling happy isn't like an answer to a question that might be put by a psychological investigator about my images or sensations, though even there the notion of *mistake* is different; for when I hesitate over my introspective reports concerning my images and sensations and sometimes revise my descriptions, this is because internal phenomena are systematically elusive and I sometimes feel that I lack an adequate vocabulary. If we call "Suddenly, I feel so happy!" an introspective statement this can only mean that it is a first-person statement that can't be checked; in this it differs from "I am wearing my new hat," which can certainly be corrected.

My first example for analysis is: "I am racked with jealousy" or "I am suffering the pangs of jealousy." We have a strong temptation to assimilate such a report-description to "I have a toothache" or "I feel dizzy." *Pace* many modern philosophers, I think it is quite harmless to say that I am introspectively acquainted with such states of affairs as my toothache or my sensations of dizziness. It doesn't seem that knowing I am jealous involves any such acquaintance with what is qualitatively distinct. Let us suppose that I do have a pang and that this is some kind of sensation, a stomach cramp or a troublesome sensation in the region of the heart. I don't identify this as a pang of jealousy because it has a peculiar quality—a *quale*—unlike other pangs. I identify it as a pang of jealousy through its connection with a pattern of behavior in an interpersonal context—for example, a triangular situation. Of course, I don't mean that on every occasion upon which I feel a pang I am at a loss to know whether it is a pang of jealousy or some other kind of pang, for I can grow to be learned in my own quirks and habits; but the standard case of identifying this emotion is one in which I do so through attention to the features of my relations with other people. Given the standard cases, there can be degenerate or parasitic cases of what looks like purely introspective knowledge.

It seems clear, then, that a report or a description of such an emotion as jealousy is not analogous to a report or description of a sensation, where it does seem right to say that some qualitatively distinct feeling is known—a pain is not a tickle. I should like to bring out the distinction in the following way.

The idea of a man who had never felt pain does not seem vacuous in the way that the idea of a man who had never had any kind of sensation does. A man who had never felt pain could no doubt acquire a concept of pain and could correctly say of others that they were in pain. All the same, we should be inclined to say that he doesn't have the concept of pain in the way we do, even if, as seems to me likely, he would be able to identify the first pain he had as pain. What about the equally imaginary but theoretically possible case of a man who had never felt jealous? It seems to me plain that he might well have our concept of jealousy in as full a way as the rest of us. He has, for example, attended performances of *Othello* and been a spectator of the domestic dramas of his friends, and understanding these situations is to know what it is to be jealous.

What he wouldn't know until he himself was jealous would be how he would feel when he was jealous. He is jealous for the first time and he says: I am sick with jealousy! He needn't mean by this something altogether metaphorical, as when a man says that he hungers for fame, or that outwardly he was unmoved but in his heart he fed on the flattery. I don't mean that if a man says he is sick with jealousy it would be appropriate to offer him a medicament. The only thing that will do is show him that he is wrong in his supposition as to how Cassio got hold of the handkerchief. This may cure him and may well take away what in him he refers to when he says he is *sick* with jealousy. The vocabulary we use about the stronger emotions, jealousy, anger, fear, strongly suggests in the patient a qualitatively distinct introspectible content, an inner disturbance not necessarily to be identified with the occurrence of inhibited impulses to strike others, beat one's head against the wall, etc. We have, quite simply, feelings that can be located in certain regions, the head, the heart, the pit of the stomach, sometimes more obscure tinglings, flutterings, feelings of nausea, etc., that pervade us without our being able to locate them with any precision. There is no clear distinction between these feelings and such specific sensations as locatable pains; indeed, they *are* sensations and what makes us characterize them as feelings of jealousy, etc., is the context in which we have them and the dispositions they are the occasions for exciting in us.

Nevertheless, as sensations their connection with the emotion that grips me is contingent or idiosyncratic. That on the occasion of feeling intensely jealous one man is dizzy, another nauseated, is not a distinction between them with respect to their jealousy. Each man may be jealous in his own way, though we mean, when we say of each jealous man that he is jealous, exactly the same thing. Suppose, though, there were *no* content of sensation, no inner disturbance? Let us imagine that out of habit, with the recurrence of a situation which has in the past provoked jealousy, a man supposes he must be jealous; but then he adverts to the fact that there are in him none of the inner disturbances that have in the past accompanied his jealous fits. His appetite is good. He likes the look of the sky. Will he decide that he is not after all jealous? I think the answer is yes; he would say something like: Suddenly, it was as though I no longer cared. I think we should be puzzled extremely by a man who claimed to be jealous and indeed did jealous things and yet steadfastly refused to admit to having any kind of inner disturbance with which his dispositions and actions were at least contingently connected. Perhaps our puzzlement here would be like that we should have if a man who had just committed a murder seemed to be more concerned about the unpleasant appearance of the blood on the trousers of his new suit than about the nature and consequences of his act. There are certain violent anomalies which cause us to wonder if this is really a case of a human agent or patient. Another way of putting it would be this. Just as we are inclined to think that thought must have *a* vehicle—words, gestures, and so on—so we are inclined to think that emotions are necessarily connected, not with *specific* inner disturbances or sensations, but with *some* inner disturbances or sensations. The claim to have emotions that have no such connections is like the claim to pure thought, to thinking without a vehicle. We are uncertain in both cases just what is being claimed. We are inclined to think that one who does jealous things with total inner calm is play-acting, not *really* jealous.

My conclusion, then, to this part of the argument is that knowing what it is to be jealous is in one way no more a matter of having a specific introspectible content than knowing what the square of 9 is. A man able to ascribe jealousy to others knows, even if he has never himself been jealous, what it is to be jealous. All the same, we want to tie *being* jealous to the having of an introspectible content of a certain kind, not this or that content, but *some* content. I think we should have to limit what would count as a suitable content. We could count nausea, troublesome sensations in the heart region, and so on; we might have difficulty over, for example, inner feelings of a kind associated with increased physical well-being. We shouldn't understand, without our being given a special explanation, one who said: I'm so jealous I could sing with happiness.

II

It seems, then, that in the case of emotions, we *name* the emotion; what we describe is what is contingently connected with the emotion. These are sensations and felt dispositions and can be described in ways that don't puzzle. For example, we can speak of shooting pains, dull aches, diffused feelings of nausea.

But sensations and emotions don't exhaust the class of things falling under the term *feeling*. I should like to take examples from Wittgenstein and Moore that suggest a further problem about the description of feeling.

Wittgenstein is arguing against the view that we know what it "feels like" to remember:

> On the other hand, one might, perhaps, speak of a feeling, "Long, long ago," for there is a tone, a gesture, which go with certain narratives of past times.[1]

And Moore writes:

> . . . the feelings which each one has about his *self*, differ in some very radical way from e.g. the pain of tooth-ache, where it is really the same thing that is painful to you and me. Is my knowledge that you are despising me unpleasant to me in the same sense in which my tooth-ache is? Certainly here the unpleasantness is *not* a quality of any sense-datum; it is not even true that the unpleasantness of the knowledge consists in its causing me unpleasant or-

1. Ludwig Wittgenstein, *Philosophical Investigations* (Oxford, 1953), II.xiii, p. 231e.

ganic sensations. But can it be a *quality*, or "tone" of my knowledge?[2]

One sees what Wittgenstein and Moore are getting at here. Certain states have a certain "tone"—it is interesting that both philosophers go to music for their metaphor. This tone seems to be neither a perceived quality nor an organic sensation; we are reduced to evocative phrases—long, long ago—coupled with the use of a musical metaphor. We are therefore faced with the problem of attempting a description of those feelings which have no content but a tone and have no connection, or no necessary connection, with any organic sensations. Of course, there is no reason why the feelings in such cases should be desired or avoided, be found pleasant or unpleasant; they may merely be had, and pleasant/unpleasant may not exhaust what we find in them. A feeling of nostalgia, for example, may be described as pleasure flavored with regret; it is bittersweet; we flee it and we seek it, and perhaps seek it more than we flee it.

I want to discuss a feeling which has, I think, a connection in its problematic character with the Wittgenstein and Moore instances: the feeling that is so central in Proust's *A la recherche du temps perdu* and which he connects with involuntary memory. I won't take the most famous example, the taste of the madeleine which provides the novel with its first case and sets the hero on his long journey into the past; but a later and more elaborately described set of instances. At the beginning of the third chapter of *Le Temps retrouvé* the (fictional) narrator enters the courtyard of the Guermantes mansion on his way to the party that awaits him.

> En roulant les tristes pensées que je disais il y a un instant, j'étais entré dans la cour de l'hôtel de Guermantes, et dans ma distraction je n'avais pas vu une voiture qui s'avançait; au cri du wattman je n'eus que le temps de me ranger vive-

2. Casimer Lewy, ed., *The Commonplace Book of G. E. Moore* (London, 1962), p. 33.

ment de côté, et je reculai assez pour buter malgré moi contre les pavés assez mal équarris derrière lesquels était une remise. Mais au moment où, me remettant d'aplomb, je posai mon pied sur un pavé qui était un peu moins élevé que le précédent, tout mon découragement s'évanouit devant la même félicité qu'à diverses époques de ma vie m'avaient donnée la vue d'arbres que j'avais cru reconnaître dans une promenade en voiture autour de Balbec, la vue des clochers de Martinville, la saveur d'une madeleine trempée dans une infusion, tant d'autres sensations dont j'ai parlé et que les dernières oeuvres de Vinteuil m'avaient paru synthétiser. Comme au moment où je goûtais la madeleine, toute inquiétude sur l'avenir, tout doute intellectuel étaient dissipés. Ceux qui m'assaillaient tout à l'heure au sujet de la réalité de mes dons littèraires, et même de la réalité de la littérature, se trouvaient levés comme par enchantement. Sans que j'eusse fait aucun raisonnement nouveau, trouvé aucun argument décisif, les difficultés, insolubles tout à l'heure, avaient perdu toute importance. Mais, cette fois, j'étais bien décidé à ne pas me résigner à ignorer pourquoi, comme je l'avais fait le jour où j'avais goûté d'une madeleine trempée dans une infusion. La félicité que je venais d'éprouver était bien en effet la même que celle que j'avais éprouvée en mangeant la madeleine et dont j'avais alors ajourné de rechercher les causes profondes. La différence, purement matérielle, était dans les images évoquées; un azur profond enivrait mes yeux, des impressions de fraîcheur, d'éblouissante lumière tournoyaient près de moi et, dans mon désir de les saisir, sans oser plus bouger que quand je goûtais las saveur de la madeleine en tâchant de faire parvenir jusqu'à moi ce qu'elle me rappelait, je restais, quitte à faire rire la foule innombrable des wattmen, à tituber comme j'avais fait tout à l'heure, un pied sur le pavé plus élevé, l'autre pied sur le pavé plus bas. Chaque fois que je refaisais rien que matériellement ce même pas, il me restait inutile; mais si je réussissais, oubliant la matinée Guermantes, à retrouver ce que j'avais senti en posant ainsi mes pieds, de nouveau la vision éblouissante et indistincte me frôlait comme si elle m'avait dit "Saisis-moi au passage si tu en as la force, et tâche à résoudre l'énigme de bonheur que je te propose." Et presque tout de suite, je la reconnus, c'était Venise, dont mes efforts pour la décrire et les prétendus instantanés pris par ma mémoire ne m'avaient jamais rien dit, et que la sensation que j'avais ressentie jadis sur deux dalles inégales du baptistère de Saint-Marc m'avait rendue avec toutes les autres sensations jointes ce jour-là à cette sensation-là et qui étaient restées dans l'attente, à leur rang, d'où un brusque hasard les avait impérieusement fait sortir, dans la série des jours oubliés. De même le goût de la petite madeleine m'avait rappelé Combray. Mais pourquoi les images de Combray et de Venise m'avaient-elles, à l'un et à l'autre moment, donné une joie pareille à une certitude, et suffisante, sans autres preuves, à me rendre la mort indifférente?

Tout en me le demandant et en étant rèsolu aujourd'hui à trouver la réponse, j'entrai dans l'hôtel de Guermantes, parce que nous faisons toujours passer avant la besogne intérieure que nous avons à faire le rôle apparent que nous jouons et qui, ce jour-là, était celui d'un invité.[3]

It may be thought that this example is too complex, too written up, to be a good example for analysis. We have first an episode, the standing on unevenly placed flagstones, which is the occasion, and perhaps a necessary cause, of a feeling of felicity ("bliss" would perhaps be the right translation of *félicité*): the feeling is associated with, perhaps mediated by, a complex of images and sensations, beginning with those sensations associated with the position of the limbs and proceeding in a rapid sequence to the "azur profond" and "des impressions de fraîcheur, d'éblouissante lumière"; and the whole coexists with a determination both "to capture the sensation" and to account for the characteristic bliss associated with this episode and with other quite different episodes in the past—a view of trees

3. *A la recherche du temps perdu* (Bibliothèque de la Pléiade; Paris, 1969), III, 866-68.

against the sky, a view of church towers, the taste of the madeleine.

Shortly afterwards, once he is in the house, there occur (somewhat improbably, I feel) two more episodes: the sound made by the knocking of a spoon against a plate by a servant; and the rough feeling of a starched napkin against the mouth. Both these episodes are carriers of felicity, bliss, occasions of multiple sensations and images. In all three cases the determination to find an explanatory hypothesis issues in an account according to which the initial sensation resembles so exactly an earlier sensation that it summons up all that was originally associated with it. This sudden return to past sensations and scenes is involuntary, is not the result of any attempt to recall the past. What of the strange bliss, the consolatory and vivifying power of the whole experience, a bliss so intense that it seems to justify the pain of life? This is given and seems to exclude both description and analysis. (Proust develops a theory out of his philosophical reading, especially of Bergson, but we needn't bother about this.) That Proust is attempting an account of a feeling which others have had seems generally accepted and we can give it a name—the Proustian feeling!

Reflection upon the Proustian examples should show us something about the possibilities and the limits of description. No one is likely to dispute Proust's power and ingenuity; it is also clear that when Proust comes to that which crowns the experience and gives it its blissful character he is driven to offer not a description which enables us to take the measure of the feeling in the way we are certainly able to take the measure of other aspects of the experience, the sensations and images— these are indeed well described or aptly referred to—but a metaphysical theory which offers a complicated explanation of why the experience is felicitous, blissful.

A possible interpretation of what Proust does would be this. There is that in our experience which is describable, the having of sensations and images. (We learn the language of sensation very early and its intelligibility rests upon there being characteristic behavior associated with sensations, and other and relevant experiences—looking in mirrors, drawing pictures—which elucidate the having of mental pictures; though it's important to remember that not everyone is able to understand the latter.) But here is a further feeling—"bliss"—which is ineffable and therefore indescribable.

Of course, if the feeling *is* indescribable we have no further duty to perform, and any thought that we haven't quite done what we ought to do would be irrational. At any rate, I think we do feel there is more to *say*, whether by way of description or not.

Why are we inclined to say that everything has been described and/or accounted for *except* the feeling of bliss? The sensations are named in a context and the conjunction of the names of sensations in this context makes up a description of the episodic experience. If a man were to say, "Give me a fuller account of the 'feeling of freshness/coolness,' for I don't yet understand," we should not attempt to give him a deeper understanding through a fuller, more detailed description; we should rather give him examples (e.g., going into the night air from a heated room) until he grasped what was being said. The relation between what is said about sensations and what is said about the feeling of bliss is, we tend to think, like the relation between what can be said about the public world of physical objects and what can be said about sensations. Sensations, too, are thought to be ineffable as compared with the geometrically and dynamically describable objects in physical space. And yet not all our sensations are nameable only; we can speak of shooting pains, dull aches, we can locate areas of itching, and there are rich resources available to those who want to describe the tastes of different vintages of wine. If the Proustian experience does defeat us it must be because it is in some peculiar way unusually and perhaps altogether resistant to description. It is named in a context and people either catch on or don't. If they don't, they are not in the position of those who don't yet understand the common language of sensation; they are rather perhaps in the position of those who are blind or stone-deaf from birth and who can certainly use the ordinary language which contains words that name sights and sounds, and use it correctly, but about whom we should hesitate if we were asked if they had the same concepts as the sighted and those with hearing. The difficulty there may be in catching on to what Proust is talking about rests perhaps upon the lack of connection between the experience of bliss and any standard behavioral or other situations. But it *does* resemble in some respects puzzles about description that can be raised about quite ordinary sensations. "Describe the aroma of coffee.—Why can't it be done? Do we lack the words? And *for what* are the words lacking?—But whence comes the idea that such a description must after all be possible? . . . Have you tried to describe the aroma and not succeeded?"[4]

Perhaps one could put the matter like this. Many situations and experiences are genuinely challenges to our powers of description and we slip into the notion that everything merely referred to is capable of further description. As we have seen, it is sometimes true that we can expand laconic references into descriptions (shooting pains, etc.). But to suppose that everything that enters into the description must itself be capable of being described would be like supposing that individual words must always be what they *sometimes* are, namely, composed of words. Not all words *could* be. Some terms, therefore, of our description must stand to the description as words stand to the sentences they compose. This is a logical requirement of any linguistic description and not a contingent fact about descriptions in some languages. If I give, even, a nonverbal description, e.g., if I describe a thing as curved by means of a gesture, the same logical requirement holds. I may of course tell you more by setting what I am describing in a fuller context, and this is what Proust does. Someone who had never come across the aroma of coffee *might* be illuminated by being told that it was like the aroma of cocoa, but sharper and less cloying, at least in the sense

4. *Philosophical Investigations*, I.610, p. 159e.

that when the man did come across the aroma of coffee he would recognize your placing of coffee at a particular place in the olfactory spectrum as apt.[5]

We may still have feelings of dissatisfaction when faced with the occurrence of "bliss" as an item of description and want to know more about it. Certainly, one can go on talking without assignable limit. One may say, as Proust does, that the experience brings with it certain consequential attitudes, such as that certain anxieties vanish or are put to sleep, or that we accept the world that up to the moment of the ineffable feeling we had found boring or hateful. But it would be misleading to identify the feeling of bliss with a set of attitudes and dispositions that we have on the occasion of having it. *Bliss* refers to an affective state in which a man is during a specifiable, if very short, period of time. To one who was still puzzled one could only say, *either:* It's evident you have never enjoyed this feeling, *or:* Have you had the following feelings which are not unlike it: how you feel coming out of a nitrous oxide trance, how you feel looking at a smoky crimson sunset over a great city, how you sometimes feel reading this passage of Wordsworth or listening to this episode in a Beethoven sonata? Here we should attempt to teach by giving what are thought to be cognate examples, as we use models and analogies and enlightening stories in every kind of teaching. But there could be no fuller *description.*

III

A strong awareness of the difficulty of giving a rich and yet comprehensible contextual account of idiosyncratic states of feeling lies behind much artistic effort, especially in literature, and may provide the hint of an explanation of one of the most used—pos-

5. I owe this point to Mr. Peter Long of the University of Leeds.

sibly abused—concepts in twentieth-century criticism: objective correlative.

Before I link this concept with the problem how we are to describe feelings I should like to make a point about the work of the novelist or the poet who is concerned with fictions in which human subjects are depicted. He is necessarily concerned with the whole range of human feeling, since it is as feeling subjects human beings are interesting to us, though their feeling is not all in them that interests us. But the ordering of feeling as presented to the reader is not identical with the feeling enjoyed and known by the character. The problem in dealing with works of the imagination is in part concerned with our own feelings that may not at all be the feelings of the fictional character(s). I take as an illustrative example a moment of some importance for Isabel Archer very early in *The Portrait of a Lady*. She is still in Albany, in her family house, and she is reflecting on the unknown future offered by her crazy Aunt Lydia, Mrs. Touchett.

> Her imagination was by habit ridiculously active: when the door was not open it jumped out of the window. She was not accustomed indeed to keep it behind bolts. . . . The years and hours of her life came back to her, and for a long time, in a stillness broken only by the ticking of the big bronze clock, she passed them in review.[6]

We are given a suggestion of a young woman full of energy and self-will, impulsive, adventurous, free, independent, at times reflective. The key image is that of the room which isn't allowed to be constricting. It isn't commonly bolted but sometimes the mere interposition of the door is intolerable and in the passion of her youth she jumps out of the window. This tells us how Isabel Archer is at this point in her fortunes. But for *us* the image of the house with the door and the window is more poignant

6. Henry James, *The Portrait of a Lady* (London: World's Classics, 1947), pp. 31-32.

and is like the first sounding of a theme in a piece of music with symphonic structure. Rooms, doors, windows are for us what they are as a result of an accumulation of impressions, perhaps as a result of the psychological structure common to most men and women in our culture. The room with the door shut is at once the place of security and of imprisonment, frustration. Through the window we look out on the world; but it is through the window that the peeping Tom of the world looks at us. The world seen through the window is ordered by the frame; it isn't that unknown and possibly menacing world that lies all round us, *behind* us. Leaping out of the window is unconventional and adventurous; it is the way a girl might elope. And the door: it is through the door that we go out to encounter our destiny; but it is also through the door that the friend and the enemy come, and the enemy disguised as a friend, the traitor; it is the gate of salvation and of doom. The weight of such ideas is there for the attentive reader, not indeed fully adverted to, but all the same *there*, establishing a tone for *our* view of Isabel Archer, not of course a tone which at this stage Isabel Archer could herself be conscious of. We note that here a quite commonplace and quite unjeweled description serves to imply a tone of feeling; the tone isn't mentioned but comes through the writing in this context; the context *expresses* the feeling (in the old sense of "express").*

This leads me into the difficult question of the "objective correlative." I quote from the first appearance, so far as I know, of the idea, in T. S. Eliot's 1919 essay on *Hamlet*.

> The only way of expressing emotion in the form of art is by finding an "objective correlative"; in other words, a set of objects, a situation, a chain of events which shall be the formula of that *particular* emotion; such that when the external facts . . . are given, the emotion is immediately evoked. If you examine any of Shakespeare's most successful tragedies, you will find this exact equivalence; you will

---

*Cod-liver oil used to be commended as being "freshly expressed."

find that the state of mind of Lady Macbeth walking in her sleep has been communicated to you by a skilful accumulation of imagined sensory impressions.[7]

I think there are many weaknesses and obscurities here. I think an idea with a promising career in front of it and a certain usefulness even now has been launched. From our point of view the important stress to note is on the impossibility of a direct description and communication of a particular kind of feeling (I don't think Eliot is using "emotion" in a very strict sense).

I take some examples from George Eliot's *Daniel Deronda*. Here is the description of Offendene, the temporary home of the Harleths:

> The season suited the aspect of the old oblong red-brick house, rather too anxiously ornamented with stone at every line, not excepting the double row of narrow windows and the large square portico. The stone encouraged a greenish lichen, the brick a powdery grey, so that though the building was rigidly rectangular there was no harshness in the physiognomy which it turned to the three avenues cut east, west, and south in the hundred yards' breadth of old plantation encircling the immediate grounds. One would have liked the house to have been lifted on a knoll, so as to look beyond its own little domain to the long thatched roofs of the distant villages, the church towers, the scattered homesteads, the gradual rise of surging woods, and the green breadths of undulating park which made the beautiful face of the earth in that part of Wessex. But though standing thus behind a screen amid flat pastures, it had on one side a glimpse of the wider world in the lofty curves of the chalk downs, grand steadfast forms played over by the changing days.[8]

Here everything is or seems to be a graceful description of a house; but there comes through the description a feeling of

---

7. T. S. Eliot, *Selected Essays* (London, 1951), p. 145.
8. George Eliot, *Daniel Deronda* (Harmondsworth: Penguin, 1967), p. 51.

maladjustment, of unfocused frustration, of something missed, of life not answering to our desires. This is precisely the frame of mind, the *tone* of mind, of the heroine. The next example is a less pure example of the objective correlative but is perhaps a more remarkable achievement.

It was half-past ten in the morning when Gwendolen Harleth, after her gloomy journey from Leubronn, arrived at the station from which she must drive to Offendene. No carriage or friend was awaiting her, for in the telegram she had sent from Dover she had mentioned a later train, and in her impatience of lingering at a London station she had set off without picturing what it would be to arrive unannounced at half an hour's drive from home—at one of those stations which have been fixed on not as near anywhere but as equidistant from everywhere. Deposited as a *femme sole* with her large trunks, and having to wait while a vehicle was being got from the large-sized lantern called the Railway Inn, Gwendolen felt that the dirty paint in the waitingroom, the dusty decanter of flat water, and the texts in large letters calling on her to repent and be converted, were part of the dreary prospect opened by her family troubles; and she hurried away to the outer door looking towards the land and fields. But here the very gleams of sunshine seemed melancholy, for the autumnal leaves and grass were shivering, and the wind was turning up the feathers of a cock and two croaking hens which had doubtless parted with their grown-up offspring and did not know what to do with themselves. The railway official also seemed without resources, and his innocent demeanour in observing Gwendolen and her trunks was rendered intolerable by the cast in his eye; especially since, being a new man, he did not know her, and must conclude that she was not very high in the world. The vehicle—a dirty old barouche—was within sight, and was being slowly prepared by an elderly labourer. Contemptible details these, to make part of a history; yet the turn of most lives is hardly to be accounted for without them. They are continually entering with cumulative force into a mood until it gets the mass and momentum of a theory or a motive.[9]

Perhaps one ought to say that this is a passage studded with objective correlatives, the dusty decanter, the texts, the "cock and two croaking hens."

The way to the description of a state of feeling is indirect, through the description of the world, not the world as metaphor, but the world as that which speaks to us of particular complexes of feeling.[10] Proust is sometimes able to do this when he is least theoretical and not trying very hard to express the ineffable. But the power and charm of the arts is that in them we discover the life of feeling that might sleep in us unregarded without their help. We find our sadness in the music, our joy in the painting, our sense of emotional balance and tranquillity in the Chinese jar, our passions in the novel or the drama. It is as though we don't understand our own feelings until we are confronted with a contrived state of affairs that isn't a direct rendering of our feelings but somehow expresses their tone and form. Wittgenstein was right in finding that "one might . . . speak of a feeling 'Long, long ago,' for there is a tone, a gesture, which go with certain narratives of past times."

9. Ibid., pp. 268-69.
10. This seems to involve sharing in a culture or acquiring one. If we can imagine a culture that is both nomadic—people live in tents—and sophisticated it would be hard for those within it to get much out of the Henry James example or the first George Eliot example. Just as the ground of our communication is our possession of a common language, so the ground of our being able to communicate complex feelings through the arts is the sharing of a common history and common ways of life. There may be no *pure* art, perhaps not even music, that can do this cross-culturally or in such a way as to transcend all cultural determinations.

The Idea of Christendom ─────────────

Unwary and inexperienced theologians seem to acquire a disposition to cast themselves with rapacity onto the dimly visible bodies of misunderstood theories. The Big Bang theory of the origin of the universe is supposed to vindicate the dogmatically certain principle of *creatio ex nihilo*, just as two generations ago Heisenberg's Uncertainty Principle was thought to do a similar service for the idea of free will. There seems to have grown up a disposition among the desperate to profit from Wittgenstein's notion of *Lebensform*, "form of life." It seems to be thought that we have here a device for rendering the various claims made by religious believers invulnerable to criticism: scientific, historical, moral, or what have you. The dogma of Transubstantiation or the doctrine of *Karma* gets its sense from the role of its linguistic expressions in the form of life, liturgical or other, of the believing community. One who stands outside the believing community stands outside the expression in question.

Professor Antony Flew and I were once seated side by side at a meeting of philosophers addressed by a well-known

─────────────────────────────────────

From *The Autonomy of Religious Belief*, ed. Frederick Crosson (Notre Dame, Ind.: University of Notre Dame Press, 1981), pp. 8-37.

philosopher of religion, later to be elevated to the episcopal chair of the great Joseph Butler. He set forward the remarkable statement: "The resurrection narratives are logically odd"; and under the pressure of the discussion, it became clear that he meant, among other things, that one couldn't raise in connection with them the crude question: Are they true or false? For once Professor Flew and I were forced into total agreement with each other. If such stratagems are to be permitted, it will turn out that believers will be told they don't mean what, historically, they have certainly meant when talking about, e.g., the resurrection of Jesus Christ; and unbelievers will be told to keep off the grass and talk to themselves in their own territory. To protect the resurrection narratives from historical criticism by labeling them "logically odd" belongs, or so it seems to me, to the same family of devices as the use of the idea of "form of life" for defensive or apologetic purposes. (I ought to add that the "unwary and inexperienced" I have in mind commonly *are* theologians, not philosophers.)

The idea of "language-game" and the idea of "form of life" are intimately connected, just because a language-game consists of "language and actions into which it is woven."[1] And "to imagine a language means to *imagine* a form of life";[2] and not only is to *imagine* a language to imagine a form of life, "the *speaking* of a language is [also] part of an activity, or of a form of life."[3] Language and actions are interwoven; this is why we have to think of language not as something which occurs *within* a given form of life but as an organic part, as it were, of the total natural history of a human group. "Commanding, questioning, recounting, chatting, are as much a part of our natural history as walking, eating, drinking, playing."[4]

We can take all such statements as enormous platitudes—

---

1. *Philosophical Investigations*, translated by G. E. M. Anscombe (Oxford: Basil Blackwell, 1953) I.7, p. 5e.

2. *PI*, I.19, p. 8e.

3. *PI*, I.23, p. 11e.

4. *PI*, I.25, p. 12e.

"Who deniges of it, Betsie?"—if we come across them in isolation, as though they were the *obiter dicta* of some relaxed and whiffling social anthropologist. Of course, they get their point from the philosophical problems they are designed to resolve or dissolve. We have also to remember that it is a Wittgensteinian principle that philosophy only states what everyone admits (or perhaps better, can be brought to admit, for this emphasizes the Socrates-and-the-slave-boy situation that is, or so he hopes, the situation of the teacher of philosophy faced with his pupils). These problems are those of the mingled Cartesian and empiricist traditions in Europe: roughly, the family of problems generated by the Cartesian principle that the mind is better known than the body (Second Meditation). Perhaps the most familiar example of this is Locke's view of how words get their meaning; they are "articulate sounds" used as "signs of internal conceptions" and made to "stand as marks for the ideas within [a man's] own mind, whereby they might be made known to others, and the thoughts of men's minds be conveyed from one to another."[5] Wittgenstein's account shows that if this were right, no one could ever learn a language, and the use of the linked ideas of language-game and form of life successfully disposes of the Cartesian-empiricist example of the bewitchment of the intelligence by means of language.

I think that in this matter Wittgenstein's arguments are satisfactory and that the dilemmas or predicaments generated by the Cartesian premise have been robbed of the interest they used to have. This doesn't mean that we are dispensed from repeating our philosophical history; although historically this cluster of problems comes from Descartes, it seems evident that such dilemmas or predicaments were known to the Greeks, and I daresay to the Chinese. This seems to be what Wittgenstein is getting at when he remarks that "the problems arising through a misinterpretation of our forms of language have the character of *depth*. They are deep disquietudes; their roots are as deep in

5. *An Essay Concerning Human Understanding,* III.1.

us as the forms of our language and their significance is as great as the importance of our language."[6] A disquietude so deep, a puzzlement that ranges over long periods of history and many different civilizations, this is for him what marks out the field of philosophical interest. If it is possible, as it is, for those equipped with the linguistic forms of Chinese to puzzle over the paradoxes of material implication, if the Greeks of the fifth century B.C. could find difficulty in seeing just how the concept of truth applies to moral statements, then it is unlikely that brisk refutations of particular epistemological theories, even those refutations that are soup boiled down from the bones of the Wittgensteinian corpus, will free us from our disposition to set ourselves philosophical problems of a kind that may turn out on investigation to be both bewitchments of the intelligence, through a failure to know whither our misunderstanding of our language is taking us, and also variations upon old themes.

I conclude, then, that there is nothing restrictive about the concept language-game/form of life, nothing, at least at first glance, that makes it impossible for Europeans and North Americans of some degree of education to grasp the meanings of individual expressions or whole sublanguages that are in the first place remote from their own experience or from their own linguistic metropolis or suburb. I am encouraged to think this by the cautionary remarks, as I take them to be, of Wittgenstein himself. In the middle of his early discussion of language-games of an elementary kind, he notes that some may have difficulty with the simplicity of his examples and may argue that such invented languages are useless as heuristic examples since they are essentially incomplete.

> If you want to say that this [the invented languages *supra* consisted only of orders] shews them to be incomplete, ask yourself whether our language is complete;— whether it was so before the symbolism of chemistry and the notation of the infinitesimal calculus were incor-

6. *PI*, I.111, p. 47^e.

porated in it; for these are, so to speak, suburbs of our language. (And how many houses or streets does it take before a town begins to be a town?) Our language can be seen as an ancient city; a maze of little streets and squares, of old and new houses, and of houses with additions from various periods; and this surrounded by a multitude of new boroughs with straight regular streets and uniform houses.[7]

I find this image full of reverberations, at least one of them provoked with intention. We are bound to think of the solemn repudiation of the ancient city, with its maze of little streets gathered round cathedral and palace, in the second part of the *Discourse on Method*. It seems possible that Wittgenstein had this passage in mind:

> those ancient cities which were originally mere boroughs, and have become large towns in process of time, are as a rule badly laid out, as compared with those towns of regular pattern that are laid out by a designer on an open plain to suit his fancy; while the buildings severally considered are often equal or superior artistically to those in planned towns, yet, in view of their arrangement—here a large one, there a small—and the way they make the streets twisted and irregular, one would say that it was chance that placed them so, not the will of men who had the use of reason.[8]

Here the unplanned city is an image of what is received from tradition, with all its irregularities, patchings, discordant themes, all that irritates and frustrates one for whom mathematics is the only science God has so far bestowed upon men. Wittgenstein is saying, as it were, that this is where we live, in the many-layered, labyrinthine city of human culture, and that there is something hopelessly wrong about the ambition to

---

7. *PI*, I.18, p. 8[e].

8. Descartes, *Philosophical Writings*, a selection translated and edited by Elizabeth Anscombe and Peter Thomas Geach (Edinburgh: Nelson, 1954), p. 15.

make the clean start, to found the geometrical city where all is clear at a glance, leaving behind us the ruins of the past.

I ———————————————————————————————————

I propose to take the idea of Christendom as a case for asking where a consideration of *Lebensform* will take us. Much of what I say will consist of observations on what Wittgenstein calls the natural history of men, and although this is not in itself what Wittgenstein or anyone else calls philosophy, it becomes philosophical if it is directed towards the solution or dissolution or even, simply, the more perspicuous rendering of those problems that won't go away when we try to handle them in accordance with ordinary critical methods.

"Christendom" I shall understand as designating a state of affairs in human history that begins in the West with Augustine, in the East of course earlier with the transfer of the Empire to Byzantium, and persists down to our own day and perhaps well into the future. It is to be identified in the main with particular spaces that contract and expand from time to time; there are what one might call fully realized expansions, as to the Americas in the sixteenth and seventeenth centuries, or frustrated expansions, as to China, Japan, and India in the seventeenth century; and there are the contractions, as in North Africa and the eastern Mediterranean. From the past Christendom has absorbed philosophies, literatures, sciences, political models, and so on, most immediately from the Hellenistic world; but it seems hard to place any limit on the openness of this particular fragment of human history to the past. It seems likely that our political forms, our moral maxims, our jurisprudential ideas, not to speak of the archaic forms that, it seems, have some role in shaping how we take our physical world—day and night, sun and moon, water and fire, cold and warmth, sexual and paternal, maternal, and filial relations—are related to strata of the common past now irrecoverable, at least in any straightforward sense. It may shake the mind to notice that Neanderthal men, with whom we may have no direct biological connection, had ceremonials for the burying of the dead.

You will have noticed that I speak of *our* political forms, moral maxims, and so on: I do this to bring out that I am using the term "Christendom" in such a way that anyone with a Western education lives within it and can't help doing so, in virtue of the legal norms, the literary fictions, the political ideas, the ways of living in community, et cetera that compel us, if I may adapt Wittgenstein, "to travel over a wide field of thought crisscross in every direction."[9] That is, "Christendom" is a complex of forms of life; how we live and move within this complex will illustrate the usefulness and the frailty of *Lebensform* as an explanatory device.

I take as my first example of a response to a part of this complex, one that is well known to literary critics. It is the violent moment in *Middlemarch* when the heroine, the natural flow of feeling blocked by her impossible marriage to the aged pseudo-scholar Casaubon, receives the attack of the Roman scene like a wound or a disease:

> after the brief narrow experience of her girlhood she was beholding Rome, the city of visible history, where the past of a whole hemisphere seems moving in funeral procession with strange ancestral images and trophies gathered from afar. . . .
>
> To those who have looked at Rome with the quickening power of a knowledge which breathes a growing soul into all historic shapes, and traces out the suppressed transitions which unite all contrasts, Rome may still be the spiritual centre of the world. But let them conceive one more historical contrast: the gigantic broken revelations of that Imperial and Papal city thrust abruptly on the notions of a girl who had been brought up in English and Swiss Puritanism, fed on meagre Protestant histories and on art chiefly of the handscreen sort. . . . The weight of unintel-

9. *PI*, p. ix[e].

ligible Rome might lie easily on bright nymphs to whom it formed a background for the brilliant picnic of Anglo-foreign society; but Dorothea had no such defence against deep impressions. Ruins and basilicas, palaces and colossi, set in the midst of a sordid present, where all that was living and warm-blooded seemed sunk in the deep degeneracy of a superstition divorced from reverence; the dimmer but yet eager Titanic life gazing and struggling on walls and ceilings; the long vistas of white forms whose marble eyes seemed to hold the monotonous light of an alien world; all this . . . at first jarred her as with an electric shock, and then urged themselves on her with that ache belonging to a glut of confused ideas which check the flow of emotion. Forms both pale and glowing took possession of her young sense, and fixed themselves in her memory even when she was not thinking of them, preparing strange associations which remained through her after-years . . . in certain states of dull forlornness Dorothea all her life continued to see the vastness of St. Peter's, the huge bronze canopy, the excited intention in the attitudes and garments of the prophets and evangelists in the mosaics above, and the red drapery which was being hung for Christmas spreading itself everywhere like a disease of the retina.[10]

I called this a violent moment because the Roman scene is received as though the soul were wounded or made sick, stricken or infected. This is a suitable image for a certain kind of induction into a way of life; the wound comes from an unwillingness, one that is all the same without interdictory force, to be brought within a form of life; the sickness, as it were a fever, of the soul comes from the wound, ever open, never quite healed. This half-entry into a form of life takes its quality from the actual situation of Dorothea with all its perplexities of thought and feeling, and here she is a more humanly representative figure than the cool observer, the one who looks in and stays outside.

10. George Eliot, *Middlemarch*, Book II, ch. 20.

She is contrasted, in the suppressed hysteria of her disturbed Puritanical maidenhood, with one for whom "Rome may still be the spiritual centre of the world"—no doubt Eliot has such a one as Newman in mind; yet although she bears "the weight of *unintelligible* Rome," the impression is deep, the effect for life. It is not as though in Rome she is faced with the otherness of Aztec temples or neolithic fortifications, mere memorials of a dead form of life; her half-entry into Rome is prepared by her education, meager though it may have been, so that the "Titanic life gazing and struggling on walls and ceilings," the "forms both pale and glowing," take possession of her, she recognizes the prophets and evangelists in the mosaics because she already has some notion of what a prophet or an evangelist is, and this is why "the excited intention" in their attitudes and garments disturbs her: it is as though they had become for her threatening realities, no longer shut up in the sacred volume, but released and hungry, with designs upon Dorothea.

Finally, the strange intimacy of the experience is represented by the magnificent image with which the passage ends: "like a disease of the retina." It is not that Dorothea is the victim of tricks of perceptive, optical illusion; such deceptions leave the one who sees aloof, uninvolved; she received Rome into the privileged organs of perception, onto the surface of the eyes, signs of the soul that get their life (in this passage) from the implied contrast with the dead marble eyes that represent the level light of pagan antiquity. It wouldn't be right to say that Rome is a complete enigma to Dorothea: an enigma doesn't trouble us in quite this sharp way. She hasn't come "into a strange country with entirely strange traditions" in which "we do not *understand* the people."[11] The effect is rather that of a dream in which a road or a room is strange and yet familiar, disturbing just because it is not simply a foreign fact. Dorothea in Rome thus may stand for one way in which we move within the complex of Christendom.

I observe in connection with this example that, trembling

11. *PI*, II.xi, p. 223ᵉ.

upon the frontier of two forms of life—one thoroughly experienced and grounded in habit, the other vaguely apprehended through visible signs that have some compelling power only because Dorothea's education provides a narrow but sufficient, if barely sufficient, ground for new apprehensions—she is filled with passion and desire, strong impulses to flee away and at the same time go forward into the not yet embraced. The images of pain and sickness bring out how wrenching and debilitating an experience it is to pass from one culture to another. Nevertheless, the "pale and glowing" forms *take possession of her*, and this is seduction rather than rape; there is that in Dorothea which reaches out with a disguised appetite for the dread forms and their half-divined intentions. The whole experience reflects a torn consciousness; the vehemence of the response seems to transcend the occasion. If we ask why this should be so, then I think one answer is that Dorothea, this "girl . . . brought up in English and Swiss Puritanism," trembles on the edge of what she takes to be absolute prohibitions. Like all human beings she has within her "a terrible, fierce, and lawless class of desires," desires that in decent people are only satisfied in dreams, in which the soul "is ready for any deed of blood, and there is no unhallowed food it will not eat"[12] (we have already noted the dreamlike quality of the experience). The charm of the mixture of paganism and Catholicism, which to her Protestant sensibility is the spectacle of Rome, is that it represents the gratification of what has been deeply repressed but has now been released in fantasy by her dim awareness of her frontier situation; but the experience is also threatening in its invitation to Dorothea to throw off the absolute prohibitions of her Protestant formation.

Well-educated people tend toward antinomianism, and it is important that Dorothea is narrowly and imperfectly educated. If she were more sophisticated the spectacle of Rome might still make her giddy, but the movement towards a foreign form

---

12. *Republic* IX.571-72, Lindsay translation.

of life would be more a flirtation, less the solemn violation of a prohibition that adultery is; indeed, the effect of sophistication might be to raise in her questions about any assertion that there are deep qualitative differences between flirtation and adultery. But Dorothea lives at the level of morality, not that of the aesthetic, where all ideas, including deeds of blood and the eating of unhallowed foods, incest and the desecration of tombs, are interesting ideas. Here the Dorotheas have even an epistemological advantage in that they are unlikely to neglect the importance of absolute prohibitions in any viable form of human life.

To pass from one form of life to another, as in conversion, is not simply to change one's point of view—"point of view" is closely linked with taking life at the level of the aesthetic—but to turn the whole of the person concerned around. Take the case of one who did not tremble on the frontier but advanced over it, passing from one form of life to another: Ruth the Moabitess. Naomi says to Ruth: "Behold, thy sister-in-law is gone back unto her people, and unto her gods. . . ." And Ruth said, "Intreat me not to leave thee, or to return from following after thee: for whither thou goest, I will go; and where thou lodgest, I will lodge: thy people shall be my people, and thy God my God."[13] The utterance that effects the transfer gets its solemnity and force from the change from the gods of the Moabites to the God of Israel, and this is no shift in a speculative point of view but the adoption of a new set of injunctions and prohibitions, though in this case it is not a wrenching experience, for Ruth "clave unto" Naomi.[14]

To be a citizen of the world is to have the capacity to pass from one form of life to another, to move from the city to the suburbs and back again, and thus also to acquire a capacity to imagine a diversity of forms of life; but just because the transitions for such a one are relatively painless, there is a tendency to fail to grasp the weight and seriousness for a given way of life

13. Ruth 1:15-16.
14. Ibid. 1:14.

of the set of prohibitions and injunctions that give it solidity and persistence through time. We see this in the crassness of aspects of social anthropology before Evans-Pritchard and in the preoccupations with formal connections of the Structuralists. Here Dorothea, trembling on the frontier, and Ruth, knowing the seriousness of abandoning her own gods but doing so happily, with a loving will, are better models, not just as better human beings, but as better, more perceptive appraisers of what is involved in so dreadful a transition.

The situation that faces Dorothea is that of a possible transition within Christendom; she endures the possibility of moving from a suburb into the twisted streets and the darkness of the ancient city. Ruth's transition, from the gods of the Moabites to the God of Israel, is more extreme, indeed, is qualitatively different.

Now, there are many transitions within Christendom, and many ways of facing them. The wanderings of the peoples in modern times, from the old to the new world and, within Europe, from the poorer south and east to the more opulent northwest, provide examples, and from such shifts in forms of life many illuminating accounts have come. The complexity of what has happened since the sixteenth century is so great that no straightforward account is possible. What is striking is the persistence of forms within forms, ways of ordering human life that recur like themes and motifs in musical structures and that, like such themes, are often subtly varied so that we may miss the identity which gathers together the variations. Take, for example, the variations on the theme of the religious life offered by the monks of the desert, those of the Benedictine tradition, and the friars that spring up with the revival of town life in the thirteenth century. And then think of the gathered communities, what Troeltsch calls the "sect-type," Anabaptists and Quakers, that correspond sociologically, for us, to the religious life in medieval and Counter-Reformation Catholicism. To think one's way through such complexities requires a power of imagination and an intellectual tact best exemplified in this century in the work of Max Weber.

One of the most interesting, though it is hard to get the description of it right—perhaps it is enough to refer to it without much description—of the transitions that are, so to speak, available to us, is that in which we pass, often within a single country, from one form of life to another simply by moving a short distance in space. Switzerland offers the most interesting and perhaps the clearest examples. If one passes from the canton of Geneva to that of the Valais, the change is palpable. The pace of life changes, things are different to the ear and the nose, even the sky seems a different sky. Life in the Valais seems relaxed and unbuttoned, tidiness seems no longer a major virtue, the image of the crucified one starts up out of the street and the hedgerow. (An American parallel would be the transition from North to South—I remember this vividly from twenty years ago: the crossing of the state line from Indiana to Kentucky.) These seem slight matters. But it appears likely that it was from the felt difference between the Catholic and the Protestant parts of Germany that the first impulse to write *The Protestant Ethic and the Spirit of Capitalism* came.

II

I want now to speak of another kind of movement or journey, that in which the form of life—strictly, complex of forms—within which a religious man exists is explored at a deeper level within itself. This is almost a mining operation. It involves separating what has been confused, articulating what has not yet been articulated or has been forgotten. It is essentially a matter of *correcting* what is taken to be, by most of those who share the form of life, the sense of what they do and say. On some views this isn't possible; it is not possible, that is, in some accounts of what Professor Kai Nielsen, irresistibly, calls "Wittgensteinian fideism." In some accounts it seems there would be difficulty in incorporating into a description (and philosophers are said to be restricted to describing)[15] any idea of a general misunderstanding, among those who share a form of life, of what it is they are engaged in as actors and speakers. The notion of a general mistake about meaning seems to have no purchase. I suppose we should be able, without abandoning "fideism," to give an account of a schism. Here the schismatics take off on their own and set up a new if related form of life with a different set of ground rules. We could also recognize that it is part of the schismatic way of carrying on that they use such concepts as "mistake" and "error" to characterize the procedures—syntax and semantic rules, if you like—of the body they have deserted, though within what language-game the philosopher is making his moves when he offers comparative descriptions of the two forms of life I am not clear.[16]

The exploratory movement I want to look at is that set out in Kierkegaard's polemical writings of 1854-55, translated and collected by Walter Lowrie under the title *Kierkegaard's Attack Upon "Christendom."* [17] Two things ought perhaps to be remem-

15. Cf. D. Z. Phillips, *Religion Without Explanation* (Oxford: Basil Blackwell, 1976), p. 41 and *passim*.

16. This is also a problem for Nielsen when he tries to show that "fideism" implies "conceptual relativism" and that therefore the entire fideist enterprise self-ignites and explodes and must end in religious skepticism. He claims, for example, that the "fideist" Christian cannot find a "conflict between accepting belief system p (Christianity) as embodying the claim Christ is the truth and acknowledging that systems, q, r, t, n, m, y, s . . . are equally legitimate forms of life." (Kai Nielsen, *Contemporary Critiques of Religion* [London: Herder and Herder, 1971], p. 110.) If "Wittgensteinian fideism" implies "conceptual relativism," then the expression "equally legitimate" couldn't occur with reference to two or more language-games. I suspect that this means that Nielsen's *reductio* argument won't work just because the thesis of "cultural relativism" can't be stated coherently. It is like the argument of those who hold that logical principles are relative to particular groups of natural languages and that Chinese, for example, is non-Aristotelian. But *this* argument is stated and its conclusion is true or false. Whether or not "fideism" and "cultural relativism" can be got out of Wittgenstein's later work is another question. I am inclined to think not. Crudely, "language-game" is a heuristic device, not a constitutive principle.

17. *Kierkegaard's Attack Upon "Christendom"* (Princeton, N. J.: Princeton University Press, 1944).

195

bered: that Kierkegaard always insisted that what he wrote, he wrote as a *corrective* (it is hard to remember sometimes that he once wrote that Christianity is the perfection of the truly human); and that he was conscious that he spoke as a dying man, that these were to be his final words.

> I have something on my conscience as a writer [this is written in 1853, before the death of Bishop Mynster]. Let me indicate quite clearly how I feel about it. There is something quite definite I have to say, and I have it so much upon my conscience that (as I feel) I dare not die without having said it. For the moment I die and thus leave this world (as I understand it) I shall in the very same second (at such a speed does it go!), in the very same second I shall be infinitely far away, in a different place where still within the same second (frightful speed!) the question will be put to me: Have you uttered the definite message *quite definitely. . . ?*[18]

What brought Kierkegaard to this point was the death of the worthy and worldly prelate, Bishop Mynster. Professor Martensen, the Court Preacher for the occasion, affirmed in his panegyric on the dead bishop that he was one of the genuine witnesses to the truth and had his place in the "holy chain of witnesses to the truth which stretches through the ages from the days of the Apostles"—"etc.," Kierkegaard adds in derision.[19] Kierkegaard begins quietly by suggesting that this is not even a kindness to Mynster, for "the genuine thing about him was that, as I am firmly convinced, he was willing to admit before God and to himself that by no manner of means was he a witness to the truth."[20] What, then, he asks, is a witness to the truth?

> A witness to the truth is a man who in poverty witnesses to the truth—in poverty, in lowliness, in abasement, and

---

18. *The Journals of Søren Kierkegaard*, selection edited and translated by Alexander Dru (London: Oxford University Press, 1938), pp. 492-93.
19. *Kierkegaard's Attack Upon "Christendom,"* p. 5.
20. Ibid., p. 6.

so is unappreciated, hated, abhorred, and then derided, insulted, mocked—his daily bread perhaps he did not always have, so poor was he, but the daily bread of persecution he was richly provided with every day. . . . A witness to the truth, one of the genuine witnesses to the truth, is a man who is scourged, maltreated, dragged from one prison to the other, and then at last—the last promotion, whereby he is admitted to the first class as defined by the Christian protocol, among the genuine witnesses to the truth—then at last—for this is indeed one of those genuine witnesses to the truth of whom Professor Martensen speaks—then at last crucified, or beheaded, or burnt, or roasted on a gridiron, his lifeless body thrown by the executioner in an out-of-the-way place (thus a witness to the truth is buried), or burnt to ashes and cast to the four winds, so that evey trace of the "filth" (which the Apostle says *he* was) might be obliterated. . . . and Bishop Mynster, says Professor Martensen, was one of the genuine witnesses to the truth.[21]

This is, Kierkegaard argues, to make a fool of God: "I would rather gamble, carouse, fornicate, steal, murder, than take part in making a fool of God."[22] If I am to twaddle in this way, that is, to say of a worldly prelate that he is a witness or, worse, that the Christian life is for all a pleasant and respectable middle-class existence under an established church and a Christian monarch, then let me "confine myself to talking about this in the parlor, over a cup of tea with my wife and some prating friends, but keep a watch on myself in the pulpit."[23] This kind of thing went on, the rhetoric ever more resourceful, the sarcasm more violent, the irony sharper, until in September 1855 he put down his pen and wrote no more. He died on 11 November 1855, refusing to receive the sacrament "at the hand of the King's officials," that is, the officers of the established church, representatives of Christendom, not of Christianity.

21. Ibid., pp. 7-8.
22. Ibid., p. 20.
23. Ibid., p. 21.

In its particular concerns Kierkegaard's polemic has to do with Denmark as, he believes, an extreme example of a general condition, especially in those Protestant countries—Scandinavia in general, and perhaps a few isolated German states—that are solidly Lutheran, with the alliance of throne and altar in good repair, and other forms of the Christian life unknown, or known only through books and travelers' tales. But his quarrel is in fact with Christendom in general; and with what Christendom had warmed in its bosom—had perhaps conceived—the middle-class democratic revolution of 1848 in which the individual is drowned in the masses, mediocrity overcomes genius and the exceptional, and a mean hedonism prevails in social and domestic life. In such a situation, as distinct from the situation in which the preaching of the Apostles was carried out, the only martyrdom possible—and how Kierkegaard hungered for martyrdom!—was, as he said more than once, that of being trampled to death by geese.

Kierkegaard's attitude to Christendom is by no means entirely negative. In *The Journals* he asks himself why asceticism has entirely disappeared from Protestant cultures, at least in an overt form.

> One phase of asceticism . . . may well be considered as over, though not . . . in such a way that subsequent ages do not require to have it inculcated again and again, and in any case how they stand in need of "grace." But in the history of the human race, or of Christianity, one phase may be looked upon as finished. First of all Christianity had to fight against violent and wild passions and in that respect educate mankind with what in the strictest sense of the word must be called asceticism. The fruit of this education is to have produced a Christian culture and civilisation. . . . this culture and civilisation has at the same time produced a development of rational understanding which is in the process of identifying being a Christian with culture, and with intelligence, desirous of a conceptual understanding of Christianity.
> This is where the struggle must come. . . . It will be a

question of establishing the validity of Christianity's incommensurability in this respect, of keeping open the possibility of scandal. . . .[24]

In his final work, then, Kierkegaard splits off the Christian witness from the ordinary physical and institutionalized life of human beings. It has to be said, even if we keep always in mind that what he writes he conceives as "a corrective," that this shows his failure, something one would not have suspected, as a dialectician. It is true that there is something ludicrous about the Danish clergy, royal officials, functioning as ambassadors of the King of Kings; but Kierkegaard forgets that *no* representation of the Divine sovereignty could be other than absurd, even obscene; this is just the kind of problem he spent so much of his life clarifying. He had always a characteristic weakness: it was noted by Theodor Haecker, who said that it was as though Kierkegaard existed as spirit and body, but not as a soul embodied. Hence his repudiation of Regina, for she offered a way—even a way of salvation, religiously speaking—for which he was unfitted, for he knew that the picture of himself as a Christian married man was a false imagination. All the same, he knew what such a life was. He puts a defense of the married state in the mouth of Judge William in *Either/Or:* "The married man . . . has not killed time but has saved it and preserved it in eternity. . . . He solves the great riddle of living in eternity and yet hearing the hall clock strike, and hearing it in such a way that the stroke of the hour does not shorten but prolongs his eternity."[25]

Only through the power of his imagination was he ever able to consider the betrothal to Regina, thinking that he too could solve the great riddle of living in eternity and yet hear the hall clock strike.

Curiously, one who was himself deeply influenced by

24. *Journals*, pp. 486-87.
25. *Either/Or*, translated by Walter Lowrie with revisions and a foreword by Howard A. Johnson (New York: Doubleday, 1959), II, 141.

Kierkegaard and who was even more extreme than Kierkegaard in his turning away from "soulish," embodied life, contrived nevertheless to render for us what is involved in the encounter of human society with absolute spirit and its claims—I mean Kafka. Whereas Kierkegaard, in this final phase in which he tries to split off the Christian witness from ordinary human life, falls into the heresies of the Donatists and Wycliffites, who thought the sacraments were invalid if they came from the hands of the fornicator or the simoniac, Kafka in *The Trial* gives us genuine officers of the Court who are nonetheless mediocre or even malicious men; their relations with women, in particular, are ambiguous; the justice they actually administer they seem not to understand. All the same, we see that they are genuine officers, for they wear their badges, and there is a sense of glory about, behind the door, up the next staircase.

I don't wish to raise the question of how far Kierkegaard was "right" in his attack upon the rootedness of a particular religious culture in Christendom, or, more accurately, upon the identification of a religious culture, that of Christendom, with the religious message set out in the New Testament, which gave it life and form. I think there is failure on his part to think his position through, even if, still, we bear in mind his being a "corrective." To wish the Church to be the tiny gathered community of the saints has about it a touch of the Manichaean, and this really does express itself in Kierkegaard's misogyny in his last phase, what Lowrie quite correctly calls "the gross disparagement of woman, expressed in terms which in his aesthetical writings he had put in the mouth of the most repulsive characters he created, such as the Ladies' Tailor and the Seducer in 'the Banquet.'" Lowrie adds: "At the bottom of all this was a feeling of horror at the thought of perpetuating a fallen race by sexual reproduction."[26] Lowrie suspects this may have been something he caught from Schopenhauer, whose work he was

26. Walter Lowrie, *Kierkegaard* (London: Oxford University Press, 1938), p. 487.

interested in at this time, but few Christians have needed an excuse to fall momentarily into the Manichaean heresy. (It is extraordinary to find, in our own time, so powerful a mind as that of Simone Weil becoming besotted with Catharism.) Again, he neglects something central in the New Testament, that the *ecclesia* is the great field in which weeds and good grain flourish together, or the great net which holds fish of every kind. The elect are to be "salt" and "light" and "leaven," that is, they exist for the others who, as meat to be cured, or living in darkness, or as the great lump of dough, are not to be despised.

But what is of interest to us is not how far Kierkegaard is just or well balanced or "right," but rather what the possibility of such an operation as that contained in *Attack Upon "Christendom"* has to tell us about the concept "form of life."

First, it brings out certain possibilities within a form of life or a loose and yet recognizably unified complex of forms of life. One of the possibilities is that of auto-criticism. It would be strange to emphasize this were it not for a disposition in us to misread Wittgenstein and think of the meanings established within a form of life as *given,* not only for the philosophical student, but also for the participant in the form. Forms of life are dynamic—all metaphors that refer to structure (as in the Marxist idea of superstructure) are dangerously misleading here— and our best accounts are betrayals, flat and photographic. The possibility of auto-criticism has to be noted, with all that it implies about innovation, new understandings, recapturings of lost positions; thus we leave ourselves free to go with the flow of life. Then, the example of Kierkegaard, as the example of every major Christian thinker, shows that there are always lines of intellectual communication running to those who on any strict interpretation stand outside the complex to which the thinker belongs. Kierkegaard always felt himself to be metaphysically related to Socrates. His teaching procedure, what he calls "indirect communication," owes as much to the Socrates of Plato as to the New Testament. He may have been a major influence upon Karl Barth, but in this respect, as touching the connection of philosophy with theology, his thought is fundamentally different.

Then, his criticism seems to show the possibility that a form of life may become moribund, even though everything empirical about the form of life remains the same, and that this can be stated *within* the dead form of life. Here is an established church in which creeds are repeated, sacraments administered, a liturgy performed, a clergy maintained, children catechized; everyone participates in this state of affairs and is satisfied with it. But it is dead even though the motions of life, or what seem to be such, are still to be observed.[27] It is one of the curiosities of our own day that as the secularizing process goes deeper, as the notion of a sacred order within and under which we live grows feebler, the sale of Bibles increases. One would be tempted to say something Kierkegaardian here; for example, that this represents the enjoyment of the Scriptures only at the aesthetic level, were it not for the grim fact that most of the newer versions are examples of and agents in the corruption of the language. I am reliably informed that in one of them—in the interest of self-preservation I haven't verified this—Jesus "puts in an appearance" on the shore of the Lake of Galilee. Such are the spurious appearances of religious vitality.

III

We may now have reached the point where the usefulness of "form of life" begins to vanish. It was primarily a device to show the impossibility of certain common positions in epistemology and to suggest, by offering simple models, the role of practices

27. I am not concerned with how far Kierkegaard was right about the Denmark of his day, but about the possibility of his having been right. That he was in fact right seems on the whole to be made plain by the present state of the Lutheran establishments in Denmark and Sweden, though not perhaps in Norway where the religious form of life is still connected with the elemental life of those who live with and from the forest and the sea.

in the acquiring and sustaining of a language. It is a valuable reminder of what to look for when we try, as we may as social anthropologists, to determine the sense of concepts employed in the culture of relatively simple human groups. We are urged to situate language in the mainfold of culture considered as "man's extra-somatic means of adaptation."[28] It is a means of penetrating the "logic" of relatively isolated or isolable practices, especially those of religious groups. But as we pursue the criss-crossings that are required to grasp any of the ideas and practices of the great family of religions and quasi-religions that persist in Christendom, as we find ourselves ranging over time and space to acquire some appreciation of the, so to speak, thickness or density of any given idea or practice as it shows itself in linguistic expressions or rituals, in styles of life, and in moral and intellectual initiatives, the explanatory power of language-game/form of life seems to vanish. It suffices for schematized accounts or parochial instances—it is useful in surveying the suburbs but not much use in the great body of the city. It will still have point in the preliminary analysis of some detail abstracted from the complex mass of social phenomena. There is perhaps no serious objection to using the expression "form of life" to stand for religious thought and behavior in general, as Stanley Cavell does,[29] though then it ceases to be a key to unlock epistemological puzzles. But in so far as "form of life" is taken as the leading clue to how we are to understand religious thought and behavior in the world religions and in civilizations, it strikes me as no more than suggestive from time to time and here and there. Further, its polemical use, against those who want to assimilate religious discourse to discourse of other kinds, tends, I believe, to obfuscation and obscurantism. I shall try to justify this presently, but before I do so, I want to say, with some fear of getting it wrong, something about Wittgenstein's

28. L. A. White, cited in Colin Renfrew, *The Emergence of Civilization* (London: Methuen, 1972).

29. See, e.g., *Must We Mean What We Say?* (New York: Charles Scribner's Sons, 1969), p. 171.

aims and to suggest that Wittgensteinian fideism, even in a more defensible form than that criticized—even guyed—by Nielsen, is discordant with these aims.

The *Remarks*, *On Certainty*, the *Philosophical Investigations*, all seem plainly concerned with language in general, and it seems at times that while new strategies and tactics have been adopted, the basic aim of the *Tractatus*, to establish the logic of language as such, has not been abandoned. I know there are dozens of proof texts that the devout, like their predecessors, the sectarian exegetes of Scripture, can cite that seem to make for the contrary conclusion. But the whole body of the work seems to be driving towards some kind of generality, and Wittgenstein himself seems to find his failure to achieve it a disappointment. He did not think his having produced in the *Investigations* "only an album,"[30] something necessarily connected with his method. This was "the best I could write." Fifteen years before, in November 1930, he wrote that what he was then writing was in spirit

> different from the one which informs the vast stream of European and American civilization in which all of us stand. *That* spirit expresses itself in an onward movement, in building ever larger and more complicated structures; the other in striving after clarity and perspicuity in no matter what structure. The first tries to grasp the world by way of its periphery; the second as its centre—*in its essence* [my italics].[31]

This position is not without support in the *Investigations*. I find myself convinced by Mr. Hacker's argument in chapters 5 and 6 of *Insight and Illusion*.[32] The texts he adduces, and his commentary on the texts, show us that Wittgenstein's "most general and recurrent positive formulation of the task of philosophy is

30. *PI*, p. ix[e].
31. *Philosophical Remarks*, edited by Rush Rhees and translated by Raymond Hargreaves and Roger White (Oxford: Blackwell, 1975).
32. (London: Oxford University Press, 1972).

the claim that its purpose is to give us an *Übersicht*, a surview or synoptic view."[33] This, Hacker argues, is concealed a bit by the Anscombe translation and other English translations of the posthumous works. Of course, the tone of writing tells us that Wittgenstein saw this task as crushing and practically impossible to carry through. But to leave open the logical possibility of an *Übersicht* means that there is nothing wrong in stating the task of philosophy as that of achieving a general and comprehensive account of the language, both city and suburbs, and also new developments marked only by trenches and sewer pipes along the roads; and therefore of the world. "Grammar tells what kind of object anything is. (Theology as grammar.)"[34]

My last task is to explain why I think the use of language-game/form of life (in the discussion of religion) is sometimes something that makes for obscurantist and obfuscatory positions. In chapters 8, 9, and 10 of *Religion Without Explanation*, Phillips, with great skill and delicacy of insight, gives us some phenomenological accounts of statements about the dead and about God, as these occur within the practice, chiefly liturgical, of religious groups.[35]

He raises two important questions, one about the dead, and the other about the ascription of existence to God.

About the dead he seems to maintain the following position. To think of the dead as living, much as they are in life, but "somewhere else," is to project fantasies. This seems to be right.

---

33. Ibid., p. 113.

34. *PI*, I.373, p. 116e.

35. These groups are not very well located, so that there is a difficulty about surrounding the instances of religious practice offered with other details, but they seem to be Protestant Christian groups; this is evident from the use made of "experience," heavy with felt connections with Schleiermacher and later Protestant theologians and with, perhaps, the use of the term in William James. They would be hard to fit into Catholicism, with its *ex opere operato* view of the sacraments and its at best cautious attitude towards the affective side of mysticism. This Catholic attitude is expressed in an exaggerated way, almost as a caricature, in Pascal, both in the *il faut parier* and in what he has to say about the role of habit in sustaining and even in providing a groundwork for faith: *Pensées*, 117-29 and 474-81 (Paris: Bibliothèque de la Pléiade, 1954).

It seems directed against the views of spiritualists, who even tell us that Uncle Harry (or whoever) is enjoying the ectoplasmic equivalents of whiskey and cigars, at least until he takes off for a higher plane; and it is not what Christians seem to believe. *Expecto resurrectionem mortuorum et vitam venturi saeculi* doesn't seem to be about Uncle Harry agitating tambourines in séances. But I understand him also to maintain that, for some reason that is never made quite clear, *all* talk about the dead, even within the religious language-game, must not contradict the "elementary fact" that the dead truly are dead,[36] that is, religious language of an approvable sort expresses the significance (Phillips says "eternal significance"—this I don't understand), for the living, of the life that has now passed away. This seems plausible if we consider, say, the veneration of ancestors in Confucianism, but it seems odd as maintained about Christianity.

One of the best-attested facts about the history of Christianity from about the second century onwards is that the dead are prayed for and to; indeed, the various forms taken by Christian eschatology from the Apocalypse of John onwards seem to presuppose and often to state explicitly that those who are dead pass into another mode of existence, and that even if they rise with Christ and in some way regain a bodily existence and with it their identities as men, the mode of existence involved is not that of everyday life. Why did the Protestant Reformers put down the practice of praying for the dead? Why did they think the practice wrong? The answer is to be found in what they understood to be the consequences of their doctrine of Grace, with the notions of predestination to glory and to damnation. And they certainly understood—how could this be denied?—glorification and damnation as involving changes in the mode of human existence. Belief in his foreordained perdition drove the poet Cowper mad. If only he had had in attendance some physician of the soul who could have explained to him that he was making moves outside the language-game to which these

36. *Religion Without Explanation*, p. 136.

206

expressions belonged! It was reserved to Dickens to provide the right predicate: we are to understand propositions about God and immortality in a Pickwickian sense.

About God and his existence: much of the force of Phillips's argument comes from his taking, as central misunderstandings, the concept of God as it occurs in the works of Hume and of the Deists. (This is a natural proceeding for a British philosopher, though it may seem strange in Europe and sometimes in North America.) What is vicious here is the notion that God's existence is to be understood as the existence of an object.[37] If this were so, then the debate between the believer and the atheist would be about whether or not this object happened to exist. For an almost uncountable number of reasons this will not work out, either as theodicy or as providing a rationale of religious belief and practice. About all this one cannot quarrel with Phillips. What strikes me as odd is that he discusses the question of what it means to say that God exists as though the considerations he cites are novel, matters that had escaped attention before Hume and Kant. (He does discuss Anselm, or rather Malcolm on Anselm.) Of course, the problem of the One who is beyond all merely being thus and thus, is to be found, in an unanalyzed form, in the Old Testament, and is a standard problem in philosophical theology for the Neoplatonists and for the Scholastics. The reasons why men in the eighteenth and nineteenth centuries become insensitive to the problem, with God as a supreme regulator, a "governor" in the technical sense, or even the chairman of the board of directors, would be worth going into; I should guess that it had something to do with the state of religious life and that here at least a scrutiny of forms of life would be rewarding.

Now, Phillips's point is that it makes no sense to say that God exists because it makes no sense to say, within religious modes of discourse, that God doesn't exist; the concept of a necessary being is parasitic upon what is said in religious dis-

37. Ibid., p. 174.

course. If one stipulates that "to exist" can refer only to objects about which it would make sense to say, even falsely, that they don't exist, then no one can have an objection, except to the usefulness of the stipulation. The stipulation strikes me as inconvenient, for since there are crisscrossings in the wide field of thought within which religious believers move, they are as likely to misunderstand "God doesn't exist" as they now, as it is believed, misunderstand "God exists" when this is said outside the religious language-game.

Two notorious features of Judaeo-Christian religious discourse seem to me to strengthen my objections to the attacks, within a philosophical context determined by the dialectic of Kant and Hume, on the notion of Divine existence. First, there is the practice of the believer in saying "Thou" to God, even if all he has to say is that truly God is a hidden God; and then there is the belief without which no one would have the courage to say "Thou," namely, that God has revealed himself. It seems to be a part of the religious language-game, as it is of most other language-games (perhaps not that of psychoanalysis), that what a man can say "Thou" to exists "over against" him, as we used to say. Consequently, Wittgensteinian fideists shouldn't be surprised if they are taken to be saying something Feuerbachian. Here is Adam Bede discoursing in that most Feuerbachian of novels:

> There's things go on in the soul, and times when feelings come into you like a rushing mighty wind, as the Scripture says, and part your life in two a'most, so as you look back on yourself as if you was somebody else.... I've seen pretty clear ever since I was a young un, as religion's something else besides doctrines and notions. I look at it as if the doctrines was like finding names for your feelings, so as you can talk of 'em when you've never known 'em, just as a man may talk o' tools when he knows their names, though he's never so much as seen 'em, still less handled 'em.[38]

38. *Adam Bede*, Book II, ch. 17.

Or here is the untheological Mr. Irwine considering the spiritual state of his flock:

> If he had been in the habit of speaking theoretically, he would perhaps have said that the only healthy form religion could take in such minds was that of certain dim but strong emotions, suffusing themselves as a hallowing influence over the family affections and neighbourly duties. He thought the custom of baptism more important than its doctrine, and that the religious benefits the peasant drew from the church where his fathers worshipped and the sacred piece of turf where they lay buried, were but slightly dependent on a clear understanding of the Liturgy or the sermon.[39]

Such are the Feuerbachian moves, to keep the scent and savor of religion, and the moral pith of it, while putting aside, perhaps sadly, "that reference to an order of goodness and power greater than any this world by itself can show which we understand as the religious spirit."[40] I don't think Wittgensteinian fideism *is* Feuerbachian, but its exponents ought, I think, to find some way of talking that makes this plainer than it is. "The abdication of belief / Makes the behavior small." So Emily Dickinson put it, happily, as so often.

---

39. Ibid., Book I, ch. 5.

40. Henry James, *Notes of a Son and Brother* in Frederick W. Dupee, ed., *Henry James: Autobiography* (London, 1966), pp. 334-35.

Newman the Liberal —————————

Leo XIII said of his appointing Newman to be a cardinal: "It was not easy! . . . They said he was too liberal."

In Meriol Trevor, *Newman: Light in Winter*[1]

This is my second attempt to work out the connections between Newman's thought and Liberalism. In the first ("Newman and Liberalism," *Cross-Currents*, Summer 1980) I took Liberalism to be something that represented for Newman a pollution or infection and also a part of the topography of nightmare, something that was, or so I tried to show, an unconsciously held presupposition of his mode of viewing the social world. This manifested itself in his refusal to *look* at the tricolor and in his resolution, as he passed through Paris on his return journey to England after his illness in Sicily, not to go into the city that was the cradle of revolution ("I kept indoors the whole time").[2] As

---

1. Meriol Trevor, *Newman: Light in Winter* (New York, 1963), p. 552.
2. John Henry Cardinal Newman, *Apologia pro Vita Sua*, edited with an Introduction and Notes by Martin J. Svaglic (Oxford, 1967), p. 42.

First delivered as a paper at a conference on Newman held at the University of Notre Dame in June 1987.

to the nightmare feeling that seems to have had some connection with the loathing of Liberalism, I took as my examples the passages in the *Apologia* in which he seems preoccupied with the figure of looking into a mirror: there is first the experience of looking into a mirror and seeing in it not one's own image but the image of a stranger or an enemy who is nevertheless in some deep way oneself; and then the experience of looking into a mirror and seeing nothing (certain uncanny creatures, vampires, for instance, are not reflected in mirrors). "If I looked into a mirror, and did not see my face, I should have the sort of feeling which actually comes upon me, when I look into this living busy world, and see no reflexion of its Creator."[3]

All I did then, I think, was to delimit an area within which it seemed profitable to examine what Newman thought about Liberalism. I suggested that in part his response to Liberalism was closely connected with the fascination of the nightmare experience and that this connection helped to determine his *affective* response to everything connected with the revolutionary convulsions that shook European society and broke the links between throne and altar (though not in England), or at least weakened the links, after 1789. My argument was that Newman's ambivalent attitude to Liberalism—that his attitude *was* ambivalent scarcely needs to be proved, though we shall look at instances later—is in part determined by factors that seem to lie below the level of full consciousness. But the tension within Newman's mind between his condemnation of Liberalism and his equally considered judgment that in fact Liberal political principles and the policies that flowed from them were to be welcomed, as being better adapted to the wellbeing of the Church in his day than any other available principles and policies, this tension was between principles both of which were attractive to Newman and judged by him as having bad and good aspects.

That there was this duality in Newman seems to be plain. His contemporary critics were on the whole a sorry lot; but both

3. Ibid., p. 216.

W. G. Ward and Manning were, whatever one may think about their conduct towards Newman, men of some acuteness of mind; and when they characterized him as a Liberal and a man whose influence was dangerous to the dominance of the Ultramontane party to whose success they sought to tie the well-being of the Church, they were not wrong. Father Ian Ker speaks of

> the central, fascinating tension in Newman between conservatism and liberalism, a rare balance of deference to tradition and openness to new developments, which achieved consummate theological expression in the mature Roman Catholic works, and the subtlety of which often eluded his contemporary correspondents.[4]

I am sure this is right and I am inclined to think that this delicate balance is one of the necessary conditions for the constructive role in theology he has in the Catholic world of today. In his later years he often exclaimed over his inability to do for the Church what in his bones he felt he could do. The conferring of the Cardinalate under Leo XIII vindicated his character and his orthodoxy in his lifetime; but his victories as a theologian have been largely posthumous.

I begin by looking at a passage in the last of the *University Sermons* ("The Theory of Developments in Religious Doctrine"). He is relying upon a familiar biblical theme, an especially strong Pauline theme: that Christian weakness is stronger than earthly power, that what is foolishness to men is a sign of God's wisdom. "St Paul, the learned Pharisee, was the first fruits of that gifted company, in whom the pride of science is seen prostrated by the foolishness of the preaching."[5] He continues:

> From his [i.e., St. Paul's] day to this the Cross has enlisted under its banner all those great endowments of mind,

4. *Times Literary Supplement*, 1 April 1983, p. 331.

5. *Newman's University Sermons*, fifteen sermons preached before the University of Oxford 1826-43 with introductory essays by D. M. Mackinnon and J. D. Holmes (London: SPCK, 1979), p. 314.

which in former times had been expended on vanities, or dissipated in doubt and speculation. Nor was it long before the schools of heathenism took the alarm, and manifested an unavailing jealousy of the new doctrine, which was robbing them of their most hopeful disciples. They had hitherto taken for granted that the natural home of the Intellect was the Garden or the Porch; and it reversed their very first principles to be called on to confess, what yet they could not deny, that a Superstition, as they considered it, was attracting to itself all the energy, the keenness, the originality, and the eloquence of the age. But these aggressions upon heathenism were only the beginning of the Church's conquests; in the course of time the whole mind of the world, as I may say, was absorbed into the philosophy of the Cross, as the element in which it lived, and the form upon which it was moulded. And how many centuries did this endure, and what vast ruins still remain of its dominion! In the capitals of Christendom the high cathedral and the perpetual choir still witness to the victory of Faith over the world's power. To see it triumph over the world's wisdom, we must enter those solemn cemeteries in which are stored the relics and the monuments of ancient Faith—our libraries. Look along their shelves, and every name you read there is, in one sense or another, a trophy set up in record of the victories of Faith. How many long lives, what high aims, what single-minded devotion, what intense contemplation, what fervent prayer, what deep erudition, what untiring diligence, what toilsome conflicts has it taken to establish its supremacy! This has been the object which has given meaning to the life of Saints, and which is the subject-matter of their history. For this they have given up the comforts of earth and the charities of home, and surrendered themselves to an austere rule, nay, even to confessorship and persecution, if so be they could make some small offering, or do some casual service, or provide some additional safeguard towards the great work which was in progress. This has been the origin of controversies, long and various, yes, and the occasion of much infirmity, the test of much hidden perverseness, and the subject of much bitterness and tumult. The world has been moved in consequence of it, populations excited, leagues and alliances formed, kingdoms lost and won; and even zeal, when excessive, evinced a sense of its preciousness; nay, even rebellions in some sort did homage to it, as insurgents imply the actual sovereignty of the power which they are assailing. Meanwhile the work went on, and at length a large fabric of divinity was reared, irregular in its structure, and diverse in its style, as beseemed the slow growth of centuries; nay, anomalous in its details, from the peculiarities of individuals, or the interference of strangers, but still, on the whole, the development of an idea, and like itself, and unlike anything else, its most widely separated parts having relations with each other, and betokening a common origin.

And this world of thought is the expansion of a few words, uttered, as if casually, by the fishermen of Galilee.

(University Sermons, p. 314)

What strikes me about this passage—what will, I believe, strike any attentive reader—is the existence of two distinct tones of thought. They do not exist side by side, so to speak, they rather penetrate each other and absorb each other, so that to take away one tone would be a ripping away that would destroy the other. The general intention of the passage is to show that from "a few words, uttered, as if casually, by the fishermen of Galilee" a vast interconnected and, in a hidden way, systematic body of Christian doctrine has arisen; and the indices, as it were, of the parts of this great and luxuriant and ever-growing body are the cathedral, the choir, the library, the ancient works housed by the library, great social movements, and all those who have gone before us, scholars, theologians, martyrs, and a great mass of other Christians, clerics and laymen. And the whole development centers upon a single *idea*.

214

The intellectual side of this development strikes Newman as very strange, stranger than the development of an ecclesiastical polity. "Stranger surely is it that St John should be a theologian, than that St Peter should be a prince." (This is to place the idea of development *within* the apostolic period, something that is to have a rich future.) It is not immediately clear what, for Newman, makes the strangeness, for the intellectual development of Christian doctrine, and its reflective understanding, are portrayed as aggressive, comprehensive, and systematic.

When Newman points to the evidences for what has been accomplished, he finds he is pointing to what is now dead or deeply sleeping. "And how many centuries did this [i.e., the absorption of the world's philosophy into 'the philosophy of the Cross'] endure, and what *vast ruins* still remain of its dominion! . . . To see its triumphs over the world's wisdom, we must enter *those solemn cemeteries* in which are stored the relics and the monuments of ancient Faith—our libraries." It is as though Newman is uttering a panegyric over a dead civiliza-tion. Ruins, cemeteries, monuments recalling what is ancient, these are what Newman's gaze encounters; it is as though he is relishing the melancholy of Piranesi's engravings of Rome. All the same, it is plainly his overt intention to astonish us with the formidable shaping power of the original apostolic preaching. The elegiac, the touch of melancholy which things past have in the recollection of them, these are elements in Newman's perception of Christendom in its present appearance; and the verdict, more a verdict of his sensibility than of his intellect, is that we are at the end of an age. Here and there the cathedral and the perpetual choir still remain; the folios of the Fathers and the Schoolmen lie on the shelves in Oxford and Cambridge, in Munich, in Tübingen, in Paris, in Louvain, though few today— even the Romans, he will later discover, are not much interested in the Fathers and the Schoolmen—read them or love them.

I turn now to Note A published as an Appendix to the second edition of the *Apologia*. Note A is a gloss on what he has to say about his development in the 1820s when, he tells us, he "was beginning to prefer intellectual excellence to moral; I was drifting in the direction of the Liberalism of the day."[6] What he gives us in the Note is more than a mere historical elucidation of what he then took Liberalism to be, as his mention of Montalembert and Lacordaire as kindred spirits shows. It is, as well as an explanation of his mind in the 1820s, also an attempt to do justice to the idea of Liberalism in its many-sidedness, as he first came across it and as he was to come across it in Catholic circles in the period of *The Rambler* and in the early Manning-Talbot-Ward campaign on the questions of Infallibility and the Temporal Power.

First, Liberalism meant for Newman in youth that reforming party in the University of Oxford (and of course outside it) which attempted with great success in a minority of the Colleges, especially Oriel, of which Newman was a Fellow, to make undergraduate education more systematic and more serious. Newman was brought into this circle through his connection with Whately, who may be said to have taught him to think for himself and to take seriously the notion of the Church as an institution existing independently of the State, and it was at this moment that he was tempted to put a higher value on intellectual excellence than moral. This he thought the characteristic failing—almost a professional deformation—of active scholars and teachers in universities. But there arose a different spirit, also a reforming spirit, which shared some of the academic concerns of the Liberals, a spirit best represented by John Keble.

> Keble was a man who guided himself and formed his judgments, not by processes of reason, by inquiry or by argument, but, to use the word in a broad sense, by authority. Conscience is an authority; the Bible is an authority; such is the Church; such is Antiquity; such are the words of the wise; such are hereditary lessons; such are ethical truths; such are historical memories; such are legal saws and state

6. Newman, *Apologia*, ed. M. J. Svaglic, p. 26.

216

maxims; such are proverbs; such are sentiments, presages, and prepossessions. It seemed to me as if he ever felt happier, when he could speak or act under some such primary or external sanction; and could use argument mainly as a means of recommending or explaining what had claims on his reception prior to proof. He even felt a tenderness, I think, in spite of Bacon, for the Idols of the Tribe and the Den, of the Market and the Theatre. What he hated instinctively was heresy, insubordination, resistance to things established, claims of independence, disloyalty, innovation, a critical, censorious spirit.[7]

Such a view captivated Newman, though it is only one of the things that made him a Tractarian. If we take, as I should do, the influence of Hurrell Froude as decisive, then Keble's affection for the old high-church tradition and his worship of established usages was simply incoherent with Froude's vision of the Church. "It was one of Hurrell Froude's main views that the Church must alter her position in the political world—and, when he heard of la Mennais, he took up his views with great eagerness."[8] Many will remember Hurrell Froude's most un-Keble-like remark: "The notion that a priest must be a gentleman is a stupid exclusive Protestant fancy, and ought to be exploded."[9]

Newman also noted that Keble's ecclesiastical Toryism had in it no principle of development, whereas Liberalism had; and with the coming to Oxford of Thomas Arnold's pupils from Rugby, Liberalism even gained in moral weight and seriousness. In fact, the future of the University of Oxford was with the Liberals. In leaving the University and the Church of England Newman stood outside both schools, that of the Liberals and that of Keble, and his later thought transcends the Liberal-Tory dialectic of the Oxford period. What remains and doesn't change

7. Ibid., p. 257.

8. Letter by Newman to Matthew Arnold, 3 December 1871, in *The Letters and Diaries of John Henry Newman,* edited at the Birmingham Oratory (London, 1961), XXV.

9. *Remains of the late Reverend Richard Hurrell Froude* (London, 1838), I, 379.

is his fierce opposition to rationalism understood as a confidence in the ability of human thought to determine religious truth, with its implicit rejection of the need for revelation. This is to banish mystery from religion and to make dogma a matter of opinion.

Note A begins from where Newman finds himself in the 1860s. As we have seen, he early introduces the names of Montalembert and Lacordaire, men he admires and with whom he is inclined to side in matters of ecclesiastical politics. He begins to find himself, after bruising himself against so many of his ecclesiastical superiors in connection with almost all the work he undertook outside the Oratory, more at ease with men of this stamp, and closer to them in matters under dispute in Catholicism, especially in the critical years 1869-1870, than he would have done had his anti-Liberalism been pure. He even uses a Tory, or perhaps Burkean, argument to explain why the difference in political labels between himself and Lacordaire is a matter of no moment. He writes that "we were both of us such good conservatives, as to take up with what we happened to find established in our respective countries, at the time when we came into active life. Toryism was the creed of Oxford; he inherited, and made the best of, the French Revolution."[10] I am not clear what Keble would have thought of this argument; of course, by this I mean I am very clear. He would have been pained.

What I have now to say has more to do with Newman's general temper of mind on a variety of theological and educational issues, and his attitude to the great historical and scientific questions of the day, than to Liberalism in relation to political questions. A first guide is provided by some extracts from his "Journal 1859-1879," first published as a whole in Father Henry Tristram's edition of the *Autobiographical Writings*.

First I note the theme which marks all the writings of the sixties and seventies, though the tone is less melancholy as time goes on. I will quote only one extended passage, an early one (1860), to illustrate the theme:

10. Newman, *Apologia*, p. 254.

Circumstances have brought a special temptation upon me of late. I have been exerting myself, labouring, toiling, ever since I was a Catholic, not I trust *ultimately* for any person on earth, but for God above, but still with a great desire to please those who put me to labour. After the Supreme Judgment of God, I have desired, though in a different order, their praise. But not only have I not got it, but I have been treated, in various ways, only with slight and unkindness. Because I have not pushed myself forward, because I have not dreamed of saying "See what I am doing and have done"—because I have not retailed gossip, flattered great people, and sided with this or that party, I am nobody. I have no friend at Rome, I have laboured in England to be misrepresented, backbitten, and scorned. I have laboured in Ireland, with a door ever shut in my face. I seem to have had many failures, and what I did well was not understood. I do not think I am saying this in any bitterness.

"Not understood"—this is the point. I have seen great wants which had to be supplied among Catholics, especially as regards education, and of course those who laboured under those wants, did not know their state—did not see or understand the want at all—or what was the supply of the want, and felt no thankfulness at all, and no consideration towards a person who was doing something towards that supply, but rather thought him restless, or crotchetty, or in some way or other what he should not be. This has naturally made me shrink into myself, or rather it has made me think of turning more to God, if it has not actually turned me. It has made me feel that in the Blessed Sacrament is my great consolation, and that while I have Him who lives in the Church, the separate members of the Church, my Superiors, though they may claim my obedience, have no claim on my admiration, and offer nothing for my inward trust.[11]

It is unnecessary to document Newman's complaints, to

11. John Henry Newman, *Autobiographical Writings*, edited with an Introduction by Henry Tristram (London, 1956).

go over once again the story of the aborted translation of the Scriptures, the lack of understanding shown towards the *Essay on Development*, the black comedy of the Catholic University in Dublin, the business about his article on Consulting the Faithful in *The Rambler*—this trouble came upon him a few days after he had written the passage I have just quoted—the quarrel with Faber, the relentless campaign against him of Manning and Talbot, and Ward. He perceives such things, but he can scarcely believe them possible. As he wrote to Acton in 1864: "It seems impossible that active and sensible men can remain still under the dull tyranny of Manning and Ward." [12] The immense success of the *Apologia* which made him a national figure, his popularity with many of the old Catholics and with such splendid representatives of an older Catholicism as Canon Walker who in his person and views suggested the Catholicism of Lingard, and Russell of Maynooth, and the redoubtable Moriarty, the Bishop of Kerry, the restoration of warm friendships with such Anglicans as Pusey and Copeland and above all Dean Church, all these mellowed him a good deal. But the ache, and the desolating sense that his intellectual powers were rusting unused, these never left him. He wrote that "as a Protestant, I felt my religion dreary, but not my life—but, as a Catholic, my life dreary, not my religion."[13]

It is hard for us quite to see the years that produced *The Idea of a University*, and the years of epistolary industry that rallied and gave a thousand arguments to the Inopportunist campaign against the proposed Infallibility decree, as wasted years. Even under the dull tyranny, an example of intellectual fastidiousness was always kept before the gaze of English Catholics.

Newman's great aim was not so much to convert men and women as "the edification of Catholics," that is, their moral and intellectual nourishment in the second half of the nineteenth century: "the Church must be prepared for converts, as well as converts prepared for the Church." He believed that among

12. *Letters and Diaries of John Henry Newman*, XXI, 84.
13. Newman, *Autobiographical Writings*, p. 254.

Catholics generally, in Rome as in England, no one had a glimmering of what this work involved.

> To aim . . . at improving the condition, the status, of the Catholic body, by a careful survey of their argumentative basis, of their position relatively to the philosophy and character of the day, by giving them juster views, by enlarging & refining their minds, in one word, by education, is (in their view) more than a superfluity or a hobby, it is an insult. It implies that they are deficient in material points. Now from first to last, education, in this large sense of the word, has been my line, and, over and above the disappointment it has caused as putting conversions comparatively in the background, and the offence it has given by insisting that there was room for improvement among Catholics, it has in two ways seriously annoyed the governing body here and at Rome—at Rome on the side of the philosophy of polemics—*I* should wish to attempt to meet the great infidel &c. questions of the day, but both Propaganda & the Episcopate, doing nothing themselves, look with extreme jealousy on any one who attempts it, and, giving him no credit for what he does well, come down with severity on any point in which he may have slipped.[14]

This, I think, explains the fierceness of the battle over the position of those Catholics who went to Oxford as undergraduates and over the whole question of university education for Catholics. Some of the Irish bishops thought Newman's ambition was to establish another Oxford on the banks of the Liffey. There is some sense in this thought, for Newman, enormously critical though he was of much in the practice of Oxford, still thought Oxford was as close to a real university as could be found in Britain. After all, as he observed to Canon Estcourt in 1860: "Catholics did not make us Catholics; Oxford made us Catholics."[15] It was the internal process of argument

14. Ibid., p. 259.
15. Wilfrid Ward, *The Life of John Henry Cardinal Newman*, two vols. (London, 1912).

in the University that advanced the Tractarian movement, and it was under the intellectual pressure of this movement that Newman thought his way through to his decision of 1845. This was only possible in so far as Oxford was a real university, with an independence of political and ecclesiastical powers sufficient to make boldness of thought a possibility. And the strength of the Oxford system then was that it had in Aristotle, Butler, and the Fathers, the staple of the formative intellectual influences on Newman and his generation, masters superior to what was available to Catholics (or used by them) in England in the 1860s.

The main difference between Newman, and Manning and Ward, was over the expediency of giving young Catholics a genuine university education and doing honest work, as scholars, in such fields as history and theology. The less important part of the discussion was over a matter that need not concern us: the moral, as distinct from the intellectual, consequences for the young men of attendance at the ancient English universities. Newman pointed out with some scorn the implication that the life of the military schools such as Woolwich, or the life of an apprentice banker or stockbroker in the City of London, was relatively free of moral danger. But the real objection was to the intellectual life of the University with all its inescapable dangers. But, Newman argues, "the cultivation of the intellect" such as is characteristic of a university has to be a danger to faith, "and where it is absolutely excluded, there is no cultivation."[16] Newman never thought that a Catholic university, if it *was* a university, could exclude this danger to faith, though it might be in a position to offer remedies.

In the same letter he passes from this point to another: that the Vatican Council has deliberately created a situation in which the intellect of the world is ranged against the Church, and it follows from this that the Church has now to deal with a multitude of intellectual difficulties, or ignore them.

16. Letter to J. Spencer Northcote, 7 April 1872, in *Letters and Diaries*, XXVI, 59.

The two main instruments of infidelity just now are physical science and history; physical science is used against Scripture, and history against dogma; the Vatican Council by its decrees about the inspiration of Scripture and the infallibility of the Pope has simply thrown down the gauntlet to the science and the historical research of the day.[17]

There is here perhaps a touch of wicked joy, as though he is saying to Manning, Talbot, and Ward, *vous l'avez voulu*, in this way of putting it. But his more serious point is that the Church is stumbling into a situation for which she is quite unprepared; and the irony of the situation is that the agitation for Vatican I and infallibility was the work of men who on principle were opposed to those modes of intellectual preparation that alone could meet the difficulties of the new age.

Except for the lectures on university topics delivered in Dublin there is little Newman was prepared to say in public by way of showing how the job he commended as necessary might be done. It isn't that he felt ill-equipped for the task. In response to an appeal by Allies that he should write a book that would traverse the same ground and issues as did Montalembert and Döllinger he replied that this would be

> against the views of a particular school in the Church, which is dominant. I cannot accept as of faith, which is not of faith. . . . I cannot fight under the lash, as the Persian slaves. . . . Never, as I know, was it so with the Church, as it is now that the acting authorities as [at] Rome . . . have acted on the individual thinker without buffers. Mere error in theological opinion should be met with argument, not authority, at least by argument first.[18]

He is disgusted by the prevailing spirit of those dominant in the English Church and in the Roman bureaucracies, especially Propaganda, and he was not a man to try to defeat the prevail-

17. Ibid.
18. Letter of 12 February 1864, in ibid., XXI, 49.

ing spirit by cunning and economical language. The assumption is common that many matters that are for Newman patently matters of opinion are matters of dogma or are so closely connected with dogmatic propositions that they have to be treated as virtually dogmatic. Such was the view of the Ultramontanes on the Temporal Power of the Papacy, such was their view of Papal Infallibility as being thought to rest upon something very like inspiration. To use modern jargon, they turned matters that were essentially functional into matters of ontology. There is a moving statement of the essential distinction between matters of opinion and matters of faith as Newman saw it, and it is especially interesting as establishing a clear connection between his Anglican and his Catholic life, in a letter to an unknown correspondent in February 1867:

> . . . I have made it a sort of resolution, ever since I ceased to be bound by the Anglican formularies, never to bind myself again to mere matter of opinion, and hitherto I have never swerved from this resolution, nor am I likely to do so, or to be asked to do so. . . . All things change but God and his Word.[19]

Some people, Acton for one, who knew what Newman's real views were, thought he ought to have been more open and fierce in his criticism of Ultramontanism. Most of those who thought in this way were laymen, such as Simpson and Acton, who had less to lose than an ecclesiastic. (As Gladsone remarked when the question of Acton's possible excommunication was raised after the Council, *They will never excommunicate an English peer!*) But Newman's behavior was rooted in what was for him a fundamental principle, and here again there is continuity between the Anglican and the Catholic Newman. For the Anglican Newman the lightest word of his bishop was heavy, and the action which in the end drove him from St. Mary's into the temporary retreat of Littlemore was the disapproval of Tract 90 by the bishops. This Newman took to be a solemn repudiation by

19. Ibid., XXIII, 50.

the Anglican bench of that interpretation of the Anglican dogmatic formulations that alone seemed to make it possible for the Catholic-minded to stay within the Church of England. In any case, obedience was high on the list of Newman's virtues. And as a Catholic he avoided those public avowals of principle that would have made him seem contumacious. For this external obedience to authority he paid a heavy price. "It is difficult to avoid the appearance of having in some respect adopted a shuffling course, when the duty of obedience decides you in one direction, and your deliberate judgment in another."[20] This undoubtedly contributed something to the common view among some Catholics and Protestants that Newman was devious and sophistical. He was in fact the most transparent of men and hated the appearance of shuffling that circumstances forced upon him. As to his Ultramontane opponents, they rarely attempted to meet Newman's arguments, when by chance they came across them, openly and as matters of argument. They were content with feeble innuendo, as for example in an 1866 letter from Manning to Talbot. "I see much danger of an English Catholicism of which Newman is the highest type. It is the old Anglican, patristic, literary, Oxford tone transplanted into the Church."[21] It is matter for astonishment, and some grief, that a man who was sensitive, far more sensitive than Newman, to the social problems thrown up by nineteenth-century capitalism, should have been quite incapable of discerning what the intellectual challenges of the day were. (But in the philosophical field Manning didn't even take on the problems of the eighteenth century. Despite Hume's conclusive criticism of the Argument for God's existence from Design, Manning believed in the force of this argument all his life.)

Newman saw that the questions on the frontier, as it were, for Christianity arose out of the impact of natural science and of historical criticism on traditional beliefs. On the whole the tactic of English Catholics was to ignore the more severe

20. Memorandum of April 1867, in ibid., XXIII, 332.
21. E. S. Purcell, *Life of Cardinal Manning* (London, 1912), II, 323.

problems. Whereas in the Church of England there were many celebrated controversies, over Darwin, over the Mosaic origin of the Pentateuch, over geology and Genesis, among Catholics remarkably little was openly discussed. This spared the Catholics some embarrassments. There is nothing so stupefyingly crass as Samuel Wilberforce's refutation of Darwin before a meeting of the British Association. There was on the Catholic side nothing corresponding to *Essays and Reviews*, no serious and open examination of the problems of biblical criticism. But although Catholics were less embarrassed by the theory of evolution and by the radical conclusions of contemporary biblical criticism than were Protestants, this was in great part because Catholics were for various understandable reasons unwilling to commit themselves publicly. In the end Catholics acted with ill-considered vigor over biblical questions; but this was after Newman's death, in the melancholy period of the anti-Modernist campaign, when Loisy and Lagrange were both put out of the seminaries.

Now, one can't argue that Newman left a great unpublished body of work on such questions. What one does find is that Newman time and again makes remarks that show a delicate sense of what is at stake in such matters.

Only a year after the publication of *The Origin of Species* Newman wrote in a notebook the following remarks:

> There is as much want of simplicity in the idea of the creation of distinct species as that of the creation [of] trees in full growth . . . , or of rocks with fossils in them. I mean that it is as strange that monkeys should be so like men, with no *historical* connexion between them, as the notion that there was no history of facts by which fossil bones got into rocks. . . . I will either go the whole hog with Darwin, or dispensing with time & history altogether, hold, not only the theory of distinct species but that also of the creation of fossil-bearing rocks.[22]

22. *The Philosophical Notebooks of John Henry Newman*, edited by Edward Sillem and revised by A. J. Bockrand (Louvain, 1970), II, 158.

This passage needs no commentary. There are some indications in the correspondence that Newman tried to calm excitement over the question of evolution, an excitement that some Catholics no doubt drew from their Protestant friends and neighbors, others from the sheer interest of the problem. Among these latter was Canon Walker of Scarborough, one of Newman's most sensible and sympathetic correspondents. Walker had sent him a work by Robert Beverley of Scarborough in which Darwin's theory is attacked. Newman in fact read very little of this work—most of the pages are uncut—but like many clever men he seems to have got a very good idea of its quality by judicious sampling. Newman writes: "I do not fear the theory as much as he seems to do. . . . It does not seem to me to follow that creation is denied because the Creator, millions of years ago, gave laws to matter. . . . If Mr Darwin in this or that point of his theory comes into collision with revealed truth, that is another matter—but I do not see that the *principle* of development . . . does. . . . Mr Darwin's theory *need* not then be atheistical, be it true or not. . . . at first sight I do not [see] that 'the *accidental* evolution of organic beings' is inconsistent with divine design—It is accidental to *us*, not to *God*."[23] A letter to Pusey is similar in tone.[24] He distances himself, so to speak, from the controversy and tries to cool it down. He professes not to know a great deal; but he also asks all the right questions and makes sharp logical points. He never "leads with his chin," but he never gives the impression that he is running away from the problem. With Pusey, who may be said to have had as much feeling for irony as a buffalo, he seems a little economical. He writes: "I have not fallen in with Darwin's book [this may not be economical: he was apt to forget what he had read]. I conceive it to be an advocacy of the theory that that principle of propagation, which we are accustomed to believe began with Adam . . . began in some one common ancestor millions of years before." He then argues that he does not believe it con-

23. Letter of 22 May 1968, in *Letters and Diaries*, XXIV, 77.
24. Letter of 5 June 1870, in Ibid., XXV, 137-38.

tradicts the sense of the biblical text, nor can he see how it is supposed to contradict Theism. ". . . if the sun does not go round the earth and the earth stand still, as Scripture seems to say, I don't know why Adam needs be [made] immediately out of dust. . . . Darwin does not *profess* to oppose religion. I think he deserves [an honorary] degree as much as many others, who have had one."[25] (Poor Pusey seems to have been anxious to know whether or not it was proper for Oxford to give Darwin an honorary degree. There was opposition to the conferment and in the event Darwin declined "on the ground that he could not stand the strain of the ceremony." Thus Oxford, perhaps characteristically, missed an opportunity to do honor to Darwin in the diocese of Samuel Wilberforce himself.)

A letter to Mivart has an additional interest, for Mivart had some qualification to speak with authority on the subject. At any rate, Newman writes of Mivart's critique of Darwin that "it is pleasant to find that the first real exposition of the logical insufficiency of Mr Darwin's theory comes from a Catholic." But he adds immediately: "In saying this, you must not suppose that I have personally any great dislike or dread of his theory, but many good people are much troubled at it."[26]

Newman saw that a future difficulty over the character of Scripture was inevitable and that therefore it was important for men to clear their minds on the subject. He did not himself do anything substantial. His best-known contribution to biblical questions is the 1883 article on Inspiration. In this he discusses the historical difficulties presented by treating Scriptural narratives that seem to be of a factual kind as though they were without error. He wants to argue that Scripture's purpose is to teach moral and dogmatic truth, not to inform us about the minutiae of history. I think it would be generally agreed that the treatment, though sensitive to genuine difficulties that at that time were taken seriously, is not very successful, though it pointed in some directions later inquiries would take. There is a more interesting

25. Ibid., XXV, 139-40.
26. Letter of 9 December 1871, in ibid., XXV, 446.

example of the way in which his mind was working on difficulties of a fundamental kind. Newman had written to Pusey concerning a difficulty raised by a contemporary man of science, Professor Richard Owen, about the ages of the patriarchs as these are stated in the Book of Genesis. The difficulty is, according to Owen's argument, that "men with lives of 800 or 900 years, *would not belong to this genus and species 'homo'* any more (I suppose) than a monkey does."[27] Pusey was ill and passed the letter on to H. P. Liddon. The controversy itself is now of no great interest. What is of interest is an indication in Newman's reply to Liddon, of the depth at which his mind was working. He writes: "It is clear we shall have to discuss the question whether certain passages of the Old Testament are or are not mythical. It is one of the gravest of questions, and we cannot spend too much time in preparing for it."[28] This is surely acute, though few were prepared in the atmosphere of that time to consider that this was even a possible matter for discussion.

The temper of Newman's mind was essentially cautious and conservative. In his Anglican years and in his first years as a Catholic he was so opposed to liberal principles that on a great variety of topics he provides rich examples of an antiliberal and illiberal disposition. He has an appetite for the wonderful (he takes the story of the Holy House of Loretto seriously), he is prepared to think—with great reluctance—that in principle the State has a right to kill for religion and to maintain—again, in principle—religious uniformity by coercive means (of course, this was also the Anglican tradition); "in heart" he sides with Wiseman in his suspicion of Rosmini's *Five Wounds of the Church*.[29] It is almost as though the petty tyrannies and cruelties to which he was subjected had an intellectually liberating effect upon him. *His* enemies were illiberal and thus he found himself encamped with *their* enemies. That he had subscribed to Garibaldi was a canard circulated by Monsignor Talbot who no

27. Letter of 3 March 1872, in ibid., XXVI, 42.
28. Letter of 18 April 1872, in ibid., XXVI, 66.
29. Letter to Faber of 23 June 1849, in ibid., XIII, 188.

doubt thought it was a great joke. But that Talbot and his friends were right in classifying him as a liberal, on general theological grounds, seems to me quite plain. The essence of this Newman is surely contained in the wonderful letter of 30 April 1871 to Emily Bowles:

> There are those who wish Catholic women, not nuns, to have no higher pursuit than that of dress, and Catholic youths to be shielded from no sin so carefully as from intellectual curiosity. All this is the consequence of Luther, and the separation off of the Teutonic races—and of the imperiousness of the Latin. But the Latin race will not always have a monopoly of the magisterium of Catholicism. We must be patient in our time; but God will take care of his Church—and, when the hour strikes, the reform will begin.[30]

30. Ibid., XXV, 326-27.

Poetry and Dialectic ————

*Non enim omne quod fingimus, mendacium est; . . . cum autem
fictio nostra refertur, in aliquam significationem, non est mendacium, sed aliqua figura veritatis. Alioquin omnia quae a
sapientibus et sanctis viris, vel etiam ab ipso Domino, figurate
dicta sunt, mendacia deputabuntur.*

St. Augustine[1]

*It haunts me like all shadows. All shades
Of meaning whipping in and out are there.
This torturer is a great lover of professors,*

*Psychiatrists, chaplains, sits on their faces' skin
But when I look at them it's on my own,
Then flies to another place, leaves me in arrears.*

Richard Eberhart, "Of Truth"[2]

---

1. S. Augustine, *Quaestionum Evangeliorum*, in Migne, *Patrologia Latina*,
XXXV, 1362.
2. Richard Eberhart, *Burr Oaks* (Chatto and Windus, 1947).

This was my Inaugural Lecture when, in 1961, I was appointed to the
Chair of Philosophy at the Univerity of Leeds.

Philosophy is essentially, irredeemably, hopelessly dialectical. This is its glory and its shame: its glory, because it is in and through the play of dialectic that the powers of the mind are most fully known and manifested; its shame, for it is precisely the enchantment of dialectic that seduces us, so that we fall into sophistry in a moment. Everything can be brought within the dialectical situation, nothing is exempt from it. We can conceive of no thesis which could not be put to the question, no response to a question which could not generate further questions. The description and analysis of concepts, the central task of philosophy since it first detached itself from mythopoeic thinking, presents us with a limitless process, sinuous, fluid, surprising in its sudden starts and turns, flashing and glittering, beginning from any point we choose and having no assignable term. Now, because philosophy can put everything to the question, it tends from time to time to show a certain roughness and even savagery towards other types of discourse; and is by way of response roughly and savagely treated in its turn. Pride in the traditions of the community and devotion to the gods of the city, these have always feared what they took to be the corrosive effects of the dialectic, so that the indictment of Socrates, that "Socrates is guilty of not believing in the gods in whom the State believes, and of introducing other strange divinities; . . . and of corrupting the young men," represents a recurring moment in the history of philosophy. The rediscovery of dialectic in the twelfth century presents us with another paradigmatic man and situation in Abelard faced with his accusers; and if in the modern age, in liberal societies at least, the martyrdom of the philosopher is most likely to be that martyrdom feared by Kierkegaard, that of being trampled to death by geese, the philosopher, insofar as he is faithful to his vocation and does not pervert the instrument of dialectic to defend the idols of the tribe or paper over the cracks in fashionable arguments, is still a man on the margin, ambiguous, of doubtful loyalties, taken to be lukewarm by fervent believers and, by average sensual men, passionate about trivial issues and fine distinctions.

A matter on which philosophers have been inclined to be passionate is poetry. The relationship between these two modes of discourse, the dialectical and the poetic, resembles in Plato and perhaps in other philosophers that type of relationship between men which is characterized by the coexistence and interpenetration of love and hate. If the poet is driven out of the good society, it is only after he has been crowned; for in virtue of his gift he is sacred and wonderful; what he says may be destroyed by the dialectic, but his words are memorable. They are incantations of power drawn from a hidden source and having, therefore, that awful quality which belongs to all that comes up out of the darkness of the earth, the abode of demons and the shadows of men who were once alive; or if, since Apollo has two homes and two faces, the words of the poet fall from the heavens, in falling into the region of mutability their heavenly origin is obscured and can only be recovered if they perish in the fire of dialectic.

In our own period the tension between poetry and dialectic slackens. Poetry is the object of liking and despising, not love and hate. The poet is no longer feared or admired as a messenger of the infernal or heavenly powers. He is now a purveyor of elegant fictions, acceptable if you happen to like his fables and jingles—they may help to pass the time—but a man to be classed with tumblers and comedians rather than with philosophers, men of science, and entrepreneurs. As late as Milton it was possible to speak of poetry to persons other than men of letters as a central human activity and one as indispensable to life as bread; but with the coming of the middle-class revolution philistinism becomes the philosophical orthodoxy. By this I do not mean that all philosophers have been insensitive to poetry, still less that there have not been attempts by poets and critics—one thinks of Blake, Wordsworth, and Coleridge—to work out the rationale of poetry within our culture; but the theory of poetry current in the philosophical schools has been such as to make it appear that the implicit claim of poetry to be a central human activity has no ground.

To say that poetry moves in the sphere of delight and not of truth seems at first unexceptionable; and this is orthodoxy in Bacon and Hobbes; it lies behind the celebrated attack upon poetic discourse in Sprat's *History of the Royal Society*, an attack motivated by the fear that the energies of poetry impel it beyond the sphere of delight into that of truth, where it is a trespasser. What it may in the end come to is brought out by Locke who, as one would expect, produces a mean-spirited gloss upon the tradition. He considers the case of the child with "a poetick Vein":

> . . . if he have a poetick Vein, 'tis to me the strangest thing in the World that the Father should desire or suffer it to be cherished or improved. Methinks the Parents should labour to have it stifled and suppressed as much as may be; and I know not what Reason a Father can have to wish his Son a Poet, who does not desire to have him bid Defiance to all other Callings and Business; which is not yet the worst of the Case; for if he proves a successful Rhymer, and gets once the Reputation of a Wit, I desire it may be considered what Company and Places he is like to spend his Time in, nay, and Estate too: For it is very seldom seen, that any one discovers Mines of Gold or Silver in *Parnassus*. 'Tis a pleasant Air, but a barren Soil. . . .[3]

Whatever is overthrown by dialectic can be set up again only by dialectic. If, therefore, we find unwelcome the conclusion that poetry is something optional, decorative, well enough when we have no serious business in hand but not to be mentioned in the same breath as money, power, and scientific discovery—unwelcome and, on purely intuitive grounds, absurd—we must take up the argument again and see if a patient analysis can give us grounds for thinking that truth is applicable to poetic discourse and for putting that value upon it which

3. John Locke, *Some Thoughts concerning Education*, para. 174.

belongs to those types of discourse in which we make plain to each other and to ourselves the character of human life and of its predicaments.

II

I shall say that the making of poetry is the making of fictions. To say this may strike us as too strong, or as not strong enough. It will appear to be too strong if we reflect that there is no reason why true narratives should not be cast in poetic form; and not strong enough, if we note that the class of fictions is wider than the class of poems. The latter difficulty will, I hope, disappear when I explain what I take to be the peculiar character of poetic fictions; but the former difficulty is the harder to meet. Andrew Marvell, for example, wrote:

> *He* nothing common did or mean
> Upon that memorable Scene:
>> But with his keener Eye
>> The Axes edge did try:
> Nor call'd the *Gods* with vulgar spight
> To vindicate his helpless Right,
>> But bow'd his comely Head,
>> Down as upon a Bed.[4]

This is an account of the execution of Charles I. In what sense is it proper to class it as a piece of fiction? In the following sense. If we were to take it as a piece of historical narrative, then a number of questions would be appropriate that are not appropriate. The historian speaks in his own person and is responsible for what he says in general and in detail; and this is why the historian can tell lies and makes mistakes. Now, if the speaker here were Marvell in his own person, it would be appropriate to test his account by asking, for example, what

4. Andrew Marvell, "An Horatian Ode upon Cromwell's Return from Ireland," *Miscellaneous Poems* (1681).

evidence there was that Charles looked at the axe, did not make a speech in defense of his constitutional right, and placed his head upon the block as he might have placed his head upon a pillow. I dare say that what Marvell here says is fair enough as an account of what an observer might have confirmed as not conflicting with anything that happened in Whitehall that day; but this, if true, is accidental to the poem and neither adds to nor subtracts from the poem considered as something made by Marvell. But how do we know that this isn't an attempt at historical narrative in verse or that, if it is, the question of its reliability as such a narrative is so irrelevant that it is proper to class it as a fiction? First, the class of fictions is wider than the class of false or imaginary accounts. A particular piece of poetic narrative or a particular incident in a novel may indeed be, as we say, founded on fact and may not conflict with what is commonly taken to be the order and character of past events. This is nothing to us unless there are unmistakable signs that the intention of the author is historical; and that what we are confronted with is verse or a novel warrants a presumption, though of course a rebuttable presumption, that the intention is not historical. Second, and this is what may strengthen the presumption to the point where it cannot be rebutted, the signs of poetic fiction are those formal structures that can be shown by analysis to be integral to the poetic effect but without function so far as historical narrative is concerned. (Of course, the matter is much more complicated than this. In particular, we might well inquire why it is we might want to say of a particular historian that he is "a great artist," thus appearing to classify him with the poets and the novelists; and the answer would be that he *is* a maker of fictions, though not on that account a liar.) As to there being fictions we should not wish to call poetic, these will be fictions having little formal interest, where *how* the thing is said doesn't matter: the excuses of schoolboys, the compliments of courtiers, the vows of lovers. Each of these might by a person of talent be raised to the level of poetic discourse; but the more successfully this was done, the less would be our interest in it merely as excuse, compliment, vow, conceived and expressed in a particular situation; and the greater its formal interest, the more it would tend to be loosened from the situation which was its living context, thus passing into that world of poetic fictions where the remarks of Dr. Johnson and of the father of Miss Elizabeth Bennet are equally at home.

It will be seen that my use of "poetic" is a wide one; that it covers not only verse but verbal fictions of every kind, novels, plays, fairy-stories, polished anecdotes, witticisms, and so on. This is, I think, an extension of the sense of "poetic" Aristotle has in mind in his *Poetics*; and it is worth noting that at the beginning of his book he looks for a moment at a problem closely resembling the problem I have just been considering. He finds that many people want to call "poetic" any metrical composition. "Even if a theory of medicine or physical philosophy be put forth in a metrical form, it is usual to describe the writer in this way; Homer and Empedocles, however, have really nothing in common apart from their meter; so that, if one is to be called a poet, the other should be termed a physicist rather than a poet."[5] That is, the sense of poetry in which Aristotle is interested is that which takes as the distinguishing characteristic of the poetic activity what he calls *mimesis*; and this in part at least overlaps with what I call the making of fictions. Further, it will be remembered that when Aristotle later makes his difficult remark that "poetry is something more philosophic and of graver import than history,"[6] he prefaces it by saying that what Herodotus put into verse would still be history and not poetry.

Before I come to the special problems of poetic discourse I wish to say something on a more general problem concerned with all verbal discourse: the problem of how words and expressions and sentences of various logical types get the sense they have. I do not wish to offer a solution of this problem, but rather to indicate the impossibility of what is often taken to be the solu-

5. *Aristotle on the Art of Poetry*, translated by Ingram Bywater, with a Preface by Gilbert Murray (Oxford, 1920), pp. 24-25.
6. Ibid., p. 43.

tion; for what is often, and wrongly, taken to be the right solution is connected with certain gross errors in poetic theory.

There is a persistent tradition in our thinking about language, and it is one that has remained vigorous in the face of heavy attacks in recent years, that a thought is one thing and the way it is expressed another. Campbell is in the tradition when he writes in his *Philosophy of Rhetoric* (a work that went through many editions—it is the work that was lying on the table beside Hume when Boswell paid his famous call on the dying philosopher) that "there are two things in every discourse which principally claim our attention, the sense and the expression; or in other words, the thought, and the symbol by which it is communicated."[7]

Now, this view cannot be wholly absurd, for we are strongly inclined to agree with it as soon as it is propounded; it seems to chime in with our most natural prejudices in the matter. Faced with the fact that there are different ways of saying the same thing within a language, and between languages, it seems to us quite right to say that where P^1 and P^2 are roughly interchangeable sentences, they have in common the thought they can both be used to express. Indeed, it could scarcely be wrong to say this. What is often taken to follow from this truism is something that seems all right when we are talking about or reflecting upon, as distinct from *using,* a sentence, namely, that to the distinction between the sentence and the thought it is used to express, and we must make this distinction if we admit that P^1 and P^2 express the same thought, there corresponds a distinction of objects standing in a certain relation one to the other: the thought; and the sentence which gets its meaning through "standing for" the thought.

It is to Locke that we must once more turn, this time for the supremely commonplace expression of the theory:

> Man . . . had by nature his organs so fashioned, as to be fit to frame articulate sounds, which we call words. But

7. George Campbell, *The Philosophy of Rhetoric* (seventh ed.; 1823), p. 47.

this was not enough to produce language; for parrots, and several other birds, will be taught to make articulate sounds distinct enough, which yet, by no means, are capable of language. Besides articulate sounds therefore, it was farther necessary, that he should be able to use these sounds as signs of internal conceptions; and to make them stand as marks for the ideas within his own mind, whereby they might be made known to others, and the thoughts of men's minds be conveyed from one to another.[8]

That Locke is here talking about two sets of objects, words and sentences (which acquire meaning by having the relation of "standing for" to ideas), and thoughts, is made clearer in a later part of the *Essay concerning Human Understanding:*

> . . . we must observe two sorts of propositions that we are capable of making. First, mental, wherein the ideas in our understanding are without the use of words put together, or separated by the mind, perceiving or judging of their agreement or disagreement. Secondly, verbal propositions, which are words, the signs of our ideas, put together or separated in affirmative or negative sentences.[9]

Locke's view is variously wrong, but I must content myself with two arguments against it. First, no one when challenged is prepared to say that he is acquainted with anything at all corresponding to Locke's story. It *must* be like that, we sometimes hear; never, I think, Yes, that's how it is. The "must" is here significant. It suggests that we are not being given an introspective account, but an account of what is held to follow logically from our talking about propositions as expressing thoughts. A genuine introspective report would be something like: When I divided 762 by 3 it was as though there were red blobs dancing about inside. Now, another might say: When I divided 762 by 3 it was as though a sewing machine were going

8. John Locke, *An Essay concerning Human Understanding,* III, 1.
9. Ibid., IV, 5.

very fast inside me. And still another might say: I've tried very hard to introspect and I have absolutely nothing to report. But if they all rap out, when asked to do this piece of division, 254, we have the best possible evidence that they are expressing the same thought. Locke's argument gets its apparent force from its seeming to be a description of what goes on when we introspect; but it is a pseudo-description—not a *misdescription* of what goes on, but rather what we take to be a description but isn't so. Again, if Locke's account of what it is for words and sentences to have meaning were correct, it would be impossible ever to teach anyone the meaning of a word or a sentence. But this is absurd, for we do teach people the meanings of words and sentences. If sounds get their significance from being the "signs of internal conceptions," then we could only teach their significance by showing another both the sound and the internal conception of which it is the sign. But Locke says that "the thoughts of men's minds" are "conveyed from one to another" *by words.* Thus, we could not *show* that relation which, according to Locke, transforms sounds into words; therefore, we could never make a sound that would for another count as a word. The argument is self-contradictory.

To talk about a sentence and the thought it expresses is clearly allowable, for we can translate at least some English sentences into sentences in other languages, and we can also have two different English sentences that express the same thought. For an example of the former I take the last paragraph of *Le Rouge et le Noir:*

> Madame de Rênal fut fidèle à sa promesse. Elle ne chercha en aucune manière à attenter à sa vie; mais trois jours après Julien, elle mourut en embrassant ses enfants.[10]

A recent translation into English runs as follows:

> Madame de Rênal was faithful to her promise. She did not attempt in any way to take her own life; but, three days

10. Stendhal, *Le Rouge et le Noir* (1830).

after Julien's death, she gave her children a last embrace, and died.[11]

It would seem hard to say that here we do not have the same thoughts in the original and in the translation. Of course, the two passages are not *equivalents*. Resonances, flavors, atmospheres, that are attached to the French expressions are not so attached to the English. In an attempt to give the force of "mais trois jours après Julien, elle mourut en embrassant ses enfants," the translator has departed from a literal rendering and gives us "but, three days after Julien's death, she gave her children a last embrace, and died." This slight dislocation of the order of the French sentence indicates that the translator is using stylistic devices that belong to English and not to French in an effort, necessarily vain but all the same worth making, to give us an equivalent as well as a translation. But the same point could equally be made in cases where two English sentences may be said to express the same thought and where, at the same time, there is plainly no equivalence. This may easily be verified by comparing archaic and modern translations of the Scriptures.

To talk about the sentence and the thought it expresses is allowable; but we have no warrant for the inference that here there are two objects, as it were, the sentence and the thought. We cannot talk about a sentence as now expressing, now not expressing, a thought; for if it did not express a thought, have a sense, we should not know enough to characterize it as a sentence. What would a sentence without a sense be? We are tempted to answer: a succession of noises, or a series of marks in some material; but if this were all we knew we should have no ground for saying it was a sentence. We may distinguish between a cheek and the bloom upon it; but there is no inference from this distinction to the existence of two independent objects, so that the bloom upon the cheek could exist apart from the cheek. I do not wish to argue, for I do not think it is true,

11. Stendahl, *Scarlet and Black*, translated and with an Introduction by Margaret R. B. Shaw (Penguin Books, 1953), p. 511.

241

that words are the only bearers of sense, the only vehicles of thought, though they are certainly the most common; but the notion that there can be thought quite apart from a vehicle of thought is a superstition, so far, at least, as human thinking is concerned; and while we may suppose that there is thinking other than human thinking, we could not say in what this thinking consists.

Locke's view of the relation between thinking and using language lies behind, provides a justification for, the theory of poetic discourse I now wish to criticize. This theory has taken a beating at the hands of literary critics in recent years and has even been given a special name: the heresy of paraphrase. Nevertheless, it is highly influential at all but the most sophisticated levels; and some discussion of it is necessary before we can consider what it means to speak of truth in poetry. It is the theory that *what* is said in a poem is one thing, *how* it is said another.

The theory has seemed most obviously correct in the case of didactic poetry and in the case of those poems which give us an exposition of some quasi-systematic view of nature or of human affairs. Pope prefaces his *Essay on Man* with some remarks in this tradition. He writes of the *Essay* as "forming a *temperate* yet not *inconsistent*, and a *short* yet not *imperfect* system of Ethics. This I might have done in prose; but I chose verse, and even rhyme, for two reasons. The one will appear obvious; that principles, maxims, or precepts so written, both strike the reader more strongly at first, and are most easily retained by him afterwards. . . ."[12] Pope's idea is that thoughts are like naked bodies. They may be seen for what they are through the diaphanous medium of prose; or they may have their features emphasized and made more attractive by the pretty and revealing clothes of verse. Pope is less than just to his own achievement in the *Essay*. He expresses the same idea, though this time more subtly and with some awareness of other possibilities, in the *Essay on Criticism:*

12. Alexander Pope, *An Essay on Man* (1734), "The Design."

True Wit is Nature to advantage dress'd;
What oft was thought, but ne'er so well express'd;
Something, whose truth convinc'd at sight we find,
That gives us back the image of our mind.[13]

Here, as well as the image of a body dressed to advantage, we have the image of the expression of thought as bringing out sharply the lines of the thought so that it "gives us back the image of our mind," displays in all its brightness the thought we have been peering at, and not seeing properly, in the depths of the mind. (This latter image has its value; for it suggests, what I shall later argue is a fundamental characteristic of much poetry, that it is a means of self-knowledge.)

The shadow of this theory remains long after the practice of criticism seems to have shown that a serious defense of it is impossible. The greatest of the romantic critics, Coleridge, held it to be true of poetry "that whatever lines can be translated into other words of the same language, without diminution of their significance, either in sense or association, or in any worthy feeling, are so far vicious in their diction."[14] The contrary view seems to underlie Arnold's characterization of poetry as "a criticism of life"; and the common nineteenth-century view of Shakespeare as a great didactic writer, a sage, the wisest and best of men, rests not only upon the belief that straightforward inferences of a moral and religious kind may be founded upon his work but also, or so I think, upon the belief that the meaning of the plays can in some way be stated, in a nonpoetic mode of discourse, outside the plays.

We may allow that the practice by critics of the method of close textual analysis has made the old theory highly implausible, since this practice has shown that to elucidate the sense of a poem involves showing how the sense is determined by the particular order of words, succession of images, covert references and allusions, even, in some instances, typographi-

13. *An Essay on Criticism* (1711), lines 297-300.
14. Samuel Taylor Coleridge, *Biographia Literaria* (1817), ch. 1.

cal devices, in the poem under analysis. It is these words in this order that constitute the poem; and the sense of the poem, a sense that can be elucidated but not stated, is so entirely a function of a particular verbal structure that it seems impossible to maintain, what Pope certainly appears to maintain in the passage I have already quoted, that a poem consists of a core of meaning that could be stated in a series of propositions and, surrounding the core, a set of embellishments delightful in themselves and having, in relation to the propositional meaning, the function of highlighting and emphasizing what the poet wishes to single out as being of peculiar interest. All this has been shown by a number of brilliant critics from whom Mr. Cleanth Brooks (the originator of "the heresy of paraphrase") in the United States and Mr. William Empson in Britain may be picked out as sufficiently exemplary.

But, we may ask, does it *have* to be like this? If we allow that it is a characteristic of at least some expressions in ordinary discourse that they can be translated without loss of meaning either into other expressions in the same language or into expressions in another language, how can we be sure that poetry is *essentially* such that this can never properly be done in the case of poetic discourse? After all, the kinds of poetry most in fashion in the last thirty years, the work of Donne and Marvell, of Hopkins, Eliot, and Yeats, lend themselves easily to the method of close analysis; but it does not follow from its being impossible to offer adequate paraphrases of these specific kinds that the thing is impossible in relation to other specific kinds. What holds of a species does not necessarily hold of the genus. From the marine habitat of whales or the manner of movement of bats we cannot legitimately infer anything about the habits of all mammals. Some further argument is necessary if one wishes to hold (as I do) that belief in the possibility of paraphrasing poetic discourse is always a heresy, no matter what the poem in question may be.

My argument is that it follows from the nature of poetic fictions as such that belief in the possibility of paraphrase is always heretical. I have already suggested that it is characteristic of a fiction that certain questions cannot appropriately be asked about it. We cannot ask how many children Lady Macbeth had; or what courses Hamlet pursued at the University of Wittenberg; or what kind of caterpillar caused the sickness of the rose in Blake's poem; or whether Mr. Jingle's talking, in the year 1827, about the 1830 Revolution is or is not a case of extrasensory perception. We are tempted to suppose we can ask such questions because poetic discourse moves in the mode of possibility; so that nothing can be said poetically that would not be appropriate in discourse of another kind. If we say

> The king sits in Dunfermling toune,
> Drinking the bluid-reid wine,[15]

this has the sense it has because the state of affairs it feigns to describe is a possible one; and we could use the same expression, or an expression of the same type, to refer to an actual state of affairs. If one says

> I wish I were where Helen lies!
> Night and day on me she cries;
> And I am weary of the skies,[16]

then this could be said truly and sincerely by a man in such a situation. Similarly, poetic discourse can have the form of an exhortation, a command, a scientific generalization, a moral judgment, a thesis in theology, a philosophical theory. Whatever can be said in forms of discourse which have straightforward applications can be said poetically in the mode of possibility. A distinction between the poetic and other kinds of discourse is that some of the entailments that belong to other kinds of discourse are, in poetic discourse, cut.

15. "Sir Patrick Spence," in Thomas Percy, *Reliques of Ancient English Poetry* (1765).
16. "Fair Helen of Kirconnell," in Sir Walter Scott, *Minstrelsy of the Scottish Border* (1802-03).

245

Now, I wish to argue to the impossibility of paraphrase from the fact, if it is a fact, that in poetic discourse the normal entailments are cut. But before I advance what I think to be a persuasive argument, I wish to examine a doctrine that appears to be a presupposition of much criticism: the doctrine that poetic is distinguished from other discourse by certain empirically determinable characteristics, roughly, the presence of paradox and ambiguity. A critic has said that poetry is saying two or more things at once.[17] An example of what is intended would be the last stanza of Blake's moving and beautiful poem, "London":

> But most thro' midnight streets I hear
> How the youthful Harlot's curse
> Blasts the new born Infant's tear,
> And blights with plagues the Marriage hearse.[18]

Ambiguity: we can read "the youthful Harlot's curse" in two ways, as a cry (this would link it with "every Infant's cry of fear," "the Chimney-sweeper's cry," and "the hapless Soldier's sigh" of the earlier stanzas), and as the plague of which she is the victim and bearer; and "Blasts the new born Infant's tear" could be read as meaning that the tear is accursed from the beginning and not innocent, and also that it is dried up by the hot breath of the curse. Paradox: this is exemplified by the expression "the Marriage *hearse.*" Certainly, paradox and ambiguity can be identified in much of the poetry that moves us most deeply, and the critic can show that the power of such poetry to move us is connected with the successful employment of these devices. But paradox and ambiguity could only be the essentially distinguishing marks of poetry if we did not have a use for paradox and ambiguity in other forms of discourse. This is plainly false. Someone once said to me, perhaps by way of warning, that a professor's life can too easily, through a preoccupation with ad-

17. I believe this was Mr. F. W. Bateson. I cannot trace the reference.
18. William Blake, "London," *Songs of Experience* (1794).

ministrative duties and the work of committees, degenerate into a life of *busy idleness*. We have learned to speak of success as "the bitch-goddess." I need not multiply examples. Even if we were to establish inductively that paradox and ambiguity are much commoner in poetic than in other forms of discourse, this would not affect my conclusion. For we could easily imagine a society where the opposite was true, where the poetry was comparatively limpid and other forms of discourse were crackling with paradox and knotty with ambiguity.

Let me further explain what I mean when I say that in poetic discourse some of the entailments that belong to other kinds of discourse are cut. I have already indicated that it would make no sense to ask a certain range of questions about narrative or descriptive poetry. To return to my earlier example, if Shakespeare tells us that Hamlet studied at Wittenberg it is inappropriate to ask what courses he studied and whether or not his teachers found him an apt pupil. These would be utterly appropriate questions if the statement about Hamlet and Wittenberg were made historically, just as there would be circumstances in which it would be appropriate to point out that Bohemia is landlocked. Again, if I write yet another poem on the *carpe diem* theme and exhort the young and beautiful to take their opportunities, I am not *advising* anybody to behave in a certain way. A final example: it might be poetically defensible to write a poem which had built into its structure some features of the pre-Copernican cosmologies; and to one who objected one would need only to reply that this was not a contribution to *Nature*.

My question now is: Granted that it is an essential characteristic of poetic discourse that the normal entailments, in the sense I have illustrated, are cut, does it follow that how things are said in poetic discourse, and what is said, are inseparable in ways they are not in other forms of discourse? (Of course, we cannot even in other forms of discourse always separate the *how* from the *what*. But this raises other issues.) My answer is that it does so follow. When we, for example, describe the world, how we describe it has much to do with the *force* of our description, very little—provided we make no syntactical blunders—to do with its *accuracy*. It has been argued that a true fact-stating sentence is through its form uniquely fitted to the state of affairs the user of it asserts to be the case; but no one has ever succeeded in showing that this is true of sentences in a natural language; and if we could make it true by convention in an artificial language, as no doubt we could, whatever was said in such a language could be said otherwise in a natural language; and we could also explain the convention. Descriptive uses of language, then, insofar as we are concerned, not with the force and resonance they have, but with their character as assertions that such and such is the case, may be translated or paraphrased. Again, to shift to another kind of discourse, it seems plain that there is more than one form of words in which I could state the principle of the Identity of Indiscernibles and that two such forms could be said to have the same meaning. Finally, it seems, so far as the giving of moral advice goes, immaterial whether I tell someone that he ought to pay his debts or whether I tell him that he is obliged to restore what he has borrowed. What are the features of such uses of language that make them susceptible of paraphrase? In the instance of descriptive uses where the intention of the user is to say that something is the case, what makes a sentence true or false is whether or not what is asserted to be the case is the case; and the form of the assertion is not uniquely tied to what is asserted to be the case. If, as I suppose, the principle of the Identity of Indiscernibles lays down limiting conditions for identification through predication, it gets its sense, not through the particular linguistic form in which it is stated, but through its being implicated in the logical properties of predication in a language. And a piece of moral advice is an exhortation to a certain course of action in the light of an established situation; and once again there is no unique tie between the form of the advice and the description of the action recommended. Briefly, what all these instances have in common, and what makes such uses susceptible of paraphrase, is that in each case the adequacy of what is said is governed by some state of affairs, prior to and independent of what is said. The character of the world, predication, a situation out of which the obligation to pay one's debts arises, these are prior to what may be said about them.

Now, the adequacy of what is said in the form of poetic fiction is not, in any straightforward sense, governed by any state of affairs prior to and independent of what is said. Fictitious descriptions are neither true nor false in the way real descriptions are true or false and this follows from their being fictions. Just as to dream that I make a promise is not to make a promise, for I do not do anything in a dream, I only dream that I do this or that, so to give a fictitious description is not to give a description, though a fictitious description has the form of a description, just as the promise I dream that I make has the form of a promise. It follows from this that I could not give an *alternative* poetic description, for there could be no criterion (as there would be in the case of a real description) for deciding whether or not the alternative description had succeeded. The poetic description has the form of a description; but it exists only as *this* description, these words in this order. What is said and how it is said are thus not distinguishable in the way they are in other forms of discourse.

III ——————————————————————————————————

My conclusion is not that truth has no application to poetic discourse but that the way in which it has application remains to be discussed. One pseudo-solution need not trouble us: the view that poetic statements get their sense from, and find their application in, a metaphysical shadow-world which stands to the statements of poetic discourse as the world of nature and human affairs does to the statements of other forms of discourse. There is so constant a witness to the view that in some sense, one yet to be explored, poetic discourse has a relation to the world of nature and human affairs, that a resort to a metaphysical shadow-world would be only a last desperate rescue operation, all other possibilities having been exhausted. When Mr. Graham Hough remarked (in *Regina* v. *Penguin Books Limited*) that "one of the things one would wish to take into account [in assessing the value of a novel] is whether it is a true and sincere representation of an aspect of life,"[19] he was enunciating a critical commonplace that goes back to antiquity and has been current in every age. Here romanticism and classicism are at one. "Poetry is the image of man and nature." Thus Wordsworth in the Preface to *Lyrical Ballads*, summing up the whole tradition.

"Image," "representation," these are the central concepts we have to elucidate, together with their many corollaries, "faithfulness," "accuracy," "truth," "sincerity," and so on. If we can know what it is for a poetic fiction to "represent" an aspect of life, to present us with an "image" of man and nature, then we shall know what it is to say of a poetic fiction that it is a faithful representation, a true image.

A representation or image of something will differ in more than one way from what is represented. A "perfect" representation would not be a representation but the thing itself. If I make a noise which is so like the hooting of an owl that it deceives those who hear it, and this includes any owls that may be listening, then I have made the noise an owl makes. If I try to explain to another through bodily gestures, speech, and so on what it is for a man to be angry and get so carried away by my own performance that I try to throttle someone, then it is not that I am imitating an angry man—I *am* an angry man. If, being a bachelor, I ask a lady to marry me and put this on paper, saying to myself that I am only playing at making a proposal of marriage, I *have* proposed marriage, and the lady in question will have good grounds for bringing an action for breach of promise should I attempt to extricate myself from the engage-

19. *The Trial of Lady Chatterley,* The Transcript of the Trial edited by C. H. Rolph (Penguin Books, 1961), p. 42.

ment by explaining that I was only playing at making a proposal. These things are not representations: they are the things they declare themselves to be. Of course, we can only fall into the error of thinking there could be, in the sense illustrated, a "perfect" representation where the medium of representation is identical with what is represented. A hoot like the hoot of an owl is a hoot, and so *mutatis mutandis* in the other instances. Then there is the kind of representation which is a trick, ink-blots made of glass and foaming glasses of stout made of rubber that one can buy from joke shops, and *trompe l'oeil* painting, like the fiddle on the back of the door at Chatsworth. These really are representations and their "perfection" consists in their tricking us for the time being into thinking they are the real thing. There is something disagreeable in representations of this kind; they arouse the expectations that the real things would arouse; and then we are suddenly let down. We can take pleasure in contemplating things that are not representations; and we can take pleasure in contemplating representations that are plainly such, whether they are representations of things that we like to contemplate or of things that in themselves we find repulsive. We do not take pleasure—or we take only a perverse pleasure—in those representations that are at first taken to be the things they represent.

A representation, then, to count as the kind of representation we are concerned with in the arts, and this is a general point about the arts and is not peculiar to the art of poetry, must be evidently distinct from what is represented. This is indeed a consequence of what I said earlier about its being a characteristic of poetic discourse that in it the normal entailments are cut. When we are in some doubt as to whether or not the normal entailments *are* cut, as in certain ways of presenting the blinding of Gloster in *King Lear*, we are uneasy; and if by some strange chance the actor playing Gloster were to have his eyes put out in reality and not in mime we should say this was not a theatrical performance. And, to reverse the argument, if we suspect that someone is pretending to show emotions, and not feeling them, we say of him that he is being theatrical; and the vice of this lies not in his offering us a representation but in his offering us a representation with the intention of deceiving us.

The possibility, then, is excluded that we should be able to appraise a poetic representation as true or faithful on the ground that we have been tricked into mistaking the representation for the thing represented. Of course, except in theatrical performances, the art of poetry does not lend itself to trickery. A poetic account of a battle cannot be mistaken for a battle. Even in lyric poetry the fictional character of the speaker is indicated by the formal devices, rhyme, meter, or other, which are not characteristic of other types of discourse. To make a declaration of war in verse is no doubt possible; but its being in verse would be *prima facie* evidence that the normal entailments were not intended. Equally, my earlier argument has excluded the possibility that a poetic representation may be thought to be true or faithful by reason of its being an accurate account of some happening or some series of events, or an accurate report of a state of mind, or a faithful picture of some natural phenomenon. Poems may be any of these but their character as poems cannot be understood as such accounts, reports, or pictures. It is not necessary to visit the Lake district or the valley of the Wye before one can evaluate Wordsworth's nature poetry. Attempts to find the originals of Albertine and Gilberte have a certain interest, of the detective-story kind, but they cannot affect our judgment of Proust's novel. We may suspect there is self-revelation of a kind in Shakespeare's dark comedies, but whether this is so or not, the critical problems they present remain the same. It is truistic that poetry of some merit can be written only by men who have contemplated the natural and social worlds in a more or less perceptive way, and equally truistic that a minimum of experience has to be had before we are capable of responding to what they write; but no particular poem is related to a particular state of affairs as a map is to a piece of country mapped, or a narrative of events to the events themselves. We could test the accuracy of the map by going over the piece of country in question; we could test the accuracy of a narrative by questioning witnesses, examining photographs, searching for footprints. There can be no such short and easy way to test the truth or the faithfulness of a poetic fiction.

I hold that when we use such a term as "truth" in the language of poetic appraisal we do so in various ways and employing different criteria in different cases. This would not be an altogether unexpected result, for the same thing holds in other fields. My grounds for asserting that I feel tired, that the blackbirds have begun to nest, that *apartheid* is morally wrong, that the sum of the angles of a Euclidean triangle is equal to two right angles, are very different. Similarly, if I wish to maintain the truth of such poetic representations as *King Lear*, Grimm's fairy story *The Juniper Tree*, the second of Pope's *Moral Essays* ("Of the Characters of Women") and Mr. Allen Tate's *Ode to the Confederate Dead*, it is very unlikely that the same criteria will be usable in each case. But it will not follow from our saying that there is truth in *King Lear* and truth in "Of the Characters of Women," and having quite different grounds for saying so in the two cases, that we are confused, any more than we are confused in saying that the blackbirds are nesting and that *apartheid* is morally wrong and that both statements are true, even though our grounds for saying they are true are not of the same kind in the two cases.

One of the reasons we may have for ascribing truth to a poetic representation is that it reveals to us the character of our inner feelings and dispositions; and by this I do not mean that it describes accurately inner feelings and dispositions of which we could give a satisfactory account independently of the poetic representation. For reasons I have already given, it will not do to say that the truth of the poem lies in its "matching" a state of affairs of which we have prior and independent knowledge.

We have the idea that the inner life may be described through introspection. We habitually talk of our feelings, passions, dispositions, capacities, in terms that suggest that introspection is to the mind and heart what sight and the other senses are to the world of nature. It is one of the great and, I believe, permanent advances recently made by philosophers in this country to have shown that this account, the monstrous offspring of Cartesian dualism and British empiricism, is impossible. The confusions in the account are legion, and they provided the later Wittgenstein with many of the problems that are central to his *Philosophical Investigations,* a rich mine whence many lesser philosophers have carried away their portions of precious ore. I will give an illustrative instance in which the impossibility of our learning to characterize the inner life through introspection may be brought out. It is impossible for me to wonder if I am in pain, though of course I may in a particular instance be in some doubt as to how I should classify a sensation; and pain is certainly something "inward," since it makes no sense to speak of my exhibiting my pain to another. How do I learn to identify one of my sensations as a pain? The force of this question is brought out if we note that it is a prior condition of my applying the concept of pain to my own case that I should already know the meaning of the word "pain." But to say that the word "pain" has a meaning is to imply that it is a unit in the public language and that my uses of the word and the uses of the word by others have the same range. For reasons I have already given, the meanings of words cannot be taught by showing that they "stand for" hidden processes of thought and feeling, since we only have the public language in which to talk about our thoughts and feelings. The conclusion, then, is that just as we can only say that others are in pain by noting their behavior (and listening to what they say), so in our own case we learn to characterize our own sensations of pain only through learning the behavioral criteria for ascribing pain to others and to ourselves. Sensations, then, do not bear their names on their faces. If we could not learn the criteria for deciding when others are in pain we should be unable to apply the concept of pain to our own case. What holds of sensations such as pain holds also of emotions such as fear and anger, except that in the case of emotions the concepts are linked even more closely and plainly with incipient or actual behavior than in the case of sensations.

All I have shown so far is that we could not learn to identify and describe our sensations and emotions through introspection alone, that we could not say *what* we were feeling without words that have sense in the public language. It is also true that we could not describe the world of nature and human affairs without the use of language. I now go on to say that understanding what it is we see or feel is necessarily connected with being able to give some account, not always one so adequate or so complete as we would wish, of what this is. It is not that we first understand and then articulate our understanding through a conceptual scheme. Such an articulation *is* understanding. Talk about the inner life is always in terms of concepts made by us as embodied intelligences, not as intelligences contingently and—as has been thought—by misfortune connected with the bodies we happen to have; and even if in one sense each of us has his own private theatre, the performances that go on within the private theatre are not the substance of the life of the mind nor are the various happenings within it the play of jealousy, ambition, desire, love, hate, fear, joy, upon which the poet discourses. When, at the end of *The Waste Land*, Mr. Eliot depicted each man as imprisoned within his own consciousness, he gave us an image of man dwelling within the haunted palace of the Cartesians;[20] but the palace is in ruins and the ghosts have departed.

20. I have heard the key
    Turn in the door once and turn once only
    We think of the key, each in his prison
    Thinking of the key, each confirms a prison

   "The Waste Land," T. S. Eliot, *Collected Poems 1909-1935*
                                  (Faber and Faber, 1936), p. 77.

   It is significant that Mr. Eliot glosses the text with an extract from F. H. Bradley's *Appearance and Reality*. Bradley writes: "My external sensations are no

The observation that we should none of us have fallen in love if we had not first read about it is commonly taken to be cynical and to carry the implication that the state of feeling, "being in love," is artificial and silly and is produced in us by an unhealthy diet of poems and romances. It can be understood quite otherwise; and in a sense that brings out the function of the poetic representation in revealing to us the character of our feelings and dispositions. We cannot mistakenly believe we are in love, though we may be quite mistaken in supposing we love the person we are in love with; but the ability to characterize our own state as one of being in love depends upon our having criteria for deciding when others are in love; and these criteria we get from a particular cultural tradition mediated to us in a thousand ways. We could not be in love and not know it, for, as I have already argued, having feelings that can be identified and described is not separable from the conceptual activity of identification and description. If the other animals can be said to have feelings, as they can certainly be said to have sensations, such feelings must be quite other than ours, and cannot be said to be known in reflection. All we could say would be that in them there is an experienced—though even "experience" may be misleading—unity of inner movement and outward behavior; for what is characteristically human, the inhibition of the overt manifestation of feeling (striking or embracing or whatever), so that we have the feeling but do not show it in behavior and may not even betray it in our faces or in our posture, has in them no counterpart.

Characterizing our state of feeling, and so bringing it about that it is *this* state of feeling, is done through the application of concepts that are, so to speak, drawn from the common stock;

less private to myself than are my thoughts or my feelings. In either case my experience falls within my own circle, a circle closed on the outside; and, with all its elements alike, every sphere is opaque to the others which surround it. . . . In brief, regarded as an existence which appears in a soul, the whole world for each is peculiar and private to that soul."

and thus when we are in love we are in love as others are in love, just as when we suffer pain we suffer as others do. Nevertheless, because each of us is himself and not another, unique in his history and in his relations to others, a characterization of our individual feelings through concepts drawn from the common stock leaves us with a sense of injustice; for the feelings are rendered, not in their particularity, but in respect of their likeness to the feelings of others. There is no complete remedy for this sense of injustice. But it may be diminished and made to seem of no account through the poetic representation (and, no doubt, in other ways too). The consolation of the poetic representation of human love is that it reveals to us that condition of feeling we share with others—it gives us "the image of man and nature"—but not, or not wholly, as articulated in the common run of concepts, but as articulated in a particular concrete representation that speaks to us and for us in our individual situation, and only *through* this to and for our common humanity. It belongs to the poetic representation that it is wholly individual, these words in this order, and that no paraphrase can be given; so that although we know that this poem that speaks to us and for us speaks also to and for others, it is still as though it speaks to us alone. Further, whereas states of feeling characterized through concepts drawn from the common stock may be characterized in mechanical and simple terms, the rendering of a state of feeling through the complexity and inner richness of the poetic representation brings it about that the state of feeling so rendered is itself complex and rich, and valuable on this account; for we can place no limit upon the possible achievements of the poetic representation, a state of feeling that is complex and resistant to characterization and on that account burdensome and frustrating, may be rendered clear and powerful when there is revealed to us a unity in the complexity, a unity we should otherwise have missed.

There is much in our inner life, in our relations with other persons, and in that obscure sense of what is deeply serious which is the ground of our capacity for religious and moral discourse, that we understand fitfully and with difficulty; and steady introspection gets us no farther. But just as we learn what it is to suffer pain, not merely through having pains but also through learning to use the language, so we can learn to understand the inner life in its complexity, and the life of society into which it flows and from which it draws much of its substance, through the poetic representation. A poetic representation is like a concept in that it is something made by man through which we articulate what would otherwise lie beyond our understanding; and just as a concept is not a *picture* of reality which gets its sense from that slice of reality it pictures, but an instrument of understanding, so that truth belongs to the concept only in the act of judgment, in the same way the poetic representation finds its truth in its proved capacity to further our understanding of ourselves and our society. "The image of man and nature" is not a symbolic transcript of something that is merely *there:* it is an instrument of knowledge.

It would be out of place here to attempt a detailed account of how a particular poetic fiction can function as an instrument of knowledge and of how, as thus functioning, it may be accounted "true." This is work for a professional critic and there are many examples readily available. What I will do is to remind you of a crucial instance of the capacity of poetry to do for one man what I have argued it can do for the generality of men. In a dark moment John Stuart Mill came to believe that "the flaw in [his] life, must be a flaw in life itself." From this state of dejection he was rescued by the poetry of Wordsworth. It is worth noticing the precise terms in which Mill describes what Wordsworth's poetry did for him:

> What made Wordsworth's poems a medicine for my state of mind, was that they expressed, not mere outward beauty, but states of feeling, and of thought coloured by feeling, under the excitement of beauty. They seemed to be *the very culture of the feelings* [my italics], which I was in quest of. In them I seemed to draw from a source of inward

joy, of sympathetic and imaginative pleasure, which could be shared in by all human beings. . . .[21]

That discipline of the sensibility and the mind to which the art of poetry, largely understood, contributes in a unique fashion enables us not only to understand ourselves; we also learn to look upon the human scene in such a way that, in the degree permitted to us by our talents, we draw from our vision representations which, though their primary and original reference is personal, speak for all men in the same predicament. Nothing could be more personal, more tied to one particular place and time, than Henry James's passionate note on his visit in 1904 to that graveyard in Cambridge, Massachusetts, where the members of his family were buried and where, twelve years later, his own ashes were to be placed. Intensely personal, wholly particular in its reference, it nevertheless displays in a supreme way that combination of consummate artistry with deep and penetrated feeling which makes it a wonderful example, for my purposes, of poetic representation; and of poetic truth, for here James finds in himself "not this or that particular man, but mankind."[22]

Isn't the highest deepest note of the whole thing the never-to-be-lost memory of that evening hour at Mount Auburn—at the Cambridge Cemetery when I took my way alone—after much waiting for the favouring hour—to that unspeakable group of graves. It was late, in November; the trees all bare, the dusk to fall early, the air all still (at Cambridge, in general, so still), with the western sky more and more turning to that terrible, deadly, pure polar pink that shows behind American winter woods. But I can't go over this—I can only, oh, so gently, so tenderly, brush it and breathe upon it—breathe upon it and brush it. It was the moment; it was the hour; it was the blessed flood of emotion that broke out at the touch of one's sud-

21. John Stuart Mill, *Autobiography* (London, 1949), p. 125.
22. Thomas Hobbes, *Leviathan*, "The Introduction."

den *vision* and carried me away. I seemed then to know why I had done this; I seemed then to know why I had *come*—and to feel how not to have come would have been miserably, horribly to miss it. It made everything right— it made everything priceless. The moon was there, early, white and young, and seemed reflected in the white face of the great empty Stadium, forming one of the boundaries of Soldier's Field, that looked over at me, stared over at me, through the clear twilight, from across the Charles. Everything was there, everything *came;* the recognition, stillness, the strangeness, the pity and the sanctity and the terror, the breath-catching passion and the divine relief of tears. William's inspired transcript, on the exquisite little Florentine urn of Alice's ashes, William's divine gift to us, and to *her*, of the Dantean lines—

> *Dopo lungo esilio e martirio*
> *Viene a questa pace*—

took me so at the throat by its penetrating *rightness,* that it was as if one sank down on one's knees in a kind of anguish of gratitude before something for which one had waited with a long, deep *ache.* But why do I write of the all unut- terable and the all abysmal? Why does my pen not drop from my hand on approaching the infinite pity and tragedy of all the past? It does, poor helpless pen, with what it meets of the ineffable, what it meets of the cold Medusa-face of life, of all the life *lived*, on every side. *Basta, basta!*[23]

I said that in this passage James represents to us "not this or that particular man; but mankind," and in this lies the truth of the representation, in its capacity to increase the under- standing of our common nature. Such performances are

23. *The Notebooks of Henry James,* edited by F. O. Matthiessen and Ken- neth B. Murdock (New York, 1947), pp. 320-21. It is worth noting that James prefaces the passage with the remark—he sees the whole scene and mood as standing "in the path like a waiting lion," a challenge, that is, to his art—"that to present these accidents is what it is to be a *master:* that and that only." I would argue that he solves the problem of representation in presenting it.

wonderfully intelligent; but they are so much more than this that one understands why people have so often spoken of the poetic performance as though the words of the poet were not his own but those of the god; or, with Coleridge, of the activity of the poetic imagination as transcendental; or as the expression of an inner glory. It is true that there is in "this life . . . no manifestation of glory coming from human beings except in products of art."[24] But if this is not a manifestation of an inner glory, and it is not, poetry and music, beyond the other arts, show us that there is the transcendent and that human life, that same life which displays "the cold Medusa-face," is open to the altogether beautiful—*tam antiqua et tam nova*[25]—and to the love in whose depths the greatest of the poets saw the scattered leaves of the universe bound together in a single volume.[26]

24. Miss G. E. M. Anscombe has kindly allowed me to make use of this expression from an unpublished paper by her. I also owe to her the idea that the glory of art is not a manifestation of an inner glory in human beings.

25. *Sero te amavi, pulchritudo tam antiqua et tam nova, sero te amavi* (St. Augustine, *Confessions*, X, 27).

26.   Nel suo profondo vidi che s' interna,
        legato con amore in un volume,
        ciò che per l'universo si squaderna. . . .

Paradiso, canto xxxiii, lines 85-87